Building Our Best Future

Thinking Critically About Ourselves and Our World

TEACHERS EDITION

Deanna Kuhn

© 2018 Wessex Press, Inc. All rights reserved.
www.wessexlearning.com

Library of Congress Cataloging-in-Publication Data

Kuhn, Deanna

    Building Our Best Future – Teachers Edition / Deanna Kuhn

        p. cm.

   ISBN 978-0-9990649-7-9 (hardcover)
             978-0-9990649-8-6 (softcover)

    1. Building Our Best Future. I. Title: Thinking critically about ourselves and our world. II. Deanna Kuhn

Design/Production: Anna Botelho

Cover image: Created by Freepik

Copyright © 2018 by Wessex Press, Inc., New York, NY, USA. All rights reserved. This publication is protected by copyright and permission should be obtained from the publisher prior to any prohibited reproduction, storage in a retrieval system, or transmission in any form or by any means, electronic, mechanical, photocopying, recording, or likewise. For information regarding permission, write to Wessex Press, Inc. at *contact@wessexlearning.com*.

Table of Contents

Part One. Teachers' Introduction 1

    Chapter 1   Introduction 3

Part Two. The Thinking Plan 9

    Chapter 2   Developing a Position 11

    Chapter 3   Investigating the Alternative 15

    Chapter 4   The Showdown 21

    Chapter 5   Sharing Your Thinking 29

    Chapter 6   What is Good Evidence? 33

Part Three. The Decision Topics 41

    Chapter 7   A Personal Future 43

    Chapter 8   A Community Future 83

    Chapter 9   A National Future 129

    Chapter 10   A World Future 171

Part Four. For Teachers 195

    Chapter 11   Assessing Student Growth:
                          What Can this Curriculum Accomplish? 197

Part One

■ ■ ■

Teachers' Introduction

The fact that this book has captured your attention already says a good deal about you as a teacher. Here are a few things likely true of you:

1. You have been intrigued by talk of "21st century skills" and you would like to think you are preparing your students for the adult world they will encounter.
2. You are concerned that much of what we ask them to learn doesn't seem to "stick" beyond the immediate moment and setting.
3. You are concerned that a good deal of what we try to teach them doesn't seem as if it will be of great use to them in their adult lives.
4. You want them to be able to think and learn independently, because you think this is what they will need to do as adults, but you aren't sure how to develop these skills.
5. You want them to be practiced in collaborating with peers to think through issues and address problems, as they will need to do so as adults.
6. You want them to be able to recognize what they need to know and to ask the questions that will enable them to find it out.
7. You want them to see themselves as someone who has the tools and disposition to inquire and learn and contribute to addressing difficult issues.
8. You think it's critical to prepare young people to assume roles as citizens of an increasingly troubled world.
9. You listen to your students at least as much as you talk to them, and you're okay with the noise of students talking with one another in the classroom.
10. You encourage your students not to accept the first answer and to ask themselves and one another, "Could it be otherwise?"

If most of these statements are true of you, this book will likely prove a resource to you and your students, even though there is great flexibility in how you and they will use it. As teachers of ELA, social studies, or science, there are many demands on you already as to what you should accomplish in the classroom and across the school year. Yet, if you answered yes, you value the goals that positive answers to these questions reflect, and you are eager to coordinate demands already in place with these goals. We present a case here that you can do that. In Chapter 11 we review the evidence that indicates that the measurable outcomes of middle- and high-school students' engagement with the activities presented in this book are not in fact at such great odds with the more standard curriculum goals. Students' literacy gains have been well documented. They become better speakers, as well as better expository writers. If English is a second language, they make gains in mastery of it. They become skilled in drawing on evidence to support and weaken arguments. They become more reflective about their own and others' thinking. They more often ask themselves and others, "How do I know? and "How do you know?"

In Chapter 11 we present tools for assessing these skills in your own students, in particular in the final individual "Position" essays they are asked to produce to summarize their thinking on a topic. You will likely already have rubrics in place for assessing students' expository writing that you want to continue to use. In the assessments suggested here, the emphasis is on the quality of the thinking that underlies the writing.

The first six chapters of this book are the same chapters that appear in the student edition of the book, supplemented by margin notes to you on implementing the activities being suggested to students. Chapters 7-10 contain the specific topics proposed to students as topics for their contemplation. In the student edition, each is accompanied by potential questions related to the topic that they might like answers to, along with reflective questions that will guide them in thinking about the answers. They are also encouraged to formulate their own questions as they delve deeper into the topic. Students are guided in how to obtain answers, accessing the website and numerical codes provided for each question. (Students enjoy having to electronically access answers to their questions and the electronic format enables us to update answers when new evidence becomes available.) In this teachers' edition, for convenience current answers appear with the questions, along with an internet URL source from which an answer was derived, providing more detailed information that will be available to students who wish it.

The chapters begin with topics that focus on the students' own personal decision making and then progress to topics of wider scope. There is no right order for engaging the topics. In some cases, students can develop their skills without going beyond the personal topics (Chapter 7). In others, students may skip these topics entirely and begin with those in the later chapters. Students ideally will have a say in the topics they engage. Even more important, however, students should choose the side they will take in debate of the topic (even if they later change their position). They need to feel they are practicing the real-life decision making they will do as adults, and getting better at it as they do so.

You as a teacher will also have considerable decision-making capacity with respect to how you make use of this book in your own classroom. Teachers' circumstances and goals vary greatly, as do the circumstances and capabilities of the particular students they teach. If your students work within only one of the topic chapters, or even with only a single topic, and perhaps with different topics entirely, the gains they make will hopefully be clear enough that both you and your students conclude the investment has been warranted.

Chapter 1

■ ■ ■

Introduction

We all wonder what our future holds. Some people are satisfied just to wait and see what happens. Others understand that they can play a major role in shaping their own future — they don't need to just wait and let it happen to them. Building your own future means making lots of decisions — many small ones and some big ones. Some decisions are just about your own life. Others involve the community you live in, your country, and even the whole world.

In history classes, you learn about the decisions individuals and countries have made in the past and the consequences of those decisions. In other social studies classes you also learn about the decisions that have become laws and affect how people live today in your local area and in your country. But you often lack time in these classes to think about decisions regarding the future. How might the choices and decisions that we live with today be different? How could we make them better?

With this book you have an opportunity to think about such decisions, for yourself and together with your classmates. You can use the book starting with the topics you choose, one involving a decision about only your own future or one that involves the future of your community, your country, or your world. For each decision, you will be called on to think carefully and deeply about it, for yourself and with your classmates, sharing your ideas with one another and finding answers to questions that will help you to make the best decisions — decisions that will help to build the best possible future.

In the first part of the book, we draw on a topic from the list below to illustrate a plan you can use for thinking deeply about the topic together with your classmates, so that by the end you will feel confident that you are able to make a good decision about the issue it raises — that is, a decision that takes into account the available evidence related to the topic and considers it from many different perspectives. You can then use this plan to consider any and all of the other topics in the lists below. You can also select other topics not on the list that you think are important ones worth thinking about.

NOTE 1.1

A final chapter in this first part of the book offers a close look at different kinds of evidence you can consider in investigating a topic. That chapter begins with a quiz you can take to see what you already know about evidence. How do we know what different kinds of evidence help to strengthen a claim we make and which kinds can be criticized as weak? You may want to turn to this chapter first, or you can go to it at any point as you investigate some of the topics below.

Here now are some topics to choose from, all of them concerned with ways to make the future a better one, for you and all of the other humans on our planet. The second part of the book takes you to the investigation of each of these topics.

NOTE 1.2

NOTE 1.3

A Personal Future

College v. work first. When you finish high school, you have the choice of going right to college or of working for a few years first.

Effort. You are very good in one school subject and don't do well in another. Should you put most time and effort in being at the top of the class in your good subject or in getting better in your poor subject?

Co-ed v. single-sex school. You are starting at a new school this year and you have the choice of attending a single-sex school or a school attended by both boys and girls.

Course choice: Foreign language or elective. Your school gives you the choice of studying a foreign language or taking one of many other electives of special interest to you (such as dance, a sport, a musical instrument).

After-school activity: School work or volunteer. Your school gives you two choices for an activity during the last period of the day: Attend study hall to do homework and get extra help or volunteer at a nearby community center to help poor children and the elderly.

After-school job. You have been offered a job in a store evenings from 5 to 9 pm. Should you take the job?

Exercise: Team or individual. Your school has sports teams that require daily practice after school and Saturdays. Or you can exercise on your own and do different things after school.

Summer activity. You have the choice of a summer job or a sports camp.

Nutrition. You like soda and think it's okay to have a couple a day as long as you have a good diet overall. Or you can decide soda does nothing good for you and it's best to avoid it.

Alcohol. You have an opportunity to try an alcoholic drink to know what it's like. Or you decide it's safest to avoid alcohol entirely and not risk starting with it.

Spend or save. You have received an unexpected gift of money from a relative. You have the choice of spending it or saving it.

A Community Future

Education: Curriculum. Should the town high school have a standard course of study for all students or allow students some choice of what to study?

Education: Leaving age. Should students be required to attend school until age 16 or age 18?

Education: Homeschooling? Should a family arriving from a foreign country be permitted to educate their child at home and not send the child to school?

Education: Teacher pay. Should all teachers receive the same pay or should teachers with more skill or experience be paid more?

Driving. Should teens be permitted to get drivers' licenses at age 16 or age 18?

Drinking. Should young people be permitted to drink alcohol at age 18 or age 21?

Juvenile v. adult court for teen offenders. Should teens who commit serious crimes be tried in regular adult court or a special court for juveniles?

Town sports teams. Should town taxes help to pay the cost of community sports teams? Or should they be paid for entirely by the families who use them?

Public transportation. Should town taxes help to pay the cost of buses and trains or should the cost be paid for entirely by the people who use them?

Sales tax. Should the town charge a sales tax on everything people buy? Or should the town get the money it needs from a tax on people's earnings?

Soda tax. Should an extra tax be charged on soda purchases?

Rent control. Should the town limit how much rent a landlord can charge?

Elderly care. Should adults be required to care for their elderly parents or should government funds be used to do this?

A National Future

Voting rights. Should everyone be allowed to vote or should voters be required to show they have studied the candidates and issues?

Voting age. Should the age one is eligible to vote be 16 or 18?

National service. Should high school graduates be required to do some community or military or international service (such as the Peace Corps)?

Health insurance. Should individuals be required to have health insurance they pay a monthly fee for?

National curriculum. Should all schools in a country have the same required school curriculum or should this be left up to local communities?

Animal research. Should animals be used in research to test new medical procedures, drugs or other products?

Social security tax. Should people be required to pay a social security tax from each paycheck that will provide money when they retire, or should people save on their own for their retirement?

Drugs. Is use of illegal drugs best reduced by educating people about its dangers or by making drugs less available?

Tobacco. Is smoking best reduced by educating people about its dangers or by charging a very high tax on purchase of cigarettes?

Capital punishment. Should the death sentence be used to punish serious crimes such as murder?

Abortion. Should it be against the law for a woman to undergo a medical procedure to end a pregnancy?

Euthanasia. Should it be allowed to help someone who wants to end their life?

A World Future

Aid to other nations. Should a powerful nation intervene to help another nation in trouble or focus only on its own problems?

United Nations. Should the United Nations be made more powerful or less powerful than it is now?

Space exploration. Should nations cooperate or compete in exploring outer space?

Immigration. Should a nation allow people from other countries to come live in their country based on what they can contribute or how bad life is where they come from?

Population control. Should countries whose population is growing too rapidly to feed their people try to reduce growth by educating people about the benefits of smaller family size or by a government policy that restricts family size?

Organ sales. Should paying or receiving money for a body organ such as a kidney be allowed?

Weapons of mass destruction. Some countries are believed to have or be developing weapons powerful enough to destroy all humanity. Should efforts be made to stop them by using persuasion or by using force?

Charity. Your family wants to make a donation to help children. Should they give money to a family they know whose parent has just lost their job or should they send it to a community in Africa where children are starving?

Teacher notes

1.1 Unless your students are already accustomed to working together in small groups where points of view differ, you may want to have some preliminary class discussion on doing so most productively. Points for discussion:

   a. Until you argue about it with others, you most likely don't really know what you think about something. Others introduce what you haven't thought of. We thus need to think and talk about the topic both with those who agree with us and those who disagree with us.

   b. Arguing, done properly, is good, not something undesirable to be avoided. It accomplishes something important.

   c. Worthwhile discussions involve reasons. Opinions without reasons are worth little. We need to be sure why we claim what we do. We can only convince others with reasons. We also need reasons for disagreeing with what another person says.

   d. Arguing well with others takes time and effort. Don't expect fast agreement.

   e. The most important skill to develop: LISTEN carefully to what the other person is saying. You can try describing it back to them to make sure you have understood.

   f. Disagreement is fine. Just remember, criticize IDEAS, not people.

1.2 Chapter 6 is designed to develop critical skills in students' thinking about evidence. However, it stands apart from the rest of the book and can be engaged in at any point. Teachers will want to look at it and make a decision as to where best to fit it in.

1.3 Some teachers and students may want to concentrate only on the Personal topics in Chapter 7. Others may want to skip those and go directly to topics in the subsequent chapters. Teachers who are inclined to go directly to the most complex topics of national and international scope in Chapters 9 and 10 may want to consider beginning with one or two topics from the earlier chapters for two reasons. First, it is worthwhile for young teens to experience personal decisions as ones amenable to and warranting thoughtful debate. Second, it is wise for teachers to know their students well and students to know one another well, so as to become aware of any personal vulnerabilities individual students may have before discussing highly controversial and potentially personally salient topics as immigration or abortion. Nonetheless, we have found young teens eager and more than ready to consider such topics. Before addressing them, they should have the norms of civil discourse (in particular the "Criticize ideas, not people" motto) well mastered. A thoughtful discussion of what topics are suitable for classroom discussion can be found in D. Hess & P. McAvoy's 2015 book *The political classroom* (Routledge). These authors recommend as potentially appropriate any topics that are authentic in being currently deliberated in the political sphere and offering a rich set of reasons to support contrasting perspectives.

Part Two

■ ■ ■

The Thinking Plan

Chapter 2

■ ■ ■

Developing a Position

You're ready to get to work. In this chapter we introduce a plan, although in the classroom your teacher may ask you to modify it in ways that will best suit your class. We can use as a sample topic one of the decisions you will need to make about your personal future: When you finish high school, should you go right to college or work for a few years first? Or you and your classmates may begin with another topic from the suggestions in Chapter 1 or with a topic of your own choice.

Choosing your position

NOTE 2.1

The first and very important thing you will need to do is to choose your initial position on the topic. In the case of the sample topic, do you think it will be better to go right to college when you graduate from high school or to work for awhile first? You may not have thought much about this and be unsure. You can change your position later as you think more about the topic. But right now you probably already have an idea of which option you think will be better. So choose that one for now.

Generating reasons

You and your classmates who make the same choice on this topic will form a team. The team's first task will be to identify some reasons that this choice is a good one, better than the one made by classmates who made the opposite choice and will form another team.

Each team should meet together, most likely in small groups to begin and then joining together as a whole team to share reasons. The two teams should meet in different corners of the room or ideally in different rooms if they are available.

Your best reason. Once you have organized into teams, begin by working silently, with each team member coming up with what seems to you like the most important reason for choosing the position you did. Write your reason on a 5" × 7" index card. For the sample topic of College vs. Work first, you would begin with "College right away is the better choice because…" or "Working first is the better choice because…"

NOTE 2.2

Share your reason. Work with the teammate seated next to you and share your reasons with each other. Work first on one person's reason and then on the other person's. Does the other person understand your reason? Do you understand theirs? Are the reasons by any chance the same reason (even if the words are a little different)? In this case, combine them on one card.

Rewrite reasons. Now look at each card and decide if there is a simple, fewest-words way to say that reason. Rewrite this simple version of the reason at the bottom of the card in capital letters and circle it. (This will make it easy to quickly identify it.)

Share rewritten reasons. Now let everyone on your team see all the reasons. Pass them around until everyone has seen each reason. Are you surprised by how many different reasons there can be for the same decision?

NOTE 2.3

Find other possible reasons. In person or by email, you may want to ask other people in your life — family members, relatives, friends — what their position on this topic and their reasons are. You can then make a new card for this reason if you don't already have it. (If the person you ask takes the opposite position, save their reasons for later; they will become important.)

NOTE 2.4

Evaluating reasons

How many reasons? How many different reasons does your team have for its position? That's the next thing you'll need to figure out. Two cards may have the same reason (even if the words are a little different).

If you wish, you can do this first in small groups and then repeat as a whole team. First choose a **group leader** and a **group scribe** to record. The leader asks each group member to read the fewest-words versions of their reasons. The scribe records the reason on a small (3" × 5") index card and pins it on a large posterboard everyone can see (or on an electronic board if you have one, or on a blackboard with tape will do).

Now the leader calls on a second person to read a reason. The group must decide "Is this the same reason as already posted or a different reason?" If it's the same reason, the scribe should record it on a card and pin it on top of the reason already there. (You can keep the card that says the reason best showing on top.) If it's a different reason, pin it somewhere else on the board. Continue until all reasons are on the board. (If you've been working in small groups, you'll need to repeat this activity as a whole team, getting all your reasons onto one board, so you know exactly how many **different** reasons your team has.)

What does your team think of these reasons? Now your team needs to decide what you think of these reasons. How good are they in making a case for your team's position on the topic? Remember, the other team is doing the same thing to make a case for their position. Each team wants to make sure they have the best possible reasons for their position.

You can discuss reasons first in small groups and then as a whole team. A way to do this is to move the reason cards around on the board, once the team agrees, putting the best reasons near the top of the board, the so-so reasons in the middle, and the not-so-good reasons near the bottom. But in order to agree about this, you need to have **reasons for reasons**. What makes this reason a good one and another reason a not-so-good one? Talk it over and be sure you agree.

NOTE 2.5

Supporting reasons with evidence

One answer to the last question is that a strong reason has evidence to support it. What is **evidence**? It is specific information about the way things are in the world. Evidence can help to make a reason more likely to be a correct one. For example, information that people without college degrees find it hard to get good jobs is evidence that helps to support the decision to go right to college. (It is also evidence **against** the decision to work before college.)

Information serves as evidence only if it helps to support (or weaken) a claim someone makes. So, rather than starting by looking for just any information about your topic, start by thinking about what information might support your position and its reasons. (Some information could weaken your position, making it less likely to be a good one.)

NOTE 2.6

A good way to do this is to think of a question whose answer might help support your position. For each of the topics suggested in this book, we will identify some possible questions and give you the opportunity to get answers to them. But equally well, you might think of other such questions. In this case your teacher or other person can help you to find an answer.

Working first in small groups, you can begin with either your own questions or a choice from the list provided for the topic in this book. Ideally, you should end up with a combination of questions and answers of these two kinds. In choosing questions from the list, your group should begin with questions whose answers you think will be most helpful to you. You can then get the answer by entering a code for that question. But before you do, talk about what the answer is likely to be and what it will mean. How will it help you?

NOTE 2.7

Once you have an answer to a question, ask yourselves again if it helps to support one of your reasons. If you agree it does, your scribe can write a short version of this evidence on a **post-it note**. Later, your team can attach this note to one of the reasons on your board.

Once each small group has several evidence post-it notes, meet as a whole team and take turns presenting them to the team. If the whole team agrees the evidence helps support one of the team's reasons, you can attach the post-it note to that reason on your team's board. Sometimes evidence can support more than one reason. In this case, your scribe can make a second post-it copy of the evidence, so a copy can be attached to each reason.

Evaluating reasons supported by evidence

Now that your reasons have evidence attached to them, your team should go back and re-evaluate these reasons. Should they still have the same position on the board or should any of them be moved? Make any moves you agree on.

NOTE 2.8

Considering the alternative

Finally, as a team look overall at your position, its reasons and its evidence. How good a case do you make? Remember that while you have been building your case, the other team has been doing the same thing. In the next chapter, we encounter and begin to think about their case.

For now, spend a few minutes trying to anticipate what their reasons will be. Whatever they are, you are going to need to address them.

Teacher notes

2.1   There is much to be gained by allowing students to choose their own side of an issue, rather than be assigned to one (a practice more common in debate as practiced by high school and college debate teams). The thinking they are doing to support a position should be genuine, not an exercise. One practical objective is to achieve approximately equal-size teams taking each side of an issue. You can solicit initial opinions in a written straw poll, leaving a middle category of "undecided" as an option. Students selecting this option can then be asked to join the team with the smaller number of members. If an initial straw poll is too uneven, with a large majority choosing one side, you may wish to move to another topic. Another possibility is to reformulate the decision alternatives slightly in a way likely to draw more advocates of the less favored position and readminister the straw poll.

2.2   Materials for this phase: 3"×5" & 5"×7" index cards, small post-it notes of a chosen color to attach to them, and a board of some sort to display them on.

2.3   The objective is to insure reasons are expressed clearly enough to be understood by all and to be usable later on.

2.4   This activity is optional but can help to expand the reason set.

2.5   The objective is to encourage students' reflection on their reasons and their recognition that some may be stronger and thus more persuasive than others. Depending on group size, it can be done at the team level or initially in smaller groups.

2.6   The objective here is for students to become aware of the critical role of evidence and to become increasingly skilled in connecting it to their reason claims.

2.7   The rationale for the question-and-answer format is for students to anticipate the purpose of the information they obtain. You will be able to judge whether students are able to start off with questions of their own or need to first see such questions modeled by consulting the provided list. You will also be able to judge what help they need in securing answers to student-generated questions and what adult guidance to provide. They will also need to recognize that some of their questions are so broadly or vaguely expressed as to require reformulating before answers can be sought (e.g., "Do students like college?").

2.8   Time to complete these activities will vary greatly by students' skill and time available. Two to three class sessions allows the sequence in this chapter to be completed at a comfortable pace.

Chapter 3

■ ■ ■

Investigating the Alternative

NOTE 3.1

You're now ready for the next important step — hearing the ideas of others who don't agree with you on this topic. Work with one of the members of your team as a partner in this activity, so you can talk about what you're hearing from members of the other team. You and your partner will talk to pairs from the other team, one pair at a time. Your teacher can help to organize the rotation, to make sure that each pair on a team has talked to every pair on the other team.

Engaging the opposition

A useful way to share ideas with the opposing team is to have a conversation with them electronically — a "Chat" method you are likely already familiar with for talking to friends. This way, you will have a record in front of you of exactly what each of you said. You can then look back at it, rather than rely just on your memory. (If you don't have an electronic medium, you can do the same thing using a "Pass the Pad" method — one side writes what they have to say and then passes the pad to the other side to respond.)

NOTE 3.2

Even though it's electronic, you and your partner will be having a conversation with the other pair. The most important feature of a conversation — one that separates good ones from bad ones — is that in good conversations each side listens very carefully to the other side. But that is not all — in addition to listening to what they say, you need to respond to it. In the same way, you will want them to respond to what you say.

First turns

You can flip a coin to decide whether you or the pair from the other team will begin. If you begin, do so by stating your position and one of your best reasons along with any evidence you have to support it. The other pair should then respond by saying what they think of your reason. Since they don't agree with your position, they will likely say what they think is wrong with your reason and why it is not a good enough reason for choosing your position. What they should NOT do is to ignore what you have said and just state their own position and reason. Just saying one position is better doesn't make it so. The two positions and the reasons for each need to be **compared**.

Once the other pair has responded to what you have said, they may want to then introduce their own position and a reason (and evidence) for it.

Later turns

Now it is your turn again, and you will have two different things to do. First, and most important, you must respond to what the opposing pair has said about your position and reasons. If they have criticized it, do you have a **comeback** — a way of taking the sting out of their criticism by criticizing their criticism, also called refuting it? Maybe you think it doesn't apply, or doesn't make sense, or doesn't have evidence to support it. In other words, it doesn't really weaken your position. Or maybe for now you don't have such a comeback, which will make this an especially important criticism to remember and think about.

The second thing you have to do is to consider what the opposing pair has said about their own position and their reasons (and evidence). Do you have any criticism of these — any reasons as to why what they have said is not a good enough reason for choosing that position? Let them know that now.

For each of these tasks, take your time before responding and **talk it over** with your partner. Together you are likely to come up with better ideas on how to respond to the other pair than either of you would alone.

Continuing the conversation

You can now continue taking turns, being sure to do the things we have described during each of your turns. You can continue criticizing things the opposing pair say, as long as each side has criticisms to make and you are having a genuine **debate** — one that does not simply repeat what has already been said. Be sure always that you **only criticize ideas**, never the person who said them.

You can also introduce new reasons from the set your team has prepared, giving the other side something new to deal with.

Whether you are questioning what the opponents have said or introducing new points of your own, keep your communication brief. The opponents don't want to get a long essay from you that includes all sorts of different ideas. Make one point and then give them a chance to respond.

You may run out of time or run out of things to say, in which case it is time for the conversation to end. With practice in debating, you will likely find your conversations getting longer over time.

NOTE 3.3

Starting a new conversation

The next thing, most likely at a new time, will be for you and your partner to start a conversation with a different pair from the other team. Likely you will find that they have different things to say than the first pair, and you will have a new conversation going. Some of their ideas you may have already heard, but you are likely to hear new ones from each new pair you talk to, ones that need new responses from you.

Continuing to ask questions

As you and your partner are conversing with each of the opposing pairs, new questions are likely to occur to you that you would like answers to, in order to strengthen your arguments and question the opponents' arguments. A good time for you and your partner to do this is while you are waiting for the other pair to respond to what you last said. Does something they have said make you think of a new question you would like to have answered? You can also review the questions suggested with the topic and decide if you would like an answer to one of those. At first, your search for evidence was focused on information that could support your position. But now that you know more about the other side's position, perhaps you are wondering whether some of the claims they make are really correct — whether they have evidence to support them.

You can of course ask them this during the conversation. But you can also find out for yourself by asking questions and getting answers about matters that have to do with their side, not only your own. Think of your own questions or look again at the questions on the list for this topic. Before finding an answer, think about what the answer will mean. After you have an answer, and while waiting for your opponents to respond, you can talk about whether to add this evidence to one of the reasons on your board. Have your scribe write a short summary of it on a post-it note and you can always decide later.

NOTE 3.4

Reflecting

After you have had conversations with a few pairs from the other team, it will be a good time to start summing up. A good time for you and your partner to work on this summing up is while you are waiting for the other pair to respond to what you last said.

The reflection sheets that appear here you can use for this purpose. They are of two types, one having to do with your side and the other having to do with the other side. Take time with your partner to prepare separate reflection sheets for what you think to be each side's most important reasons. These are going to be helpful to you in what will come next.

NOTE 3.5

Team members _____
Date _____

Let's think...Starting with the other side's argument

One of the other side's MAIN ARGUMENTS was:

_____
_____
_____
_____

Our COUNTERARGUMENT against their argument was:

_____
_____
_____
_____

Give a specific example of an improved, more effective COUNTERARGUMENT.

_____
_____
_____
_____
_____

Team members _____
Date _____

Let's think...Starting with our argument

One of our MAIN ARGUMENTS was:
_____
_____
_____
_____

Their COUNTERARGUMENT against our argument was:
_____
_____
_____
_____

Our COMEBACK was:
_____
_____
_____
_____

How can this COMEBACK be improved? Is there a more effective comeback?
_____
_____
_____
_____

Teacher notes

3.1 This can be done easily by numbering each pair by team and number, e.g., A1, A2, A3, A4, A5, A6 and B1, B2, B3, B4, B5, and B6. Then make a 6×6 (or appropriate size, depending on number of pairs) grid with As across the top and Bs down the left. The boxes inside the grid can then be checked off as you announce the pairs who will converse that session, e.g., A1 with B1, etc. At the next session, move over one, so that A1 is with B2, A2 with B3 … A6 with B1, and check off the appropriate boxes.

3.2 Many different platforms can be used for this purpose. The simplest is a shared Google Doc document that the opposing pairs alternate adding to. You need only a secure electronic connection for this purpose, with no need for connection to the internet. Just remind students to save frequently. Similarly any device will serve as hardware, the simplest being inexpensive netbooks. Or the Pass-the-Pad method mentioned in the text can be used.

3.3 Do not be concerned if initial dialogs are produced slowly and are not rich in content. They improve quickly with experience. Remind partners to discuss and jointly decide on a response before entering and sending it.

3.4 Remind students at each dialog session to continue asking questions. If there is not time for them to discuss the answer to a question, this can wait until a later time. Encourage scribes, however, to get a short summary of it onto an evidence post-it note, so it doesn't get overlooked.

3.5 Materials: Multiple copies of the reflection sheets included in this chapter. The reflection sheets highlight a benefit of the electronic method. Students can now review and reflect on the conversation as a whole. The two forms shown can be alternated across dialog sessions. Remind students as necessary to work on the reflection sheets. They will be useful in the next phase.

Chapter 4

■ ■ ■

The Showdown

You and your partner have now had the chance to discuss this topic with all or most of your classmates whose position on this topic is opposite yours. Some of these discussions maybe went better than others and you likely learned more from some than others. Now it's time to do some summing up and to prepare for what will be the major event — what we can call the "Showdown." Both teams will come together as a whole group to argue face-to-face in favor of their decision as the better one compared to their opponents' choice.

To best do this, each team will need to be ready with all of their thinking about both their own position and about the other side's position. The first step, then, is to get ready for the Showdown.

NOTE 4.1

Preparing for the Showdown

You have already done a lot of work on your own position and reasons to support it, even though you may have discovered some new reasons or changed your thinking about old reasons after hearing what opposing team members thought of them. So let's start with the other major task — summing up the opposing team's reasons for their position and deciding how you are going to address them.

Other side's reasons. One way to do this is to get the other-side reasons up onto a posterboard in the same way you did with your own reasons. The **Reflection sheets** you prepared about their reasons will be helpful to you now. First in small groups and then as a whole team, have a leader ask for short versions of the other side's reasons that you heard during the dialogs and have on your Reflection sheets.

The scribe can then write each different short-version reason on a small index card to put on the **Other-side posterboard**. If you've been working in small groups, you'll need to repeat this activity as a whole team, getting all the reasons onto one board, so you can see exactly how many different reasons the other team has and what they are. (If you have duplicate cards with the same short-version reason, put the version that says it best on the board.) You also should add an evidence post-it note with any **evidence** you've seen for this reason.

NOTE 4.2

Countering the other side's reasons. But you're not finished. Look at each of the other-side reasons on the board and share ideas as to how you can best counter that reason, that is, identify problems with it that make it not a strong reason, that take away its power. (Is a claim it makes true? Is there evidence it is true? Does the claim lead directly to a conclusion in favor of the position?) This is where the work you did on your **Reflection sheets** during the conversations again can help you.

Discuss as a group and decide what your best counter is to each other-side reason on the board. Have your scribe write a short version of this counter on a post-it note and attach it to the reason. (Use a different color post-it than the color you used for evidence post-its.) You may decide you have two different counters that both help to weaken the other side's reasons. In this case, include both. Again, if you've been working in small groups, you'll need to repeat this activity as a whole team, considering all the possible counters and deciding on the best one or two.

Why is it important to do this? During the Showdown, the other team will be using these reasons to support their position. You will need to respond to them, on the spot. Having your counters organized and ready to respond to whatever reason they bring up will be a big help.

Own-side reasons. Once you are confident you have responses ready for all of the other-side's reasons, you can turn to the second part of preparing for the Showdown: Looking again at your Own-side reasons. Each of them is an argument you are making to support your team's position. You may want to rearrange them on your board if you've changed your mind about which ones are most important. Now you can ask: Which reasons will make our case best in the Showdown? These are the ones to focus on.

Other side's counters. But now you have another job. You have heard counters to your reasons in your conversations with pairs from the other team. Your Reflection sheets will help you to remember these. Remember, you may have heard more than one good counter of each of your main reasons — your arguments. Have your scribe write on a post-it note a short version of each counter that you think threatens your position and attach it to the reason. (Use a different color post-it than the color you used for evidence post-its and the same color you used for your counters to the other side. Then you'll recognize this color as the color of counters.) On the next page is a sketch of what you are working toward. Prepare one of these for each of the reasons you think you will use in the Showdown. Again, repeat this activity as a whole team if you need to.

At this point, now that you've considered criticisms of them, as a whole team you can talk over and decide which is your best argument, second best, and so on. You may want to rearrange your board to reflect any changes in your decisions about this. Or you may want to wait to do this until you've completed the last step, below, in order to judge how well you can save your reasons from the criticisms made against them.

Chapter 4 ■ The Showdown   23

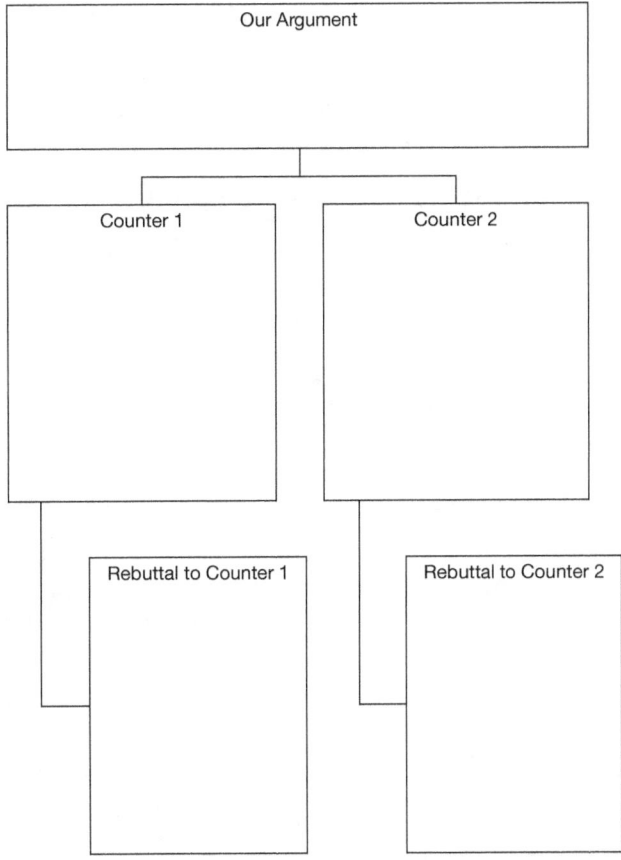

Comebacks (rebuttals). There's still one more step, shown in the lower part of the sketch above. Why do you want to know the other side's counters to your reasons? It's important because in the Showdown you are going to need to try to save your reason with a comeback. Think of a comeback as a criticism of a criticism, or an argument against an argument, also called a **rebuttal**. You have each of your side's reasons on the board, with the other side's main counters of each one attached. What can you say to each of these criticisms to take the power or "sting" out of it and save your argument?

Discuss this until everyone agrees what the best comeback will be to save this reason. Ask your scribe to write it on a post-it note (use a third color, so as not to confuse it with evidence post-its or counter post-its) and add that post-it to the bottom of the counter post-it that is already on your board.

NOTE 4.3

Review. This has been a lot of thinking work, but now you're finally ready for the Showdown. Go over your Own-side board and your Other-side board once more to be sure everything is organized. Your team will be able to have these with you during the Showdown. On the following page are pictures of how your two boards might look.

During the Showdown you will not have a partner with you as you take turns with your teammates debating face-to-face with a member of the other team. Your team members will be in the background, ready to help you if you need it. You should think now about which of your side's reasons you want to use first when it is your turn and you have the chance to introduce a new reason. Go over it in your mind to be sure you are ready with it, and remember the person you are talking to from the other team will likely criticize your reason, so you need to be ready with a comeback.

Photos. *Partially completed 'Our Arguments' and 'Their Arguments' boards illustrated for the sample topic of College v. Work First.*

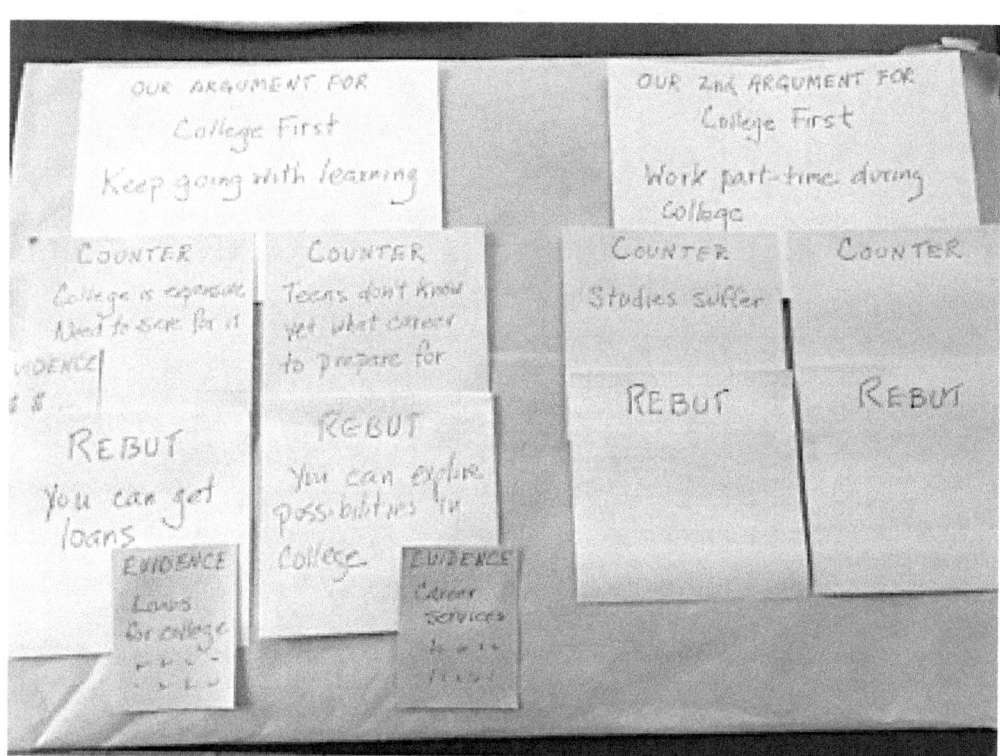

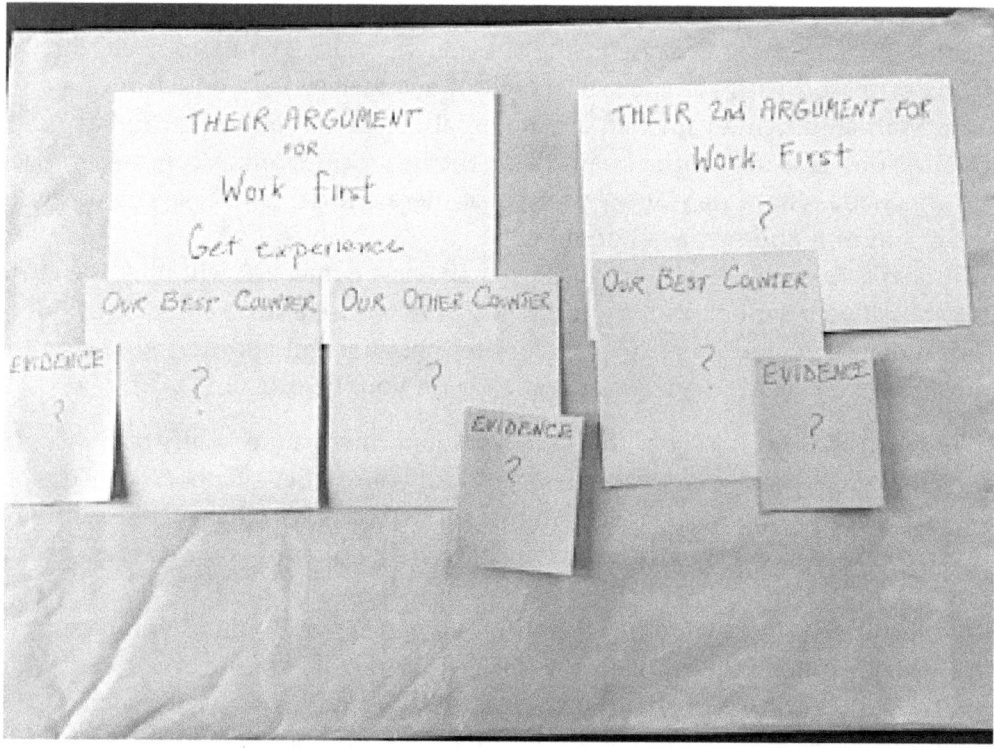

Conducting the Showdown

There are many ways to conduct a whole-class Showdown debate. The guidelines offered here you or your teacher may want to change in a few ways to best meet the needs of your class. Just go over the rules very carefully and be sure everyone agrees on them before you begin.

Each team should assemble on opposite sides of the room. Depending on group size, half the team members of each team can be the "on duty" team members. The other half will be the "advisory" group. Midway through the Showdown, the "on duty" group and the "advisory" group switch roles, so every team member gets the chance to be on duty. The advisory half of the team pays close attention to what is going on and takes notes on what is being said. If they have suggestions to make to help their on-duty teammates, they can deliver notes to them, but otherwise they don't speak.

Hot seats and hot tables. The "on duty" team members take turns going to the center of the room one at a time, where two "hot seats" are placed, and sitting in one of them. The team can decide in advance, or as they go along, the order in which they will take turns going to the hot seat. A member of the other "on duty" team takes their place in the other hot seat.

NOTE 4.4

The remaining on-duty members of each team sit at their own "hot table" (with their advisory teammates sitting at their own table behind them). Those seated at the hot table have the posterboards from their earlier work (one for own-side position reasons and one for other-side position reasons) displayed on the table in front of them, so they can refer to them. The team member who goes to the hot seat, however, does not take anything with them — only what is in their head.

Starting off. A coin can be tossed to decide who speaks first. When new people take their places in the hot seats, the other team gets to go first. The teams then alternate going first each time new people come to the hot seats.

Responding. Once a person in the hot seat has finished speaking, the person in the other hot seat has two tasks. One is to respond to what the opposing hot seat member has said. Do you accept it or do you have criticisms of it? Once you have responded to your satisfaction, you can bring up a new point of your own.

These tasks are much the same as the tasks you had in the electronic dialogs themselves. The only differences are that then only the other pair heard what you said and you had plenty of time to consult with your partner and think about what to say. Now you have to think faster and you have a bigger audience. But do not think you are entirely alone. Your whole team is there to help you, which they can do by calling huddles.

Huddles. Any member of the "on duty" half of a team is free to call a "huddle" whenever they think it would be helpful to consult with one another. The person in the hot seat may feel they are stuck for the moment about how best to respond to the opponent in the other hot seat and would like to have help. Or the on-duty members sitting at the hot table may think their teammate in the hot seat needs help and want to suggest something to say.

NOTE 4.5

In either case, the person wanting a huddle waits for the person speaking to finish their sentence and then calls out clearly, "Huddle." Then everything stops and the persons in both hot seats go back to their team's table to talk about strategy. When they are finished, the hot-seat speakers return to their hot seats, hopefully with some new ideas.

Timing. You will set rules in advance about the time everyone has to do their jobs. A suggestion is to allow three (3) minutes for a given pair to be in the Hot Seats. Someone needs to have a stopwatch and be a timekeeper. At the end of the time period, they should allow the person speaking to finish their sentence and then call "Time."

NOTE 4.6

When a huddle is called, the clock stops. It starts again only when both speakers have returned to their hot seats. A suggested time limit for huddles is one (1) minute. You may also want to impose a limit of one huddle per each set of speakers.

Hopefully, there will be time overall to continue the Showdown until every team member has had the opportunity to take a turn in the hot seat.

Reminder. See the box for a reminder of Do's and Don'ts.

DO	DON'T
✔ Speak slowly and clearly and loudly enough to be heard. If you can't be heard, what you say won't matter. ✔ Listen well to what is said. ✔ Address and counter what your opponent says. ✔ Take time to think about the best response before speaking. You do not gain an advantage simply because you respond quickly or loudly. ✔ Use only words to communicate, not facial expressions, laughter, or other sounds.	✘ Ignore what your opponent says. ✘ Fail to respond to your opponent while there is still time on the clock. ✘ Raise your voice at your opponent or fail to give them a chance to respond. ✘ Speak unless you are in the hot seat.

The most important DO is this: Do treat your opponent with respect. Criticize ideas, not people.

Reflecting on the Showdown

Wait until another day to reflect on the Showdown. An excellent way to do this is to view a video of it, a little at a time. In doing this, remember the guidelines above: Treat every person with respect. Criticize ideas, not people. Use only words to communicate. For each pair of speakers you view, you can evaluate whether each response was a strong one or a weak one. If weak, what would have been better? When you view your own turn, think about what you would do differently in another Showdown.

NOTE 4.7

You may have had a judge judging the teams' performance and assigning points for strong and weak moves. Or your teacher may have played this role and have feedback to give you. Whatever the ways in which you do it, this reflection is an opportunity for you to learn very important skills in thinking, communicating,

NOTE 4.8 and discussing. In the next chapter we turn to a final one — your taking a final position on the topic in writing.

Teacher notes

4.1 This task is conceptually demanding, so you want to motivate students by emphasizing that this hard work is necessary to be in the best possible position for their team to do well in the Showdown.

4.2 The value of this task is not simply a procedural one of eliminating duplicates and reducing the set to a core. Reflecting on whether two ideas are the same or different one is an excellent way to think deeply about them.

4.3 Materials: Small post-it notes of three different colors. Consistent colors for the different post-it functions (such as blue for evidence, pink for counters, and yellow for rebuttals) is a good idea so students will quickly come to recognize their function by their color.

4.4 Devoting one class session to the Showdown is typically sufficient time to allow most team members a turn in the hot seat. Teachers will decide whether the teams are able to organize an order of turns on their own or whether this needs to be arranged in advance with teacher assistance. Typically there are some students who are reluctant to take this role. They can be reminded they will have the support of their teammates (via the "Huddle" procedure) and may become less hesitant over time. It is not essential, however, that every student play this role.

4.5 Huddles are brief but likely noisy. A teacher may wish to suggest a huddle if a student in the hot seat appears to be struggling.

4.6 Time limits can be adjust to fit students' skill levels. Another possibility is to give a pair in the hot seat the option after two minutes of continuing for another minute or being replaced by a new pair.

4.7 Reflection is best done at a later session when students have a little distance from what they have just done. A supplement or alternative to viewing a video of brief excerpts from the Showdown is to provide students a written transcript of such excerpts. This facilitates their reflection. Teacher comments should be adjusted to fit the students' level of experience. For more formal scoring methods, see the teacher guidebook with accompanying video by Kuhn, Hemberger, & Khait, *Argue with me* (Routledge, 2016). These, however, should be employed flexibly to match students' level.

4.8 For topics in the Personal decision chapter, you will want to emphasize that it does not follow that the position of the stronger team is the position that is best for anyone, simply because one team made better arguments for it than the other team. It only highlights that anyone making this decision for themselves needs to consider all of the arguments made and weigh them for themselves.

Chapter 5

■ ■ ■

Sharing Your Thinking

You've finished the Showdown and spent some time reflecting on it. One or the other team may have been declared a winner if you had a judge who added and subtracted points for each side's strong and weak moves. In any case, whether or not one team was declared a winner, both sides expressed many important ideas and shared criticisms of these ideas. You, as an individual, may even have changed your views and come to a different conclusion about the topic than your earlier one. Whether your decision has stayed the same or changed, one thing is certain: You now have a lot more thinking underlying your decision than you did at the outset.

Before you leave this topic for now, there is one last important step to take. You can share your thinking with others who have not studied the topic and may want to make a decision about it. Your doing so will be helpful to them, but it will also benefit you. Pulling together all your thinking about the topic will make it clearer to you in your own mind just why you have come to the position you hold.

NOTE 5.1

A very good way people sometimes share their thinking about a topic important to them is by writing a short piece about it as a Letter to the Editor or an Op-Ed article that they submit to a newspaper, either a local one in their community or a national one. Or they can submit it to an on-line blog or website that shares ideas about life today. Here we suggest you write such a piece. Once you have worked carefully on it, gotten feedback, and revised it, you could submit it to one of these places. Or a school newspaper might be a good place. Get some advice about a good choice.   You can write your piece by yourself, to express entirely your own position. We suggest you try this first. Then you can try the more challenging task of writing jointly with a partner.

Transforming your thinking to writing. Beginners sometimes find hard putting their thoughts in writing on a blank page. But it needn't be if you have thought carefully and deeply about the topic, by yourself and especially in exchange with others, as you now have done. The thinking that gets exchanged between people can get transformed onto the page. Imagine as the reader of what you write one of your classmates from the opposing team. Just don't expect to get it exactly right first time. Write, then read what you have written. Think about how to say it better. Think about how it connects to what has come before and what should follow. Then write again, and repeat this process several times, looking at gradually bigger and bigger chunks of what you have written.

The box below gives you some specific guidelines.

The thinking:

Have you communicated strong, clear reasons in favor of your position? What is your evidence? Could someone argue against these reasons? Anticipate what they could say and include a response to it.

Have you addressed the other side's position? What arguments/reasons support their position? What evidence do they have? Can you challenge their position? Are their arguments as strong as yours? If not, why not?

Have you connected your points into an overall argument in which you weigh both sides and take a final position?

The writing:

Make it short but rich. Letters to the Editor cannot be long. Yours should be a maximum of 300 words. You may want to write more at first, then work at eliminating extra words and getting what you have to say into the fewest words you can, without losing any of your meaning.

Have you communicated clearly to your reader? Is each sentence written clearly enough to make sense to the reader? Does each sentence connect to both the previous one and the next one, to make a meaningful paragraph?

Include the date, the salutation (Dear Editor) and your signature, and print your name and the name of your school clearly.

Once you have finished your writing, read it over playing the role of someone reading it for the first time. You are likely to find changes you want to make. After you are satisfied with it, give it to someone else to read. See if they find it easy to understand and convincing. Based on their comments, you may want to do some more revising that will make your piece stronger.

Writing with a partner. If you go on to write a second piece with a partner, you have a good chance of making the piece you wrote even better. If you do this, however, do NOT choose the partner you worked with during the dialogs on this topic. Instead, take on the harder task of writing with a partner from the other team, one who reached a conclusion opposite yours.

This task may sound impossible, but it's not. The purpose and goal of what you write will just be somewhat different. Now you are not simply trying to make a case for the side you support. Instead, you are trying to introduce both sides of the issue to someone who is not familiar with it and thus has thought little about it. What you write will be useful to someone who is going to debate the topic (but we don't know which side they'll take).

To do this you need to work with your partner to lay out all the issues and reasons connected to the topic. You already have a lot of material to work with. What are the major reasons in favor of one side? What evidence supports them? What are their weaknesses (what counters to them are there?) Are there comebacks (rebuttals) that address these weaknesses?

Now answer the same questions for the other side. But both of you should work on both sides, making sure all reasons, evidence, counters, and rebuttals are stated clearly and fairly. Remember you must agree on everything you write. (One of you can't write one part and the other person write the other part.)

There is no one right way to organize what you write. For example, you may want to lay out all the reasons and evidence for one side, then all the reasons and evidence for the other side, before going on to counters and rebuttals for each. Or you may decide on a more back-and-forth structure of claims, counterarguments, and rebuttals. Don't forget to back up all claims with evidence.

Once you have finished your writing, and have read it over as a new reader would, ask others to read it and see if they find it clear and fair to both sides. Does it favor one side unfairly by not including all the negatives of that side and both positives and negatives of the other side? There may be still more changes you can make.

NOTE 5.4

Finally, think back to your initial decision about this topic. What was the thinking behind your decision then? What is it now? You will likely realize that a lot more is in your mind now.

Teacher notes

5.1 The materials students have produced from their preceding work on the topic should be available. Students may need to be reminded that these are only a resource. Emphasize that what they write needs to fit into an overall, connected argument. In some cases students will be able to do this final task as a homework assignment; in others it may lead to better work as an in-class activity.

5.2 The preceding collaborative work on the topic lays the groundwork for this more common activity of having students read one another's work. Now they are accustomed to peer feedback and evaluation and better able to appreciate its value.

5.3 Again, the preceding collaborative work on the topic lays the groundwork for this activity. However, it is best to undertake it only after the student has written an individual piece. An intermediate step of writing first with a same-side partner is a possibility.

5.4 See Chapter 11 for suggestions regarding teacher feedback and assessment of students' writing. Also useful may be Chapter 5 in the teacher guidebook by Kuhn, Hemberger, & Khait, *Argue with me* (Routledge, 2016).

Chapter 6

■ ■ ■

What is Good Evidence?

In working on the topics in this book, you have come to realize the importance of evidence. It begins simply as information and becomes evidence once you identify how it can serve to support or to weaken a specific claim. But all evidence is not equal. There are many different kinds of evidence. You have probably noticed that some of the evidence you identified seemed stronger, more convincing to you, than other evidence.

In this chapter, we explore different kinds of evidence and what makes some kinds stronger and more convincing than other kinds. We do this with the exercise that follows, the "**Yes, But**" challenge. Work on it with a partner.

Do Vaccinations Cause Learning Disabilities?

An online group is encouraging parents not to have their young children get injections of vaccines to protect them against diseases like polio and measles. The group says these shots can cause learning disabilities (LDs).

You have been asked by a medical society to write an article arguing that this claim is wrong and that the vaccines are NOT a cause of LDs. You do a lot of research for your article and you come across a lot of information that might support your position that the vaccines do NOT cause LDs. Your article must be a short one, however, so you can't use all the evidence you've found. In the space you have, you want to include only the best, strongest evidence. For each possible piece of evidence below, decide whether you will use it.

With your partner, look at each of the pieces of information about vaccinations and learning disabilities (LDs) that appear below, one at a time. Reach a **decision** with your partner about whether you should use this piece as evidence in your report: YES, NO, or MAYBE. (You'll have a chance to change your mind later.) Then answer the **question** following it: Is there a reason someone could give for not finding this evidence very convincing? What might this reason be?

After you and your partner have come up with the best possibilities you can, you then can check your answer against one that some careful questioners came up with.

34   Part Two ■ The Thinking Plan

To access these answers, open your internet browser to *www.axcessvids.com* (bookmarking it is a good idea so you'll have it easily available): enter the code shown next to your question.

Talk about the answer with your partner, see if you agree, and keep it in mind. Your discussion will help you decide whether this is good evidence. Then go on to the next piece of evidence and do the same things.

On a later occasion, do this exercise again with a different partner. See how much agreement you and this partner now have about the strength or weakness of each piece of evidence. And you can make a final decision about the evidence to use in a report. Finally, you may want to have a whole-class discussion to see if everyone agreed on the best evidence to use in the report.

Information about Vaccinations and Learning Disabilities: Is It Good Evidence?

1. Most infants and children in developed countries have vaccinations. Would you use this evidence? [*circle one*]

   YES   NO   MAYBE (*if nothing better was available*)

   Is there a reason someone could give for not finding this evidence very convincing? What might this reason be? Code 749d

2. A pediatrician who has cared for hundreds of children claims that the vaccines do not cause LD (learning disabilities). Would you use this evidence? [*circle one*]

   YES   NO   MAYBE

   Is there a reason someone could give for not finding this evidence very convincing? What might this reason be? Code 759d

3. Most children do not have LD. Would you use this evidence? [*circle one*]

   YES   NO   MAYBE

   Is there a reason someone could give for not finding this evidence very convincing? What might this reason be? Code 978d

4. A medical association states that the vaccines do not cause LD. Would you use this evidence? [*circle one*]

   YES   NO   MAYBE

   Is there a reason someone could give for not finding this evidence very convincing? What might this reason be? Code 413d

5. Some doctors say children's flu and fevers cause LD. Would you use this evidence? [*circle one*]

   YES   NO   MAYBE

   Is there a reason someone could give for not finding this evidence very convincing? What might this reason be? Code 962d

6. **Some scientists say lack of sleep causes LD. Would you use this evidence?** [*circle one*]

    YES   NO   MAYBE

    Is there a reason someone could give for not finding this evidence very convincing? What might this reason be? Code 113d

7. **Maybe it's not the vaccine itself that causes LD but the needles to inject them that break the skin and cause infection. Would you use this evidence?** [*circle one*]

    YES   NO   MAYBE

    Is there a reason someone could give for not finding this evidence very convincing? What might this reason be? Code 764d

8. **There exist several documented cases of children who had vaccinations and have LD. Would you use this evidence?** [*circle one*]

    YES   NO   MAYBE

    Is there a reason someone could give for not finding this evidence very convincing? What might this reason be? Code 525d

9. **There are many cases of children who had vaccinations and don't have LD. Would you use this evidence?** [*circle one*]

    YES   NO   MAYBE

    Is there a reason someone could give for not finding this evidence very convincing? What might this reason be? Code 442d

10. **Maybe it's not the vaccine itself that causes LD but giving the vaccine when the child is too young to withstand it. Would you use this evidence?** [*circle one*]

    YES   NO   MAYBE

    Is there a reason someone could give for not finding this evidence very convincing? What might this reason be? Code 170d

11. **There are many cases of children who had no vaccinations and do have LD. Would you use this evidence?** [*circle one*]

    YES   NO   MAYBE

    Is there a reason someone could give for not finding this evidence very convincing? What might this reason be? Code 453d

12. **In a study of 100 children who had vaccinations, 10 later had LD. Would you use this evidence?** [*circle one*]

    YES   NO   MAYBE

    Is there a reason someone could give for not finding this evidence very convincing? What might this reason be? Code 824d

13. **In a study of 50 children who did not have vaccinations, 5 later had LD. Would you use this evidence?** [*circle one*]

    YES NO MAYBE

    Is there a reason someone could give for not finding this evidence very convincing? What might this reason be? Code 434d

14. **In a study of 50 children who had vaccinations and 50 who didn't have vaccinations, 5 children in each group later had LD. Would you use this evidence?** [*circle one*]

    YES NO MAYBE

    Is there a reason someone could give for not finding this evidence very convincing? What might this reason be? Code 423d

15. **In a study of 1000 children who had vaccinations and 1000 who didn't have vaccinations, 98 children in each group later had LD. Would you use this evidence?** [*circle one*]

    YES NO MAYBE

    Is there a reason someone could give for not finding this evidence very convincing? What might this reason be? Code 761d

Only the above statements and questions appear in the student text. The following list of model answers appears only in the Teachers' Edition.

1. Most infants and children in developed countries have vaccinations.
   YES BUT *That doesn't tell us whether the vaccinations cause LD.*

2. A well-known pediatrician claims that the vaccines do not cause LD (learning disabilities).
   YES BUT *This is only one doctor's opinion. How does he know?*

3. Most children do not have LD.
   YES BUT *That doesn't tell us whether vaccinations cause LD.*

4. A medical association states that the vaccines do not cause LD.
   YES BUT *They haven't said how they know this. They could be wrong.*

5. Some doctors say children's flu and fevers cause LD.
   YES BUT *Vaccines could still also cause LD.*

6. Some scientists say lack of sleep causes LD.
   YES BUT *Vaccines could still also cause LD.*

7. Maybe it's not the vaccine itself that causes LD but the needles to inject them that break the skin and cause infection.
   YES BUT *You don't know if this is correct unless you try giving it a different way.*

8. There exist several documented cases of children who had vaccinations and have LD.
   YES BUT *Something else may have caused their LD.*

9. There are many cases of children who had vaccinations and don't have LD.
   YES BUT *Many children who had vaccinations do have LD.*

10. Maybe it's not the vaccine itself that causes LD but giving the vaccine when the child is too young to withstand it.
    YES BUT You don't know if this is correct unless you try giving it at a later age.

11. There are many cases of children who had no vaccinations and do have LD.
    YES BUT Many children who had vaccinations do have LD.

12. In a study of 100 children who had vaccinations, 10 later had LD.
    YES BUT You don't know if the vaccination caused their LD.

13. In a study of 50 children who did not have vaccinations, 5 later had LD.
    YES BUT You don't know how this compares to children who did have vaccinations.

14. In a study of 50 children who had vaccinations and 50 who didn't have vaccinations, 5 children in each group later had LD.
    YES BUT That's not enough children to be sure. It could be different for others.

15. In a study of 1000 children who had vaccinations and 1000 who didn't have vaccinations, 98 children in each group later had LD.
    That's impressive evidence. Let me think about that.

Another Evidence Challenge: Smoking and Cancer

If you did well in identifying the "Yes, Buts" that leave some kinds of evidence open to criticism, you're ready for a new challenge task. It appears below.

Does Smoking Cause Cancer?

You have been asked by a medical society to write an article challenging the claim made by The League of Tobacco Growers that smoking does not cause cancer. They say they have a lot of evidence that supports their position. For each piece of evidence can you challenge it with a **YES BUT** that questions how good that evidence really is?

1. Many people of all ages smoke.
   YES BUT...

2. A doctor who has practiced for many years says there is no certain link between smoking and cancer.
   YES BUT...

3. Most people never develop cancer.
   YES BUT...

4. A large, successful tobacco company has challenged the connection between smoking and cancer.
   YES BUT...

5. Some doctors say environmental toxins are a major cause of cancer.
   YES BUT...

6. Some scientists say poor diet causes cancer.
   YES BUT...

7. Maybe it's not what's in cigarettes that causes cancer but the paper they're wrapped in.
   YES BUT...

8. Several verified cases exist of heavy smokers who developed cancer.
   YES BUT...

9. There are many cases of heavy smokers who never developed cancer.
   YES BUT...

10. Maybe it's not smoking itself that causes cancer but just smoking too much.
    YES BUT...

11. There are many cases of people who have lung cancer but never smoked.
    YES BUT...

12. In a study of 50 smokers, 5 later developed lung cancer.
    YES BUT...

13. In a study of 100 non-smokers, only 10 later developed cancer.
    YES BUT...

Finally, describe the study you would do to settle the matter.

Summing Up

After you and a partner have completed this task, have a class discussion about the features of evidence that make it strong or weak, whatever the particular topic. Here are some categories to look for, in the common case in which the claim is that A causes B.

There is an explanation of how A could cause B.
Many people say A definitely causes B.
An expert says that A definitely causes B
A is rare.
A is frequent.
B is rare.
B is frequent.
There are cases of A occurring along with B.
There are cases of A being absent and B also absent.
There are cases of A occurring without B.
There are cases of B occurring without A.
In cases of A, B occurs a certain percentage of the time.
C can cause B.
B occurs more often when A is present than when it is absent.

None of these findings tells us with certainty that A causes B. The last one comes closest, but even it doesn't provide absolute proof. Something else — a C — could also be present along with A and be the real cause. Sometimes experiments can be done (by removing all the possible Cs), but many times this isn't possible. The conclusion: Causality is hard to prove, and we need to be cautious and not draw quick conclusions.

Of course, not all claims are about cause and effect. But a great many are, and thinking about evidence for them will give you practice in thinking carefully about evidence.

Answers for smoking scenario.

1. **YES BUT** That doesn't tell us whether smoking causes cancer.
2. **YES BUT** This is only one doctor's opinion. How does he know?
3. **YES BUT** That doesn't tell us whether smoking causes cancer.
4. **YES BUT** They haven't said how they know this. They could be wrong.
5. **YES BUT** Smoking could also cause cancer.
6. **YES BUT** Smoking could also cause cancer.
7. **YES BUT** You don't know if this is correct unless you try a different wrapping.
8. **YES BUT** Something else may have caused their cancer.
9. **YES BUT** There are many cases of heavy smokers who do get cancer.
10. **YES BUT** You don't know if this is correct unless you also study light smokers.
11. **YES BUT** Many smokers get cancer; non-smokers' cancer could have another cause.
12. **YES BUT** You don't know what caused it; you need to compare to non-smokers.
13. **YES BUT** You don't know why; you need to compare to smokers.

Final Q: To settle the matter you need to compare cancer frequencies in similar groups of smokers and non-smokers.

Part Three

■ ■ ■

The Decision Topics

Decisions &

Questions to Answer

Chapter 7

■ ■ ■

A Personal Future

In this and the next three chapters, we go back to each of the topics suggested in Chapter 1. For each, some possible questions are suggested that you might want to ask. Their answers may be helpful to you as evidence to support (or weaken) one position or the other on this topic. In this chapter, we begin with the Personal topics, in Chapter 8 the Community topics, in Chapter 9 the National topics, and in Chapter 10 the World topics. You along with your classmates will decide which topics to work on and in what order. There is no single right order to work on them. You may want to start with those closest to your own life, or you may want to jump right in to topics that affect the whole world.

For each topic, the questions listed in the chapter are certainly not the only ones to ask, but they are a beginning. You will think of questions of your own to ask and make a note of these. You can gradually add more as they occur to you and then get help in finding answers.

For each question you want to ask, whether your own or a suggested one, first think about how the answer will help you. How will you be able to use this information? How can you make it work for you as **evidence** that will support (or weaken) a position on the topic. This is the question you will need to ask first about your chosen question, before searching for an answer to it. Once you have an answer to a question, you will need to think about how good it is as evidence and indeed whether it is even evidence at all. At some point you will want to spend time on Chapter 6, which will help you think about what makes good evidence.

The internet is one place to look for answers to your own questions, but keep in mind that not everything you find on the internet is true. In fact, most of what you find there are claims without any evidence at all, and these claims often contradict one another. So you must think carefully about any statements you find, who made them and why, and what evidence exists that they are correct.

Of the suggested questions, how do you know which ones to ask first? There is no one right answer. For each question you consider, just think first about how an answer may become something you can use as evidence. Once you have the answer, if it seems useful, you can write a short version of it on an evidence post-it that you will be able to attach to a reason and perhaps use later.

44   Part Three ■ The Decision Topics

Finally, remember it is as important to ask questions about the other side's position as it is about your position. If you want to show that your position is the better one, the only way to do that is to compare them. And the only way to do that is to know a lot about each of them.

So, you're ready to get started. In the rest of this chapter are topics and questions you might ask about them, having to do with your personal future. Once you have chosen one, go to the page it appears on. Then you can begin the activities described in Chapters 2-5.

When you are ready to ask one of the questions listed with the topic, first think about your question by answering the question below it (How can you make use of this information in your argument?). **Then open your internet browser to *www.axcessvids.com* (bookmarking it is a good idea so you'll have it easily available): enter the code shown next to your question, and you will find an answer (one based on the best available evidence at this time), along with internet sources for further information (verified at publication time). Think again about how you might use this answer and keep a note of the question and answer so you'll be able to use it later.**

Here again is a list of possible topics to choose from about a personal future:

> **DECISION. College v. work first.** When you finish high school, you have the choice of going right to college or of working for a few years first. (p. 46)
>
> **DECISION. Effort.** You are very good in one school subject and don't do well in another. Should you put most time and effort in being at the top of the class in your good subject or in getting better in your poor subject? (p. 48)
>
> **DECISION. Co-ed v. single-sex school.** You are starting at a new school this year and you have the choice of attending a single-sex school or a school attended by both boys and girls. (p. 51)
>
> **DECISION. Course choice: Foreign language or elective.** Your school gives you the choice of studying a foreign language or taking one of many other electives of special interest to you (such as dance, a sport, a musical instrument). (p. 54)
>
> **DECISION. After-school activity: School work or volunteer.** Your school gives you two choices for an activity during the last period of the day: Attend study hall to do homework and get extra help or Volunteer at a nearby community center to help poor children and the elderly. (p. 58)
>
> **DECISION. After-school job.** You have been offered a job in a store evenings from 5 to 9 pm. Should you take the job? (p. 61)
>
> **DECISION. Exercise: Team or individual.** Your school has sports teams that require daily practice after school and Saturdays. Or you can exercise on your own and do different things after school. (p. 65)
>
> **DECISION. Summer activity.** You have the choice of a summer job or a sports camp. (p. 69)
>
> **DECISION. Nutrition.** You like soda and think it's okay to have a couple a day as long as you have a good diet overall. Or you can decide soda does nothing good for you and it's best to avoid it. (p. 73)
>
> **DECISION. Alcohol.** You have an opportunity to try an alcoholic drink to know what it's like. Or you decide it's safest to avoid alcohol entirely and not risk starting with it. (p. 76)
>
> **DECISION. Spend or save.** You have received an unexpected gift of money from a relative. You have the choice of spending it or saving it. (p. 79)

Only the questions appear in the student edition. Students select a question, respond to the preliminary question about it (How can you make use of this information in your argument?), and then access an answer electronically. These answers and sources are printed for convenience only in this teachers' edition. (See Chapter 11 for an explanation of the symbol in parentheses following each answer.)

DECISION. College v. work first. *When you finish high school, you have the choice of going right to college or of working for a few years first.*

Questions about College

1. Is college expensive? Code 307d
2. Do most families have enough saved to pay for college? 792d
3. Do most good jobs require college? 510d
4. Do college graduates earn good salaries? 865d
5. Do most teens know what career they want to prepare for in college? 483d
6. Do teens benefit from living away from home? Code 123d

Questions about Work

7. Can new high school graduates find jobs? 200d
8. Do new high school graduates' jobs pay well? 352d
9. Can high school graduates fail to find jobs? 804d
10. Do teens enjoy working? 372d
11. If teens work first, do they go to college later? 565d
12. What do teens do with money they earn? 903d

Add questions of your own:

13. _____

14. _____

15. _____

Questions about College

1. Is college expensive?
Yes and getting more so. In the US, a few community colleges offer free courses but most charge tuition from $10,000 to more than $30,000 per year. [C–]

https://www.nytimes.com/2015/09/13/magazine/is-college-tuition-too-high.html

2. Do most families have enough saved to pay for college?
In 2015, only 45% of US parents with children under age 18 saved for college. More than half of the parents said they don't have enough money to save for college. [C–]

http://news.salliemae.com/sites/salliemae.newshq.businesswire.com/files/doc_library/file/HowAmericaSaves2015_FINAL.pdf

3. Do most good jobs require college?

Yes. It is estimated that by year 2020, 35% of all jobs will require at least college education. High paying jobs such as those in science and engineering always require at least a college degree. [C+]

https://cew.georgetown.edu/wp-content/uploads/2014/11/Recovery2020.ES_.Web_.pdf

4. Do college graduates earn good salaries?

Yes. In cumulative earnings over an entire career, the typical bachelor's degree graduate worker earns $1.19 million, which is twice what the typical high school graduate earns. [C+]

http://www.hamiltonproject.org/papers

5. Do most teens know what career they want to prepare for in college?

Some do but many teens are uncertain about what careers they want to pursue and many change their minds. A Pennsylvania study found that one third of teens had the same career goals at age 14-15 and when asked again at age 17-18. The other two thirds had changed their minds. [C–]

https://edsource.org/2015/survey-most-high-school-students-feel-unprepared-for-college-careers/83752

6. Do teens benefit from living away from home?

It is expensive to live away from home, and teens find it hard to pay for their own housing and food. But if they do live away from home, teens may become more independent and able to take care of themselves. Studies conducted by Harvard University researchers have shown teens also hear new ideas and form their own opinions, often different from their parents' beliefs, while at college. [C+]

http://social.eli.ubc.ca/2013/02/06/advantages-and-disadvantages-of-living-away-from-home

Questions about Work

7. Can new high school graduates find jobs?

Unemployment is high among high school graduates but usually they can find a job working in retail stores such as Costco, Whole Foods market, or Starbucks. [W+]

http://www.epi.org/publication/the-class-of-2015/

8. Do new high school graduates' jobs pay well?

Usually not. Only 8% of workers who have just a high school diploma earn more than $100,000 per year. The average salary is $30,000 per year. A fast-food server job pays under $10 per hour and as low as $7 per hour in the USA. [W–]

http://work.chron.com/comparison-level-education-salary-6533.html

http://learn.org/articles/Fast_Food_Worker

9. Can high school graduates fail to find jobs?

Yes. The unemployment rate among high school graduates is about 10%. [W–]

http://work.chron.com/comparison-level-education-salary-6533.html

10. Do teens enjoy working?

Working teens report high rates of satisfaction with their jobs. [W+]

https://www.ncbi.nlm.nih.gov/pmc/articles/PMC2936460/

11. If teens work first, do they go to college later?

Some do but others don't, especially if they have good job opportunities. Economists note that when there are more jobs, people are less likely to go to college. A study by the National Center for Education Statistics found that students who postponed college for one year were less likely to enroll or to get a college degree than those who went right to college. [W–]

https://nces.ed.gov/pubs90/90346_1.pdf

12. What do teens do with money they earn?
Research has shown that teens mostly spend money they earn on personal items and activities. Some help their families. However, some of them save part of the money for later education. [W+]

https://www.ncbi.nlm.nih.gov/pmc/articles/PMC2936460/

DECISION. Effort. *You are very good in one school subject and don't do well in another. Should you put most time and effort in being at the top of the class in your good subject or in getting better in your poor subject?*

Questions about Most effort in strong subject

1. How long does it take to become an expert in a subject? Code 500d
2. Does high achievement in school raise self-esteem? 102d
3. Are students who excel in one subject more likely to get scholarships than students who are good, but not excellent, in all subjects? 644d
4. Do different students have different types of intelligences? 688d
5. What happens when students set goals based on comparing themselves to others? 896d
6. What can happen when people devote all their time to one activity? 923d

Questions about Most effort in weak subject

7. How do colleges judge grades in admitting students? 537d
8. Do people try harder when they don't do well at something? 579d
9. Is perseverance related to success? 686d
10. What is a growth mindset and how can it affect learning? 983d
11. What happens when students are praised for their effort? 549d
12. What happens when students set goals for their learning? 111d
13. Does fear of failure influence what people do? 882d
14. Does failure always motivate people to succeed? 150d
15. Does perseverance guarantee success? 379d
16. How does failure affect self-esteem? 341d

Add questions of your own:

17. _____

18. _____

19. _____

Questions about Most effort in strong subject

1. How long does it take to become an expert in a subject?
Research shows that it takes about 10,000 hours, or approximately 10 years of intense practice, to become an expert in a subject (for example, math). [S+]

http://projects.ict.usc.edu/itw/gel/EricssonDeliberatePracticePR93.pdf

2. Does high achievement in school raise a student's self-esteem?
Research shows that doing very well in school may increase the self-esteem of a student, making them feel more positive about themselves. [S+]

http://www.ricklavoie.com/Self-esteem.pdf

3. Are students who excel in one subject more likely to get scholarships than students who are good, but not excellent, in all subjects?
In the US, there are many scholarships for students who are exceptional in a specific academic area. For example, the Caroline D. Bradley Scholarship for Exceptional Children is awarded to students who score in the 97th percentile or above in at least one major academic area and exhibit a passion for learning. [S+]

http://www.top10onlinecolleges.org/scholarships-for/gifted-students/

4. Do different students have different types of intelligences?
According to Psychologist Howard Gardner, there are 9 different types of intelligences and different people have different combinations of intelligences. For example, one person can be very strong in logical-mathematical intelligence but weak in verbal-linguistic intelligence. [S+]

https://www.edutopia.org/multiple-intelligences-research

5. What happens when students set their goals based on comparing themselves to others?
Students who set goals by comparing themselves to others may avoid taking risks so as not to risk losing their standing. [S–]

http://psycnet.apa.org/journals/psp/54/1/5/

6. What can happen when people devote all their time to one activity?
Some people who focus on one subject might miss out on exploring others they might enjoy. The desire to be at the "top" has also been connected to depression, anxiety, and academic dishonesty. [S–]

http://onlinelibrary.wiley.com/doi/10.1111/j.1542-734X.2007.00499.x/full

Questions about Most effort in weak subject

7. How do colleges judge grades in admitting students?
According to the National Association for College Admission Counseling (NACAC), having good grades in all courses is among the most important factors that colleges consider when evaluating applicants. [W+]

http://www.collegedata.com/cs/content/content_getinarticle_tmpl.jhtml?articleId=10045

8. Do people try harder when they don't do well at something?
Research shows that because harder tasks require more effort, people will try harder up to a certain point to complete a hard task. [W+]

http://www.psych.nyu.edu/gollwitzer/96BrunGoll_Failure.pdf

9. Is perseverance related to success?
Research has suggested that perseverance, or continuing to try despite failures, may be the most important factor in success. [W+]

http://www.abc.net.au/radionational/programs/bigideas/the-power-of-grit-why-hard-work-is-more-important-than-talent/7641876

10. What is a growth mindset and how can it affect learning?
People with a growth mindset believe they can improve their performance by putting in effort. They welcome challenges because they see failure as an opportunity to grow and learn from experience. [W+]

https://www.fastcompany.com/3039181/why-determination-matters-more-than-smarts-in-getting-ahead

11. What happens when students are praised for their effort?
Students who are praised for their effort believe they have control over their results and that they can improve over time. [W+]

https://www.aft.org//sites/default/files/periodicals/PraiseSpring99.pdf

12. What happens when students set goals for their learning?
When students set goals based on what they will learn, they are more likely to seek challenges and see failure as a step toward mastery. [W+]

http://psycnet.apa.org/journals/psp/54/1/5/

13. Does fear of failure influence what people do?
Some people who are afraid of failing miss out on activities they might enjoy. [W+]

https://www.fastcompany.com/3039181/why-determination-matters-more-than-smarts-in-getting-ahead

14. Does failure always motivate people to succeed?
Failure does not always motivate people to succeed. If a person believes ability is fixed, failure may cause them to put forth less effort and even give up. [W–]

http://is.muni.cz/el/1451/podzim2009/bp979/um/ElliotDweck2005HandbookOfCompetenceAndMotivation1.pdf#page=71

15. Does perseverance guarantee success?
Perseverance may be very important to success, but psychologists say it is only part of the equation. A person must also have passion for what they do to be good at it. [W–]

http://www.abc.net.au/radionational/programs/bigideas/the-power-of-grit-why-hard-work-is-more-important-than-talent/7641876

16. How does failure affect self-esteem?
One study found that students experiencing failure scored lower on self-esteem tests. [W–]

http://onlinelibrary.wiley.com/doi/10.1080/00049537908254643/abstract

DECISION. Co-ed v. single-sex school. *You are starting at a new school this year and you have the choice of attending a single-sex school or a school attended by both boys and girls.*

Questions about Single-sex schooling

1. Does the presence of the other gender affect academic performance? Code 626d
2. Do students in single-sex and co-ed schools take different classes? 244d
3. Do girls' and boys' brains develop differently? 893d
4. Do single-sex schools reduce gender stereotypes about males and females? 124d
5. Are students academically more successful at single-sex schools? 266d
6. What is the effect on students of spending time with same-sex members only? 712d
7. What happens to transgender students in single-sex schools? 840d
8. Are there many single-sex colleges? 627d
9. Does limited contact with the opposite sex lead to not coping well with relations with the opposite sex in later life? 879d
10. Do differences in boys' and girls' brains cause them to learn differently? 938d

Questions about Co-ed schooling

11. Do young people need to be prepared to interact successfully with both sexes? 363d
12. Do students perform better academically at co-ed or single-sex schools? 382d
13. What is the ratio of single-sex high schools to co-ed schools? 155d
14. Do boys and girls show different math and science outcomes in single-sex vs. co-ed schools? 892d
15. How might boys and girls benefit from studying together? 540d
16. Do boys and girls behave differently in school? 367d
17. Do co-ed schools affect esteem? 368d
18. Are there physical differences in boys' and girls' development? 268d
19. Are students more distracted in co-ed schools? 706d

Add questions of your own:

20. _____

21. _____

22. _____

Questions about Single-sex schooling

1. Does the presence of the other gender affect academic performance?
One study in Korea found that peer gender affected boys' academic performance but not girls', as measured by standardized tests in reading, math, English, social studies, and science. Boys in single-sex schools outperformed boys in co-ed schools in every subject. [S+]

http://econ.tulane.edu/seminars/Lee_Gender.pdf

2. Do students in single-sex and co-ed schools take different classes?
Girls in single-sex schools are more likely to take math and science courses (often considered "boys' subjects") than are girls in co-ed schools. Boys in single-sex schools are more likely to take art, music, drama, and foreign language classes (often considered "girls' subjects") than are boys in co-ed schools. [S+]

http://www.singlesexschools.org/research-singlesexvscoed.htm

3. Do girls' and boys' brains develop differently?
Research shows that there are brain differences in development in the early years. According to one study, different parts of the brain develop in different ways and at different times in girls than in boys. Girls' brains process visual information and language earlier than boys, raising the possibility that they need different kinds of instruction. [S+]

http://www.apa.org/monitor/2011/02/coed.aspx

4. Do single-sex schools reduce gender stereotypes about males and females?
In one study, students attended either a single-sex or co-ed science class. At the end of the year, girls in the single-sex classes were less likely to agree with the common stereotype that "physics is for boys." [S+]

http://onlinelibrary.wiley.com/doi/10.1348/000709907X215938/abstract

5. Are students academically more successful at single-sex schools?
One study found that students in single-sex classes scored better than their peers in co-ed classes on a standardized test. Both boys and girls in single-sex schools were also found to be more likely to attend four-year college than their peers in co-ed schools. [S+]

http://www.singlesexschools.org/research-singlesexvscoed.htm

6. What is the effect on students of spending time with same-sex members only?
Research shows that separating children by sex leads to differences in the development of social skills and preferences between boys and girls. The study's authors say that this may make it harder for children to interact well with the opposite sex. [S–]

http://www.apa.org/monitor/julaug01/peerplay.aspx

7. What happens to transgender students in single-sex schools?
The US Department of Education aims to protect transgender students in public schools from discrimination. In recent times, single-sex private schools in the US have begun to create policies regarding transgender students as well. Some schools handle the issue on a case-by-case basis and many say that they will accept students who identify as the gender of the same-sex school. [S+]

http://www.losfelizledger.com/article/local-single-sex-schools-creating-transgender-policies/

8. Are there many single-sex colleges?
In 2016, of 7000 colleges in the US, there were 39 all-female colleges and very few all-male colleges. [S–]

https://www.insidehighered.com/quicktakes/2015/12/09/college-new-rochelle-goes-completely-coed

https://nces.ed.gov/fastfacts/display.asp?id=84

9. Does limited contact with the opposite sex lead to not coping well with relations with the opposite sex in later life?
Researchers say that separating students by gender can lead to gender discrimination and make it harder for students to deal with the opposite sex later in life. This happens because they don't have experience interacting with the other sex as equals in school. [S–]

http://www.apa.org/monitor/2011/02/coed.aspx

10. Do differences in boys' and girls' brains cause them to learn differently?
Many studies have been done, but there is not enough evidence to show that brain differences between boys and girls affect individual learning. [S–]

http://www.apa.org/monitor/2011/02/coed.aspx

Questions about Co-ed schooling

11. Do young people need to be prepared to interact successfully with both sexes?
Co-ed schools are similar to the real world, where students will interact with both sexes. There are few contexts in the US and many other countries in which the genders are separated. In a vast majority of colleges and jobs, individuals interact with both males and females. [C+]

http://www.apa.org/monitor/2011/02/coed.aspx

12. Do students perform better academically at co-ed or single-sex schools?
There are mixed findings regarding whether single-sex classes improve grades, test scores, or college acceptance rates. Researchers found that in the US, evidence showing higher academic achievement in single-sex schools is not substantial. [C+]

http://www.apa.org/monitor/2011/02/coed.aspx

https://phys.org/news/2014-02-single-sex-advantage-coed-schools.html

13. What is the ratio of single-sex high schools to co-ed schools?
In the US, less than 100 public schools are single-sex, but around 500 co-ed public schools offer single-sex classes. However, in many other countries, particularly Muslim countries, single-sex education is the norm. [C+]

http://www.apa.org/monitor/2011/02/coed.aspx

https://www.researchgate.net/publication/233036889_Single-sex_or_Co-educational_Learning_Experiences_Views_and_Reflections_of_Canadian_Muslim_Women

14. Do boys and girls show different math and science outcomes in single-sex vs. co-ed schools?
Studies shows that girls in co-ed schools perform as well as boys in math and science. These studies show that the quality of teaching, school resources, and student motivation are more important for math and science success than the gender makeup of the class. [C+]

https://www.oecd.org/pisa/pisaproducts/42843625.pdf

15. How might boys and girls benefit from studying together?
Co-ed schools provide a structured environment for boys and girls to interact with each other. Research shows that students who interact with more diverse individuals are better prepared to work with others who are different from them. [C+]

http://www.apa.org/monitor/2011/02/coed.aspx

16. Do boys and girls behave differently in school?
Boys and girls show differences in how they act, how they learn, and their abilities and interests. Although the evidence is inconsistent, boys tend to be more physically active, whereas girls find it easier to sit still in a quiet environment. [C–]

https://www.washingtonparent.com/articles/1302/coed-vs-single-sex-schools.php

17. Do co-ed schools affect self-esteem?
One study found that girls who attend co-ed schools are more likely to be more concerned about their bodies and have more self-esteem issues than girls at single-sex schools. [C–]

http://www.sec-ed.co.uk/news/self-esteem-problems-more-likely-for-girls-in-mixed-school-environments/

18. Are there physical differences in boys' and girls' development?
There are physical differences in boys' and girls' development starting at the end of elementary school, when girls are generally taller than boys. Girls also enter puberty about a year before boys do. [C–]

http://www.babycenter.com/0_raising-boys-and-girls-differences-in-development_3659011.bc

19. Are students more distracted in co-ed schools?
Many teachers have observed that girls in single-sex schools seem more focused on academics than on other common teenage concerns such as social life and appearance. Little formal research has been conducted to test this observation. [C–]

http://www.apa.org/monitor/2011/02/coed.aspx

DECISION. Course choice: Foreign language or elective. *Your school gives you the choice of studying a foreign language or taking one of many other electives of special interest to you (such as dance, a sport, a musical instrument).*

Questions about Foreign language

1. Does studying a foreign language affect school performance? Code 814d
2. Does studying a foreign language affect the brain? 784d
3. Does learning a foreign language affect attitudes and beliefs about other cultures? 682d
4. How does knowing a foreign language affect job opportunities? 390d
5. How does learning a foreign language affect social life? 766d
6. Do colleges require foreign language for admission? 517d
7. Is language learning more difficult at some ages than others? 645d
8. Are people who learned a language in high school still able to speak that language later in life? 785d
9. How many jobs require people to know more than one language? 614d
10. Do employees who speak multiple languages earn more? 721d
11. Is learning in a classroom an effective way to learn a language? 687d

Questions about Electives

12. How are electives different from regular classes? 616d
13. Do elective courses give students a chance to study things they are especially interested in? 519d
14. Do elective courses have an effect on school performance? 834d

15. Do elective courses have an effect on academic test performance? 380d
16. How do college admission officers regard electives? 898d
17. How can taking an elective be beneficial outside of school? 471d
18. Do students continue studying the subjects they took as electives? 428d
19. Does taking electives mean students take fewer core academic classes? 715d
20. Do students have equal opportunity to take elective courses? 468d
21. Are there gender imbalances in elective courses? 924d
22. Do students work hard and learn a lot in elective courses? 868d
23. What happens when only a few students are interested in an elective? 643d
24. What happens when many students are interested in the same elective? 511d

Add questions of your own:

25. _____

26. _____

27. _____

Questions about Foreign language

1. Does studying a foreign language affect school performance?
Studies have shown that students who learn a foreign language earn higher scores on standardized tests and show higher academic performance. [FL+]

https://www.actfl.org/advocacy/what-the-research-shows/studies-supporting

2. Does studying a foreign language affect the brain?
Research has shown relations between foreign language learning and cognitive skills such as memory, problem solving, attention, and intelligence. [FL+]

https://www.actfl.org/advocacy/what-the-research-shows/studies-supporting

3. Does learning a foreign language affect attitudes and beliefs about other cultures?
Research shows that people who learn a foreign language develop more positive attitudes toward that language and the people who speak it. [FL+]

https://www.actfl.org/advocacy/what-the-research-shows/studies-supporting

4. How does knowing a foreign language affect job opportunities?
Because today's world is increasingly multicultural, job candidates with foreign language skills are more likely to be hired, even if the language has nothing to do with the job. [FL+]

https://www.education.com/magazine/article/learning-a-second-language/

5. How does learning a foreign language affect social life?
Learning a second language may open up social opportunities. According to one poll, speaking a second language makes people appear more worldly, intelligent, and friendly than English-only speakers. [FL+]

https://www.education.com/magazine/article/learning-a-second-language/

6. Do colleges require foreign language for admission?
Many US colleges require that applicants have taken 2 or more years of a foreign language course. Some selective colleges prefer more than 2 years, while other colleges have no foreign language requirement. [FL+]

https://bigfuture.collegeboard.org/get-in/your-high-school-record/high-school-classes-colleges-look-for

7. Is language learning more difficult at some ages than others?
Young children can learn to speak languages as fluently as native speakers, but this window of opportunity closes around age 10. After that age it becomes harder to learn a second language. [FL–]

https://www.education.com/magazine/article/learning-a-second-language/

8. Are people who learned a language in high school still able to speak that language later in life?
According to one survey, less than 1% of US adults report that they can speak a foreign language that they learned in school "very well." [FL–]

http://econlog.econlib.org/archives/2012/08/the_marginal_pr.html

9. How many jobs require people to know more than one language?
Knowing multiple languages can make a person more desirable to employers. But very few jobs require foreign language skill. Exceptions are translating, interpreting, or teaching language. [FL–]

http://www.omniglot.com/language/careers.htm

10. Do employees who speak multiple languages earn more?
One study showed that people who spoke the most common second languages to English (Spanish and French) earned only 1-2% more than those who only spoke English. [FL–]

https://www.education.com/magazine/article/learning-a-second-language/

11. Is learning in a classroom an effective way to learn a language?
Most US foreign language classes focus more on grammar than conversation. As a result, many students cannot communicate effectively in the new language. [FL–]

https://www.forbes.com/sites/forbesleadershipforum/2014/04/22/the-best-way-to-learn-a-foreign-language-is-the-opposite-of-the-usual-way/2/#1bd9c2824df2

Questions about Electives

12. How are electives different from regular classes?
Regular classes are required. Students have choices in taking electives. Elective classes allow students to learn things they otherwise might not. [E+]

https://www.teachingquality.org/content/why-electives-matter

13. Do elective courses give students a chance to study things they are especially interested in?
Many students develop interests, such as music, that require years of practice to become proficient in. Students cannot expect to leave school as experts in a subject, but electives may allow them to gain knowledge and skills in areas of interest. [E+]

https://www.teachingquality.org/content/why-electives-matter

https://www.education.umd.edu/HDQM/labs/Alexander/ARL/Publications_files/Alexander2003.pdf

14. Do elective courses have an effect on school performance?
Taking electives can help students see overlap with their more traditional academic classes. This can lead to a richer learning experience. For example, research shows that students taking electives perform better in school. [E+]

http://www.greatschools.org/gk/articles/choosing-smart-electives/

15. Do elective courses have an effect on academic test performance?
One study showed that students taking sports or arts electives scored higher on the ACT test than others. Another study found that students taking a music elective scored higher on the SAT test than others. [E+]

http://dc.etsu.edu/cgi/viewcontent.cgi?article=3815&context=etd

http://communityunity.cfsites.org/custom.php?pageid=1161

16. How do college admission officers regard electives?
College advisors say it is important to keep a balanced course schedule. Academic subjects are most important, but taking electives shows interest in other areas that can set students apart. [E+]

https://www.princetonreview.com/college-advice/choosing-high-school-classes

17. How can taking an elective be beneficial outside of school?
After-school electives give students a useful and fun way to spend their time. For example, high school students who took a music elective engaged in fewer unhealthy activities outside of school, such as drug use. [E+]

http://www.miamiherald.com/news/local/community/miami-dade/community-voices/article59407953.html

18. Do students continue studying the subjects they took as electives?
Studies show that students are more likely to get a degree or choose a major in a class they took as an elective. [E+]

http://www.miamiherald.com/news/local/community/miami-dade/community-voices/article59407953.html

19. Does taking electives mean students take fewer core academic classes?
Not necessarily. Most US states require students to take a certain number of elective classes, just like they have to take a certain number of core academic classes. [E+]

http://ecs.force.com/mbdata/mbprofall?Rep=HS01

20. Do students have equal opportunity to take elective courses?
Schools in the US get their money from a combination of federal, state, and local taxes. In order to give students more elective opportunities, schools often need to have more local financial support. This suggests that schools serving a wealthier population are able to offer more elective courses. [E–]

https://www.publicschoolreview.com/blog/decreasing-public-high-school-elective-programs

21. Are there gender imbalances in elective courses?
Data from one school suggests that electives are the courses with the largest gender imbalances. One teacher reported that only books took his Jazz Band elective, and another said that few boys took a Peer Interaction elective. [E–]

http://thetamnews.org/features/playing-along-why-some-students-succumb-to-gender-stereotypes-and-others-dont/

22. Do students work hard and learn a lot in elective courses?
Students often report looking for easy electives that do not require a lot of work. They also say that some electives are a "waste of time" and expect little of students. [E–]

http://www.ign.com/boards/threads/what-were-the-easiest-classes-for-you-in-high-school.452949991/

23. What happens when only a few students are interested in an elective?
In some cases, if not enough students are interested in an elective, the class may be cancelled. [E–]
https://www.edgerton.k12.wi.us/cms/lib/WI01919720/Centricity/Domain/156/HSSummerSchool-RegistrationPacket2017.doc.pdf

24. What happens when many students are interested in the same elective?
In some cases, if many students are interested in the same elective, additional sections of that class may be offered. In other cases, not all students may be able to take the class. [E–]
http://www.chaminade.org/document.doc?id=775

DECISION. After-school activity: School work or volunteer. *Your school gives you two choices for an activity during the last period of the day: Attend study hall to do homework and get extra help or Volunteer at a nearby community center to help poor children and the elderly.*

Questions about School work

1. What types of support are available during study hall? Code 564d
2. How does attending study hall affect a student's time use? 701d
3. Does required study hall improve school performance? 127d
4. Do students get more homework done if they have help in study hall? 478d
5. How many hours on average do students spend on homework per night? 659d
6. Do students who attend study hall get better grades? 187d
7. Do students actually study in study hall? 905d
8. What are students' experiences like in study hall? 783d
9. Do students receive course credit for attending study hall? 755d

Questions about Volunteering

10. Are there benefits of volunteering? 837d
11. Does volunteering increase the feeling of well-being? 463d
12. Do students have enough time to do volunteer work? 252d
13. Do students who volunteer do better in school? 635d
14. Does a record of doing volunteer work strengthen a student's college application? 209d
15. Can students earn scholarships from volunteering? 971d
16. Do students who have free time after school always use it wisely? 470d
17. Is volunteering beneficial for everyone? 163d
18. Do students who volunteer in high school continue to volunteer later in life? 264d

Add questions of your own:

19. _____

20. _____

21. _____

Questions about School work

1. What types of support are usually available during study hall?
Since study hall takes place in school, students may have supports available that they would not have outside school. For example, they can ask the teacher for help or work with classmates on assignments. [S+]

https://ace.nd.edu/index.php?option=com_zoo&Itemid=1847&element=5ca6f2cb-951b-4c68-81a0-f0ae4c847fc7&format=raw&item_id=1739&lang=en&method=download&task=callelement

2. How does attending study hall affect a student's time use?
Many students who play sports, have jobs, or participate in other after-school activities may use study hall as a time to do their homework, leaving more time for after-school activities. [S+]

http://www.ctpost.com/news/article/Making-the-most-of-study-hall-377759.php

3. Does required study hall improve school performance?
One school that created a required study hall for students with missing homework assignments found that students' grades improved. Half as many students were failing classes and more students were on the honor roll. [S+]

http://www.educationworld.com/a_admin/admin/admin347.shtml

4. Do students get more homework done if they have help in study hall?
One study showed that after students started attending a study hall where they got help from a teacher, they were more likely to finish their homework than before they had the study hall. The combination of a study hall and teacher guidance improved homework completion rates. [S+]

https://eric.ed.gov/?id=ED501250

5. How many hours on average do students spend on homework per night?
One survey found that US high school students spend about 3.5 hours per night on homework. [S+]

http://articles.latimes.com/2014/mar/01/news/la-ol-too-much-homework-20140228

6. Do students who attend study hall get better grades?
One study showed that students who spent less time in study hall and more time on homework outside of school had better grades. [S–]

https://www.jstor.org/stable/27531756?seq=1#page_scan_tab_contents

7. Do students actually study in study hall?
Many students use study hall as a time to study or complete homework. However, teachers and principals have reported that many students socialize or do things other than homework in study hall. [S–]

http://www.edweek.org/ew/articles/2011/09/22/05mct_orstudyhall.h31.html

8. What are students' experiences like in study hall?
Study hall conditions vary by teacher and school. One survey showed that study halls were often very noisy. [S–]

https://ace.nd.edu/index.php?option=com_zoo&Itemid=1847&element=5ca6f2cb-951b-4c68-81a0-f0ae4c847fc7&format=raw&item_id=1739&lang=en&method=download&task=callelement

9. Do students receive course credit for attending study hall?
Some schools allow students to earn credit for study hall but many do not. [S–]

http://www.lamedeer.k12.mt.us/Policies/HS_Credit_REQ.pdf

http://www.pps.k12.or.us/depts-c/otl/syllabus/2010-11/6260

Questions about Volunteering

10. Are there benefits of volunteering?
Volunteering may help students meet people they would not otherwise meet and better understand people different from themselves. [V+]

https://www.scholarships.com/resources/public-service-and-volunteering/benefits-of-volunteerism-in-high-school/

11. Does volunteering increase the feeling of well-being?
One study found that people who volunteer to help others report better health and more happiness than those who do not. [V+]

http://eprints.lse.ac.uk/24592/

12. Do students have enough time to do volunteer work?
One survey found that 87% of US students either agreed or strongly agreed that they do not volunteer because of their busy school schedules and programs. This suggests that time spent volunteering may take away from time to do homework, sports, or other activities. [V–]

http://compositionawebb.pbworks.com/f/Reasons+why+students+and+individuals+do+not+volunteer%5B1%5D.pdf

13. Do students who volunteer do better in school?
Research shows students who report doing well in school are more likely to be volunteers than students who report doing less well in school. [V+]

https://www.nationalservice.gov/pdf/05_1130_LSA_YHA_SI_factsheet.pdf

14. Does a record of doing volunteer work strengthen a student's college application?
Volunteer work can help students stand out in a college application. This is especially true for applications to more selective schools, because most applicants have high grades and test scores. [V+]

https://www.scholarships.com/resources/public-service-and-volunteering/benefits-of-volunteerism-in-high-school/

15. Can students earn scholarships from volunteering?
Scholarships based on a record of volunteer community service are one of the most common types of scholarships awarded to college applicants. [V+]

https://www.scholarships.com/resources/public-service-and-volunteering/benefits-of-volunteerism-in-high-school/

16. Do students who have free time after school always use it wisely?
Studies show that youth are most at risk during after-school hours. Juvenile crime rates triple and teens engage in more risky behaviors. Even if they are not getting into trouble, teens are often at home watching TV, playing video games, and eating during this time. [V+]

http://www.afterschoolalliance.org/printPage.cfm?idPage=9AC3841C-B33A-5A21-1C8EE2B59468977F

17. Is volunteering beneficial for everyone?
One study suggests that volunteering is not beneficial until age 40. The study found that young people had good emotional health regardless of whether they volunteered. However, after 40 mental health was significantly better among those who volunteered. [V–]

http://www.telegraph.co.uk/science/2016/08/09/volunteering-is-not-beneficial-until-you-hit-40-study-finds/

18. Do students who volunteer in high school continue to volunteer later in life?
One study found that requiring unpaid community service work in high school may reduce the likelihood a person will volunteer later in life. [V–]

http://www.edweek.org/ew/articles/2013/08/21/01volunteer_ep.h33.html

---

DECISION. After-school job. *You have been offered a job in a store evenings from 5 to 9 pm. Should you take the job?*

Questions about Taking the job

1. How many students have after-school jobs? Code 679d
2. Do students who work have a better chance of finding jobs after they graduate? 695d
3. Can having an after-school job help students save for college? 474d
4. Does having an after-school job affect students academically? 115d
5. Does having an after-school job affect students personally? 342d
6. How do parents feel about their teen having a job? 872d
7. What do most teens spend their earnings on? 347d
8. How can having a job affect a teen's family finances? 298d
9. Do teens enjoy working? 327d
10. Do teens who work later make more money as adults? 239d
11. Do students who have free time after school always use it wisely? 427d

Questions about Not taking the job

12. Do students have enough time to work? 175d
13. Are students who work also involved in school activities? 988d
14. Does the amount of time teens spend working matter? 300d
15. Does holding an after-school job affect school attendance? 119d
16. Are teens with jobs more likely to drop out of school? 178d
17. Do students with after-school jobs have different career goals? 585d

18. How do teachers feel about teens having jobs? 794d

19. Can having a job affect a teen's personal development? 577d

20. Are teens with jobs more likely to engage in risky behaviors? 612d

21. How many hours do students spend on homework per night? 177d

22. Do teens with jobs get adequate sleep? 660d

23. What alternatives to teens have in place of an after-school job? 692d

24. Do teens need time to explore personal interests? 410d

Add questions of your own:

25. _____

26. _____

27. _____

Questions about Taking the job

1. How many students have after-school jobs?
More than two thirds of US 17-year-olds have after-school jobs — more than students in many European or Asian countries. [J+]

http://www.ascd.org/publications/researchbrief/v3n14/toc.aspx

2. Do students who work have a better chance of finding jobs after they graduate?
Students who worked during high school showed less unemployment two years after high school. Older teens have almost a 100% chance of being employed if they were employed as high school students 40 weeks or more in the previous year. [J+]

http://journals.sagepub.com/doi/abs/10.3102/00028312042002331?journalCode=aera

http://www.clasp.org/resources-and-publications/publication-1/BMOC_Employment.pdf

3. Can having an after-school job help students save for college?
Research suggests that many students who work do save money for college, although they also spend their earnings on personal items and activities. [J+]

https://www.ncbi.nlm.nih.gov/pmc/articles/PMC2936460/

4. Does having an after-school job affect students academically?
A study found that students having an after-school job had better grades, test scores, and school attendance. [J+]

http://www.ascd.org/publications/researchbrief/v3n14/toc.aspx

5. Does having an after-school job affect students personally?
A study found that having an after-school job can increase students' self-esteem and decrease the likelihood of delinquent activity. [J+]

http://www.ascd.org/publications/researchbrief/v3n14/toc.aspx

6. How do parents feel about their teen having a job?
Many parents like the idea of their children having a job because they think working can build positive character traits such as independence, responsibility, communication skills, and work ethic. [J+]

http://journals.sagepub.com/doi/abs/10.1177/0044118X90022002003

7. What do most teens spend their earnings on?
Many teens earn money so they can participate in activities with their friends. They also use their earnings for clothes, food, gas, and entertainment. Some also save their money or contribute to family expenses. [J+]

https://www.ncbi.nlm.nih.gov/pmc/articles/PMC2936460/

8. How can having a job affect a teen's family finances?
Some teens share earnings from their jobs with their families. Even if they don't, having a job allows teens to buy items for themselves that their parents would normally buy for them. [J+]

https://www.ncbi.nlm.nih.gov/pmc/articles/PMC2936460/

9. Do teens enjoy working?
Working teens report high rates of satisfaction with their jobs. [J+]

https://www.ncbi.nlm.nih.gov/pmc/articles/PMC2936460/

10. Do teens who work later make more money as adults?
Teen employment is linked to higher earnings both in the short-term and later in life. [J+]

http://www.clasp.org/resources-and-publications/publication-1/BMOC_Employment.pdf

11. Do students who have free time after school always use it wisely?
Studies show that youth are most at risk during after-school hours. Juvenile crime rates triple and teens engage in more risky behaviors. Even if they are not getting into trouble, teens are often at home watching TV, playing video games, and eating during this time. [J+]

http://www.afterschoolalliance.org

Questions about Not taking the job

12. Do students have enough time to work?
One survey found that 87% of US students said that they had busy school schedules and programs. This suggests that time spent working may take away from time to do homework, sports, or other activities. [V–]

http://compositionawebb.pbworks.com/f/Reasons+why+students+and+individuals+do+not+volunteer%5B1%5D.pdf

13. Are students who work also involved in school activities?
A study showed that young teens who worked regularly outside of school were more likely to hold leadership positions at school. However, older teens who worked regularly were less likely to hold leadership positions and were less involved in school activities. [J–]

http://www.ascd.org/publications/researchbrief/v3n14/toc.aspx

14. Does the amount of time teens spend working matter?
Having an after-school job has benefits for teens if the job occupies no more than 20 hours per week. Otherwise, studies have shown that they perform worse in school. [J–]

http://education.cu-portland.edu/blog/news/high-school-student-jobs/

https://www.ncbi.nlm.nih.gov/pmc/articles/PMC2936460/

15. Does holding an after-school job affect school attendance?
A study showed that 17-year-olds who worked many hours after school had poorer attendance than students who did not have jobs. [J–]

http://www.ascd.org/publications/researchbrief/v3n14/toc.aspx

16. Are teens with jobs more likely to drop out of school?
A study shows is a strong association between teen employment and school dropout. Teens who work more than 15-20 hours weekly are 40% more likely to drop out than students who work fewer hours or students who do not work. [J–]

http://www.sciencedirect.com/science/article/pii/S0049089X02000212

17. Do students with after-school jobs have different career goals?
One study found that students who held jobs had lower occupational and career goals. [J–]

http://www.ascd.org/publications/researchbrief/v3n14/toc.aspx

18. How do teachers feel about teens having jobs?
Many teachers complain that teens who work too many hours come to class tired, participate less in school activities, and do not have as much time to get help from their teachers after school. [J–]

https://www.ncbi.nlm.nih.gov/pmc/articles/PMC2936460/

19. Can having a job affect a teen's personal development?
Some psychologists say that having a job takes away from a teen's identity formation–their sense of who they are and who they might become. They say teens need time free from other responsibilities to think about these things. [J–]

https://www.ncbi.nlm.nih.gov/pmc/articles/PMC2936460/

20. Are teens with jobs more likely to engage in risky behaviors?
If teens work many hours, they are more likely to drink alcohol, smoke, engage in early sexual activity and to spend money on these things. [J–]

https://www.ncbi.nlm.nih.gov/pmc/articles/PMC2936460/

21. How many hours do students spend on homework per night?
One survey found that US high school students spend about 3.5 hours per night on homework. [J–]

http://articles.latimes.com/2014/mar/01/news/la-ol-too-much-homework-20140228

22. Do teens with jobs get adequate sleep?
Experts have observed that having a job can cut into the time teens need for homework. They find the time by reducing their sleeping hours. This can seriously affect their health. [J–]

https://well.blogs.nytimes.com/2014/10/20/sleep-for-teenagers/

23. What alternatives do teens have in place of an after-school job?
Teens who do not have an after-school job can utilize their free time in personal development activities such as hobbies and exercise. Some research shows that evening can be the best time for exercise. [J–]

http://www.dailymail.co.uk/health/article-55222/Why-evening-best-time-exercise.html

24. Do teens need time to explore personal interests?
Many students develop interests, such as music, that require years of practice to become proficient. Students cannot expect to leave school as experts in a subject, but free time after school may allow them to gain knowledge and skills in areas of interest. [J–]

https://www.teachingquality.org/content/why-electives-matter

https://www.education.umd.edu/HDQM/labs/Alexander/ARL/Publications_files/Alexander2003.pdf

DECISION. Exercise: Team or individual. *Your school has sports teams that require daily practice after school and Saturdays. Or you can exercise on your own and do different things after school.*

Questions about Team exercise

1. Do student athletes have fewer absences from school? Code 909d
2. Are student athletes more likely to graduate from high school? 492d
3. Are high school student athletes smarter than non-athletes? 258d
4. Do high school student athletes score higher on standardized tests? 370d
5. What can high school students gain from participating in team sports? 661d
6. How qualified are high school coaches? 850d
7. Does participating in a high school sport demand a lot of time? 595d
8. Do young students continue with a sport once they start to play it? 906d
9. Do young people have fun playing sports? 920d
10. How can coaching affect an athlete's enjoyment of a sport? 529d
11. What is the risk of injury in sports? 320d
12. How might sport participation affect a teen's physical development? 732d
13. Does it cost money to be on a sports team? 228d
14. What percentage of high school student athletes go on to play in college? 283d
15. What percentage of high school student athletes go on to play professionally? 555d
16. Are members of a student team always in the game? 208d

Questions about Individual exercise

17. How many hours of homework per night are students assigned? 322d
18. Does exercising on your own affect self-concept? 809d
19. Does exercising on your own reduce stress? 120d
20. How much daily exercise time is needed to stay in good health? 875d
21. What percentage of high school students meet exercise recommendations? 992d
22. What percentage of teens spend their out-of-school time in physical activities? 950d
23. What do teens spend their out-of-school time on? 213d
24. How much time do teens spend on media? 797d
25. Do people know good exercise techniques? 856d
26. How many people develop their own exercise plan and stay with it? 311d
27. Why do people use personal trainers? 162d

Add questions of your own:

28. _____

29. _____

30. _____

Questions about Team exercise

1. Do student athletes have fewer absences from school?
One study found that student athletes had lower rates of absences than non-athletes. [T+]

https://news.ku.edu/2014/01/15/study-shows-high-school-athletes-performed-better-school-persisted-graduation-more-non

2. Are student athletes more likely to graduate from high school?
One study showed that student athletes have higher graduation rates and lower dropout rates than non-athletes. [T+]

https://news.ku.edu/2014/01/15/study-shows-high-school-athletes-performed-better-school-persisted-graduation-more-non

3. Are high school student athletes smarter than non-athletes?
One study found that athletes perform better in school work, even though there is no evidence that athletes are smarter than non-athletes. Evidence suggests that school policies that require athletes to maintain certain academic standards in order to compete encourages students to take school seriously. [T+]

https://news.ku.edu/2014/01/15/study-shows-high-school-athletes-performed-better-school-persisted-graduation-more-non

4. Do high school student athletes score higher on standardized tests?
Student athletes have been shown to score higher on standardized academic tests than non-athletes. [T+]

https://news.ku.edu/2014/01/15/study-shows-high-school-athletes-performed-better-school-persisted-graduation-more-non

5. What can high school students gain from participating in team sports?
Experts suggest that participating in school sports has important benefits like learning time management and discipline, and handling expectations from coaches, teammates, and family members. [T+]

https://news.ku.edu/2014/01/15/study-shows-high-school-athletes-performed-better-school-persisted-graduation-more-non

6. How qualified are high school coaches?
Less than 8% of high school coaches have received any formal training in strengthening and conditioning of young athletes, emergency management of sports injuries, or first aid. [T–]

https://www.ncbi.nlm.nih.gov/pmc/articles/PMC3871410/

7. Does participating in a high school sport demand a lot of time?
Many athletes spend more time with coaches than with their family. This could leave them without time to complete their homework. [T–]

https://www.ncbi.nlm.nih.gov/pmc/articles/PMC3871410/

8. Do young students continue with a sport once they start to play it?
About 35% of young athletes quit participating in a sport every year. By age 15, 70-80% of teens who once played a sport have quit. [T–]

https://www.ncbi.nlm.nih.gov/pmc/articles/PMC3871410/

9. Do young people have fun playing sports?
One study reported that while "having fun" is the main reason most children play sports, pressure to compete may lead to stress and unhappiness for a child. [T–]

htttps://www.ncbi.nlm.nih.gov/pmc/articles/PMC3871410/

10. How can coaching affect an athlete's enjoyment of a sport?
Sometimes youth coaches use methods like punishments for poor performance, only allowing the best athletes to play, and over-celebrating wins. These practices can be upsetting to young athletes. [T–]

htttps://www.ncbi.nlm.nih.gov/pmc/articles/PMC3871410/

11. What is the risk of injury in sports?
In the US, there are 2.6 million emergency room visits every year for sports-related injuries among those aged 5-24 years. [T–]

https://www.ncbi.nlm.nih.gov/pmc/articles/PMC3871410/

12. How might sport participation affect a teen's physical development?
Teenage athletes may experience a decrease in flexibility, coordination, and balance due to their physical development, which can increase their risk of injury. [T–]

https://www.ncbi.nlm.nih.gov/pmc/articles/PMC3871410/

13. Does it cost money to be on a sports team?
Sometimes it does cost money to be on a sports team, unless the school is covering the costs. Participating in sports can be a financial hardship for some families. Costs include uniforms, equipment, participation fees, travel expenses, and footwear. [T–]

https://www.ncbi.nlm.nih.gov/pmc/articles/PMC3871410/

14. What percentage of high school student athletes go on to play in college?
Less than 13% of high school athletes go on to play their sport in college. [T–]

http://www.gcic.peachnet.edu/newsletter/dec06/dec%20outlook/athletes.html

15. What percentage of high school student athletes go on to play professionally?
Less than 1% of US high schoolers who play basketball, football, baseball, or hockey will go on to play professionally. [T–]

http://www.gcic.peachnet.edu/newsletter/dec06/dec%20outlook/athletes.html

16. Are members of a student team always in the game?
Student athletes typically spend a portion of the game sitting on the bench. The amount of time an athlete does this varies greatly. Some athletes who are benched experience long-lasting identity crises. [T–]

http://journals.humankinetics.com/doi/abs/10.1123/tsp.3.1.48

Questions about Individual exercise

17. How many hours of homework per night are students assigned?
One survey found that on average, US high school students spend about 3.5 hours per night on homework. [I+]

http://articles.latimes.com/2014/mar/01/news/la-ol-too-much-homework-20140228

18. Does exercising on your own affect self-concept?
In one study, 53% of teens reported that they feel good about themselves after exercise. [I+]

http://www.apa.org/news/press/releases/stress/2013/exercise.aspx

19. Does exercising on your own reduce stress?
In one study, 32% of teens said they feel less stressed after exercising. [I+]

http://www.apa.org/news/press/releases/stress/2013/exercise.aspx

20. How much daily exercise time is needed to stay in good health?
Health experts recommend at least one hour of regular physical activity. This can take any form that the person chooses. [I+]

http://www.apa.org/news/press/releases/stress/2013/exercise.aspx

21. What percentage of high school students meet exercise recommendations?
One four-year study of US high school students found that only 9% fulfilled the exercise recommendations made by The US Centers for Disease Control and Prevention throughout the study period. [I–]

http://www.cbsnews.com/news/teens-dont-get-enough-exercise/

22. What percentage of teens spend their out-of-school time in physical activities?
A US survey found that only 22% of teens choose to spend their out-of-school time in physical activities. [I–]

https://www.chapinhall.org/sites/default/files/publications/Issue_Brief%2005_27_09_Final.pdf

23. What do teens spend their out-of-school time on?
One US study found that 73% of teens spend their out-of-school time on activities like watching TV, listening to music, sleeping, reading, or playing or working on a computer. [I–]

https://www.chapinhall.org/sites/default/files/publications/Issue_Brief%2005_27_09_Final.pdf

24. How much time do teens spend on media?
One study found that US teens spend 9 hours a day using media. [I–]

http://www.cnn.com/2015/11/03/health/teens-tweens-media-screen-use-report/

25. Do people know good exercise techniques?
Most people who exercise on their own don't know how to begin an exercise plan. They may not be aware of how to develop a safe and effective exercise plan and often skip exercises they know less about. [I–]

http://www.acsm.org/public-information/articles/2016/10/07/benefits-of-group-exercise

26. How many people develop their own exercise plan and stay with it?
Research has shown that about half of people who develop their own exercise plan will quit within the first 6 months. [I–]

https://www.unm.edu/~lkravitz/Article%20folder/ExerciseMot.pdf

27. Why do people use personal trainers?
About 13.5% of people who go to the gym use a personal trainer. People use personal trainers for a variety of reasons, including needing to be held accountable for their actions and wanting individualized attention. [I–]

http://www.ihrsa.org/consumer-research/

DECISION. Summer activity. *You have the choice of a summer job or a sports camp.*

Questions about Summer job

1. What skills can be gained from having a summer job? Code 727d
2. Can having a summer job affect attendance during the regular school year? 935d
3. Do students who work have a better chance of finding jobs after they graduate? 400d
4. Do teens who work later make more money as adults? 480d
5. What do most teens spend their earnings on? 205d
6. Can having a summer job help students save for college? 256d
7. How can having a job affect a teen's family finances? 248d
8. Does summer employment affect academic performance? 628d
9. How do parents feel about their teen having a job? 560d
10. Do teens enjoy working? 439d
11. How common is summer employment among teens? 238d
12. How can having a job affect a teen's development? 122d
13. Are teens having jobs more likely to drop out of school? 771d
14. Do teens holding jobs have different career goals? 642d
15. Are teens holding summer jobs more likely to do well on exams? 521d
16. Are teens holding jobs more likely to engage in risky behaviors? 880d
17. Do school activities require involvement during the summer? 499d

Questions about Sports camp

18. Can summer sports camps benefit teens socially? 557d
19. Can summer sports camps benefit teens personally? 338d
20. Can summer sports camps benefit teens physically? 791d
21. Do parents think summer camp is beneficial for their children? 272d
22. Do camps offer financial aid? 435d
23. Can participating in a sports camp make an athlete better at a sport? 509d
24. How long does it take to become an expert in an activity? 723d
25. How much do summer sports camps cost? 575d
26. Can summer sports camps help an athlete get recruited for college play? 513d
27. How time consuming are sports camps? 206d
28. Do sports increase stress levels? 437d
29. Do sports pose a danger to physical well-being? 383d
30. Is too much competition bad for young athletes? 914d

Add questions of your own:

31. _____
_____

32. _____
_____

33. _____
_____

Questions about Summer job

1. What skills can be gained from having a summer job?
By having a summer job, teens can acquire time management skills, motivation, self-confidence, and responsibility. [J+]

https://journalistsresource.org/studies/society/education/impact-summer-youth-employment-academic-year-outcomes

2. Can having a summer job affect attendance during the regular school year?
One study found that students holding summer jobs had slightly higher attendance rates than those who do not. This benefit was larger for students with poorer attendance before having a summer job. [J+]

https://journalistsresource.org/studies/society/education/impact-summer-youth-employment-academic-year-outcomes

3. Do students who work have a better chance of finding jobs after they graduate?
Students who worked during high school showed less unemployment two years after high school. Older teens have almost a 100% chance of being employed if they were employed as students 40 weeks or more in the previous year. [J+]

http://journals.sagepub.com/doi/abs/10.3102/00028312042002331?journalCode=aera
http://www.clasp.org/resources-and-publications/publication-1/BMOC_Employment.pdf

4. Do teens who work later make more money as adults?
Teen employment is linked to higher earnings both in the short-term and later in life. [J+]

http://www.clasp.org/resources-and-publications/publication-1/BMOC_Employment.pdf

5. What do most teens spend their earnings on?
Many teens earn money so they can participate in activities with their friends. They also use their earnings for clothes, food, gas, and entertainment. Some also save their money or contribute to family expenses. [J+]

https://www.ncbi.nlm.nih.gov/pmc/articles/PMC2936460/

6. Can having a summer job help students save for college?
Research suggests that many students who work do save money for college, although they also spend their earnings on personal items and activities. [J+]

https://www.ncbi.nlm.nih.gov/pmc/articles/PMC2936460/

7. How can having a job affect a teen's family finances?
Some teens share earnings from their jobs with their families. Even if they don't, having a job allows teens to buy items for themselves that their parents would normally buy for them. [J+]

https://www.ncbi.nlm.nih.gov/pmc/articles/PMC2936460/

8. Does summer employment affect academic performance?
According to a researcher at Stanford University, a summer job can help boost academic performance in the classroom, especially for low income youth. [J+]

http://news.stanford.edu/2015/09/01/summer-job-benefit-090115/

9. How do parents feel about their teen having a job?
Many parents like the idea of their children having a job because they think working can build positive character traits such as independence, responsibility, communication skills, and work ethic. [J+]

http://journals.sagepub.com/doi/abs/10.1177/0044118X90022002003

10. Do teens enjoy working?
Working teens report high rates of satisfaction with their jobs. [J+]

https://www.ncbi.nlm.nih.gov/pmc/articles/PMC2936460/

11. How common is summer employment among teens?
In the US, there has been a decline in the percentage of teens (16-19 years) having summer employment, from 50% in 2000 to 33% in 2009. [J–]

https://journalistsresource.org/studies/society/education/impact-summer-youth-employment-academic-year-outcomes

12. How can having a job affect a teen's development?
Some psychologists have claimed that having a job takes away from a teen's identity formation. Adolescence can be a time free from the stresses of adult responsibilities when teens can figure out what they want to do in life. [J–]

https://www.ncbi.nlm.nih.gov/pmc/articles/PMC2936460/

13. Are teens having jobs more likely to drop out of school?
There is a strong association between teen employment and school dropout. Teens who work more than 15-20 hours weekly are 40% more likely to drop out than students who work fewer hours or students who do not work. [J–]

http://www.sciencedirect.com/science/article/pii/S0049089X02000212

14. Do teens holding jobs have different career goals?
One study found that students who held jobs had lower occupational and career goals. [J–]

http://www.ascd.org/publications/researchbrief/v3n14/toc.aspx

15. Are teens holding summer jobs more likely to do well on exams?
Students holding summer jobs have been found more likely to take more challenging tests, but they were not more likely to pass these exams than non-working students. [J–]

https://journalistsresource.org/studies/society/education/impact-summer-youth-employment-academic-year-outcomes

16. Are teens holding jobs more likely to engage in risky behaviors?
If teens work many hours, they are more likely to drink alcohol, smoke, engage in early sexual activity and to spend money on these things. [J–]

https://www.ncbi.nlm.nih.gov/pmc/articles/PMC2936460/

17. Do school activities require involvement during the summer?
Some school activities, such as certain sports or band, require summer involvement of students. Teens with summer jobs may find it difficult to participate in these activities. [J–]

http://www.tennessean.com/story/money/2014/05/17/summer-jobs-teens-weighing-pros-cons/9197677/

Questions about Sports camp

18. Can summer sports camps benefit teens socially?
Summer sports camps may provide an opportunity for teens to make friends from other states and countries with the common bond of their sport, as well as spend time with nearby friends. [C+]

http://www.ussportscamps.com/tips/multisport/five-reasons-to-go-to-a-summer-sports-camp

19. Can summer sports camps benefit teens personally?
Camps may provide opportunities for teens to try new things and build self-esteem. Being away from family and teachers gives teens a chance to practice independence. [C+]

http://www.ussportscamps.com/tips/multisport/five-reasons-to-go-to-a-summer-sports-camp

20. Can summer sports camps benefit teens physically?
Participating in a sports camp can provide teens a chance to exercise while having fun. [C+]

http://laxcamps.com/five-benefits-to-attending-youth-sports-camp/

21. Do parents think summer camp is beneficial for their children?
According to one survey, parents said camps were good for their children. They said camp their child with feeling successful, making new friends, gaining new skills, getting along better with others, and having a better idea of what they are good at. [C+]

http://www.acacamps.org/press-room/benefits-of-camp/skill-development

22. Do camps offer financial aid?
Many summer sports camps offer financial aid for athletes, ranging from full tuition coverage to partial coverage. Financial aid is typically given to athletes based on need. [C+]

http://byusportscamps.com/compliance/student-athletes/financial-aid

23. Can participating in a sports camp make an athlete better at a sport?
Sports camps can help teens decide if they would like to continue with that sport during the regular school year. With more practice a student may excel and become eligible for awards or scholarships. [C+]

http://laxcamps.com/five-benefits-to-attending-youth-sports-camp/

24. How long does it take to become an expert in an activity?
Research shows that it takes about 10,000 hours, or approximately 10 years of intense practice, to become an expert in an activity (for example, basketball). [C+]

http://projects.ict.usc.edu/itw/gel/EricssonDeliberatePracticePR93.pdf

25. How much do summer sports camps cost?
Few summer sports camps are free. Most camp prices in the US range from less than $100 to thousands of dollars, depending on the camp and length. [C–]

http://blog.prepscholar.com/summer-sports-camps

26. Can summer sports camps help an athlete get recruited for college play?
Many student athletes attend camps hoping to get "discovered" by college coaches. However, there are usually many participants at a camp, reducing the chances of getting individual attention. [C–]

http://www.momsteam.com/blog/tim-twellman/will-college-camp-help-me-get-recruited

27. How time consuming are sports camps?
Sports camps often consume a large amount of time, leaving less time for family and other activities. Sleep-away camps take all of a student's time, but even day camps can consume a large amount of time. [C–]

https://www.wsj.com/articles/SB10001424052748703724104575379011786110460

28. Do sports increase stress levels?
Research tells that sports settings can induce high levels of competitive stress in many young people. A player may not be as good as others and find it upsetting. [C–]

https://www.psychologytoday.com/blog/coaching-and-parenting-young-athletes/201407/are-youth-sports-too-stressful

29. Do sports pose a danger to physical well-being?
Researchers have found that sports injuries are common and are the leading cause of injury among teens. [C–]

https://www.ncbi.nlm.nih.gov/pmc/articles/PMC4210977/

30. Is too much competition bad for young athletes?
Too much competition can lead athletes to focus on winning. This can increase pressure and decrease enjoyment of the sport. A study also found that competition can lead to intense play and increased risk of injury. [C–]

http://www.livestrong.com/article/523284-negatives-of-competitive-sports/

DECISION. Nutrition. *You like soda and think it's okay to have a couple a day as long as you have a good diet overall. Or you can decide soda does nothing good for you and it's best to avoid it.*

Questions about Drinking soda

1. How does soda affect the brain in the short-term? Code 284d
2. Are all types of soda high in sugar and calories? 335d
3. Does drinking soda boost energy? 462d
4. Does drinking soda have any health benefits? 956d
5. Does drinking soda help digestion? 147d
6. Do no-calorie sodas affect a person's weight? 629d
7. Who conducts most of the research on soda and obesity? 913d
8. Does soda fulfill the hydration needs of the body? 552d
9. What are soda companies doing to make soda healthier? 446d

Questions about Avoiding soda

10. Can avoiding soda improve health? 273d
11. Do schools allow students to drink soda at school? 204d
12. Can drinking regular soda lead to weight gain? 105d
13. Can avoiding soda help people to lose weight? 696d
14. How long-lasting is the short-term energy boost from the caffeine found in soda? 443d
15. Is no-calorie soda a good substitute for regular soda? 514d
16. Does soda have nutritional value? 556d
17. Does drinking soda affect dental health? 230d

18. Can people become addicted to soda? 449d

19. How does soda affect the brain in the long-term? 203d

Add questions of your own:

20. _____

21. _____

22. _____

Questions about Drinking soda

1. How does soda affect the brain in the short-term?
When a person consumes sugar, as found in soda, the reward system in the brain is activated. The brain releases chemical called dopamine, which produces feelings of pleasure. [S+]

http://www.npr.org/sections/thesalt/2014/01/15/262741403/why-sugar-makes-us-feel-so-good

2. Are all types of sodas high in sugar and calories?
Most sodas are available in no-calorie types. [S+]

http://www.coca-cola.co.uk/faq/calories-in-330ml-can-of-diet-coke

3. Does drinking soda boost energy?
Most sodas contain caffeine, which gives a short-term energy boost. [S+]

http://bodyfocus.me/html/feel-great/112-want-more-energy-give-up-soda

4. Does drinking soda have any health benefits?
A study of people with constipation symptoms found that those who drank carbonated water, as found in soda, had fewer symptoms than those who drank normal tap water. [S+]

http://woman.thenest.com/health-benefits-soda-carbonated-water-3526.html

5. Does drinking soda help digestion?
Some research claims that drinking carbonated water, as contained in soda, may reduce indigestion problems. [S+]

http://woman.thenest.com/health-benefits-soda-carbonated-water-3526.html

6. Do no-calorie sodas affect a person's weight?
Researchers claim that sugar substitutes, such as those found in no-calorie sodas, have little to no impact on weight. [S+]

http://www.webmd.com/diet/features/sodas-and-your-health-risks-debated#3

7. Who conducts most of the research on soda and obesity?
Most studies that have found links between soda and obesity have been conducted by researchers who are against consuming soda. [S+]

http://www.webmd.com/diet/features/sodas-and-your-health-risks-debated#3

8. Does soda fulfill the hydration needs of the body?
According to the Mayo clinic, if not consumed in excess, soda is no different than normal tap water for hydration. [S+]

http://woman.thenest.com/health-benefits-soda-carbonated-water-3526.html

9. What are soda companies doing to make soda healthier?
Coke, Pepsi, and Dr. Pepper have announced that they are planning to reduce the calories Americans get from such beverages by 20% by marketing smaller bottles, bottled water, and diet drinks. [S+]

https://www.nytimes.com/2014/09/24/business/big-soda-companies-agree-on-effort-to-cut-americans-drink-calories.html?_r=0

Questions about Avoiding soda

10. Can avoiding soda improve health?
Avoiding soda can improve health by lowering the chances of hypertension, asthma, pancreatic cancer, and diabetes. [S–]

http://inspiyr.com/6-health-benefits-of-not-drinking-soda/

11. Do schools allow students to drink soda at school?
In Britain and France, soda sales have been banned from elementary and high schools, and many US school districts are considering or already doing the same. [S–]

https://www.ncbi.nlm.nih.gov/pmc/articles/PMC1829363/

12. Can drinking regular soda lead to weight gain?
Research suggests that drinking soda may make people want to eat more because it causes a rise in blood sugar. In one study, people who added soda to their regular diet consumed 17% more calories. Consuming more calories leads to weight gain. [S–]

https://www.ncbi.nlm.nih.gov/pmc/articles/PMC1829363/
https://www.ncbi.nlm.nih.gov/pubmed/10878689

13. Can avoiding soda help people to lose weight?
A study showed that high schoolers who reduced their soda intake maintained the same weight. Students who made no change gained weight. [S–]

https://www.ncbi.nlm.nih.gov/pmc/articles/PMC1829363/

14. How long-lasting is the short-term energy boost from the caffeine found in soda?
Research has found that students who consume caffeine are more likely to have trouble sleeping and to feel tired in the morning. [S–]

http://www.sciencedirect.com/science/article/pii/S1054139X05002582

15. Is no-calorie soda a good substitute for regular soda?
Studies suggest that the sweeteners used in no-calories soda increase risk of diabetes, heart problems, and stroke. [S–]

http://www.cell.com/trends/endocrinology-metabolism/fulltext/S1043-2760(13)00087-8

16. Does soda have nutritional value?
Soda lacks essential nutrients like vitamins, minerals, antioxidants, or fiber. Soda is said to have "empty" calories because it mainly contains sugar. [S–]

https://authoritynutrition.com/13-ways-sugary-soda-is-bad-for-you/

17. Does drinking soda affect dental health?
Drinking soda regularly causes plaque to build up on the teeth and can lead to cavities and gum disease. [S–]

https://wellnessmama.com/379/reasons-to-avoid-soda/

18. Can people become addicted to soda?
Evidence suggests that sugars, such as found in soda, can lead to reward and craving in ways similar to addictive drugs like cocaine. [S–]

https://www.ncbi.nlm.nih.gov/pubmed/23719144

19. How does soda affect the brain in the long-term?
Research has shown that drinking sugary beverages, such as soda, is associated with lower brain volume and lower scores on memory tests. Lower brain volume has been linked to higher risk of Alzheimer's disease. [S–]

https://www.nytimes.com/2017/04/24/well/eat/sugary-drinks-brain-aging.html

---

DECISION. Alcohol. *You have an opportunity to try an alcoholic drink to know what it's like. Or you decide it's safest to avoid alcohol entirely and not risk starting with it.*

Questions about Trying alcohol

1. Do teens report drinking alcohol? Code 148d
2. At what age is it legal to drink? 255d
3. Are there ever circumstances under which a person not normally allowed legally to drink can do so? 146d
4. What effects might a person experience from small amounts of alcohol? 153d
5. Are there any benefits to drinking alcohol? 355d
6. Is it legal to drink alcohol at home with a parent or guardian if they approve of it? 287d
7. Is drinking involved in any religious activities? 985d

Questions about Avoiding alcohol

8. Is there a connection between teen drinking and life success? 201d
9. How does teen drinking affect teens' school performance? 141d
10. Are there long-term physical effects of drinking alcohol? 654d
11. Are there short-term physical effects of drinking alcohol? 234d
12. By what age is brain development completed? 277d
13. Can alcohol lead to a young person's death? 582d
14. How much alcohol would it take to lead to death? 562d
15. Does trying a sip of alcohol at an early age influence teen drinking behavior? 800d
16. Can alcohol be addictive? 405d
17. How easy is it to become reliant on alcohol? 165d
18. Does family history have an influence on alcoholism? 161d
19. What are the legal consequences of being caught by authorities drinking underage? 493d

Add questions of your own:

20. _____

21. _____

22. _____

Questions about Trying alcohol

1. Do teens report drinking alcohol?
Teen drinking varies around the world. In some European countries (Austria, Denmark), as many as 80% of 15–16-year-olds report drinking in the past 30 days. In the US, this figure is about 33%. By age 18, it increases to about 65%. [+]

http://www.samhsa.gov/data/sites/default/files/NSDUH-DetTabs2014/NSDUH-DetTabs2014.htm#tab2-15b

http://resources.prev.org/documents/ESPAD.pdf

2. At what age is it legal to drink?
The legal drinking age varies by country. In the US it is 21. In most countries it is 18 or 19, but in some it is as young as 10. Some countries have no minimum legal drinking age, and in some it is illegal to drink alcohol at any age. [+/–]

http://www.who.int/substance_abuse/publications/global_alcohol_report/msb_gsr_2014_2.pdf?ua=1

3. Are there ever circumstances under which a person not normally allowed legally to drink can do so?
This varies around the world, but in some US states, rules allow people under 21 to drink in special circumstances, such as religious events, medical purposes, or if the person is with a parent or guardian. In Hong Kong, the drinking age is only enforced in public places, so minors can drink in the home. [+]

https://alcoholpolicy.niaaa.nih.gov/state_profiles_of_underage_drinking_laws.html

http://www.scmp.com/lifestyle/health/article/1511128/teenage-binge-drinking-hk-becoming-headache-amid-lack-regulation

4. What effects might a person experience from small amounts of alcohol?
With a few sips of alcohol, a person may feel slight happiness, relaxation, and a loss of shyness. There is not yet the loss of coordination that may come from larger amounts, but the person may feel a little lightheaded. [+]

http://www.brad21.org/effects_at_specific_bac.html

5. Are there any benefits to drinking alcohol?
Drinking alcohol in moderation may provide health benefits such as reducing the risk of heart disease, stroke, and diabetes. [+]

http://www.mayoclinic.org/healthy-lifestyle/nutrition-and-healthy-eating/in-depth/alcohol/art-20044551

6. Is it legal to drink alcohol at home with a parent or guardian if they approve of it?
This varies around the world and within the US. In some US states (including Colorado, Texas, and Wisconsin) it is legal for teens to drink alcohol with a parent or guardian if they have permission. In other countries such as Mongolia, it is illegal for parents to provide alcohol to their underage children. [+]

http://www.youthrights.org/issues/drinking-age/laws-in-all-50-states/

http://legacy.grsproadsafety.org/sites/default/files/ICAP%20report4.pdf

7. Is drinking involved in any religious activities?
Many religions use alcohol for ritual or ceremonial purposes. In Christianity, wine is used to represent the blood of Christ. In Judaism, kosher wine is blessed and consumed on the Sabbath. [+]

https://www.supercall.com/culture/alcohol-religious-ceremonies-around-the-world

Questions about Avoiding alcohol

8. Is there a connection between teen drinking and life success?
While success can mean different things to different people, US children who begin drinking alcohol by age 13 were found 38% more likely to become alcoholics later in life. Alcoholism can affect family relationships, friendships, work performance, and mental health. [–]

http://www.apa.org/monitor/jan08/earlydrinking.aspx

9. How does teen drinking affect teens' school performance?
Studies show that students in US states with a legal drinking age of 18 were 13 times more likely to drop out of high school compared to students in states with a legal drinking age of 21. [–]

https://www.cdc.gov/alcohol/fact-sheets/minimum-legal-drinking-age.htm

10. Are there long-term physical effects of drinking alcohol?
If people drink a lot of alcohol often, they can develop liver disease, kidney damage, malnutrition, or other health conditions. Heavy drinking can also lead to declined thinking and memory abilities. [–]

https://www.chooseresponsibility.org/frequently_asked_questions/#raised

11. Are there short-term physical effects of drinking alcohol?
If large amounts of alcohol are consumed, slower heart and breathing rates may result. The central nervous system can even shut down, causing loss of consciousness, blackout, or even death. Alcohol use can also make a person less in control of their motor skills and worsen their memory. [–]

https://www.chooseresponsibility.org/frequently_asked_questions/#raised

12. By what age is brain development completed?
The prefrontal cortex, which is responsible for abstract thinking and good judgment, is not fully developed until one's early- to mid-20s. [–]

https://www.chooseresponsibility.org/frequently_asked_questions/#raised

13. Can alcohol lead to a young person's death?
In the US, teen drinking contributes to over 4,300 deaths and 189,000 alcohol-related hospital visits each year. [–]

https://www.cdc.gov/alcohol/fact-sheets/minimum-legal-drinking-age.htm

14. How much alcohol would it take to lead to death?
A Blood Alcohol Content (BAC) higher than .3 is considered "life threatening." It would take about 8 drinks for men and 6 drinks for women (within a short amount of time) to reach this level. [–]

http://www.brad21.org/bac_charts.html

15. Does trying a sip of alcohol at an early age influence teen drinking behavior?
One US study found that young teens who had tried a sip of alcohol by 6th grade were more likely to be heavy drinkers by 9th grade. [–]

https://www.ncbi.nlm.nih.gov/pmc/articles/PMC5374474/

16. Can alcohol be addictive?
In the US, alcohol is the most commonly used addictive substance. About 1 in every 12 adults suffers from alcohol abuse or dependence. [–]

https://www.ncadd.org/about-addiction/alcohol/facts-about-alcohol

17. How easy is it to become reliant on alcohol?
A person becomes reliant on alcohol by developing tolerance, which means over time it takes more alcohol to feel the same effects. [+]

http://web4health.info/it/add-alcohol-how.htm

18. Does family history have an influence on alcoholism?
Research has shown that about 50% of the risk of developing alcoholism is due to genetic factors. This means a young person is more likely to become an alcoholic if they have an alcoholic parent. [–]

https://www.ncadd.org/about-addiction/family-history-and-genetics

19. What are the legal consequences of being caught by authorities drinking underage?
This varies around the world. In the US, if a person is caught drinking under 21, they may have their driver's license taken away or be required to pay fines or do community service. In some countries the consequences are extreme. In Saudi Arabia, a person may be sentenced to death of caught drinking at any age. [–]

http://www.nolo.com/legal-encyclopedia/underage-drinking-minor-possession-laws-33778.html

---

DECISION. Spend or save. *You have received an unexpected gift of money from a relative. You have the choice of spending it or saving it.*

Questions about Spending

1. How much money do teens spend per week? Code 828d
2. Is spending money important to teens? 360d
3. Can spending money lead to good feelings? 641d
4. What do most teens spend money on? 407d
5. Do people spend all the extra money they have on themselves? 947d
6. Are there ways in which teens can spend their money wisely? 345d
7. How has teens' spending changed over time? 396d
8. Do most teens know how to spend their money wisely? 647d
9. Do teens know how to get the best price when they shop? 637d
10. Where do teens get the money that they spend? 217d
11. Can spending lead to a person becoming a shopping addict? 497d
12. Do people spend money on things they may not need and feel regret afterward? 482d
13. How often do people plan what they are going to buy versus buying on impulse? 286d

Questions about Saving

14. Do teens save money? 329d

15. What do teens save money for? 845d

16. Do teens worry about money? 195d

17. Is college expensive? 376d

18. Do most families have enough saved to pay for college? 563d

19. Is ability to delay pleasure connected to life success? 452d

20. Are teens interested in learning about saving? 630d

21. Is money worth less over time? 473d

22. Does saving money lead to missing out on important things? 598d

Add questions of your own:

23. _____

24. _____

25. _____

Questions about Spending

1. How much money do teens spend per week?
One survey reported that American teens tend to spend around $18.50 per week on average. However, some have very little money to spend as they choose and some spend much more. [Sp+]

http://www.schwabmoneywise.com/public/file/P-4192268/110526-SCHWAB-TEENSMONEY.pdf

2. Is spending money important to teens?
Going out with friends and shopping are popular activities for teens. In one study, 61% of American teens agreed that shopping was a good way to spend time with friends and family. [Sp+]

https://www.creditdonkey.com/teenage-consumer-spending-statistic.html

3. Can spending money lead to good feelings?
Some research has shown that when people buy things for themselves that they like, they experience positive moods. [Sp+]

http://foxfellowship.yale.edu/sites/default/files/files/Money%20Buys%20Happiness%20When%20Spending%20Fits%20Our%20Personality%20(1).pdf

4. What do most teens spend money on?
Many teens spend money to participate in activities with their friends. They also use their money for clothes, food, gas, and entertainment. [Sp+]

https://www.ncbi.nlm.nih.gov/pmc/articles/PMC2936460/

5. Do people spend all the extra money they have on themselves?

People do not always spend their extra money on themselves. They often spend it in ways to help others, by donating to charity. Some also save their money or contribute to family expenses. [Sp+]

http://www.slate.com/articles/life/ft/2011/01/live_like_a_grad_student_forever.html

https://www.ncbi.nlm.nih.gov/pmc/articles/PMC2936460/

6. Are there ways in which teens can spend their money wisely?

According to experts on teenage affairs, teens can spend their money wisely through practices such as goal setting and making spending plans. [Sp+]

http://www.zelawelakids.com/blog/bid/63202/10-ways-to-help-your-teens-spend-money-wisely

7. How has teens' spending changed over time?

Between 2007-2011, teens reported spending less money than they reported previously. In 2007, 41% reported spending less than $20 per week. In 2011, this percentage increased to 55%. [Sp–]

http://www.schwabmoneywise.com/public/file/P-4192268/110526-SCHWAB-TEENSMONEY.pdf

8. Do most teens know how to spend their money wisely?

83% of teens in a survey admitted that they do not know how to spend their money wisely. [Sp–]

http://www.foxbusiness.com/features/2012/07/17/teaching-gap-83-teens-dont-know-how-to-manage-money.html

9. Do teens know how to get the best price when they shop?

According to a US survey, 72% of teens knew how to shop to get the best price when making a purchase. This dropped to only 61% in 2011. [Sp–]

http://www.schwabmoneywise.com/public/file/P-4192268/110526-SCHWAB-TEENSMONEY.pdf

10. Where do teens get the money that they spend?

Teens earn some of their spending money. But they spend about 3 times as much as they earn. The majority of their income comes from money given to them by others. [Sp–]

https://www.creditdonkey.com/teenage-consumer-spending-statistic.html

11. Can spending lead to a person becoming a shopping addict?

Psychologists have reported evidence that over time, brain reactions during shopping can lead to lack of self-control over one's spending. [Sp–]

http://www.psychguides.com/guides/shopping-addiction-symptoms-causes-and-effects/

12. Do people spend money on things they may not need and feel regret afterward?

About half of people who made unplanned purchases for items they might not need reported that they regretted it later. [Sp–]

http://www.creditcards.com/credit-card-news/impulse-purchase-survey.php

13. How often do people plan what they are going to buy versus buying on impulse?

According to a survey, 75% of Americans make impulse (unplanned) purchases. Teens reported buying on impulse more often than any other age group. [Sp–]

http://www.creditcards.com/credit-card-news/impulse-purchase-survey.php

Questions about Saving

14. Do teens save money?

According to a US survey, 38% of teens reported that they are currently saving money. [Sa–]

http://www.statisticbrain.com/teenage-consumer-spending-statistics/

15. What do teens save money for?
Most teens save money for college, for emergencies, or for bigger purchases such as an iPod, computer, or car. [Sa+]

http://www.schwabmoneywise.com/public/file/P-4192268/110526-SCHWAB-TEENSMONEY.pdf

16. Do teens worry about money?
Research has shown that money can be a source of worry for teens. The majority in a US group reported that they are worried about not having enough money, either now or in the future. [Sa+]

https://www.creditdonkey.com/teenage-consumer-spending-statistic.html

17. Is college expensive?
Yes and getting more so in the USA. A few community colleges offer free courses but most charge tuition from $10,000 to more than $30,000 per year. [Sa+]

https://www.nytimes.com/2015/09/13/magazine/is-college-tuition-too-high.html

18. Do most families have enough saved to pay for college?
In 2015, only 45% of parents with children under age 18 saved for college. More than half of the parents said they don't have enough money to save for college. [Sa+]

http://news.salliemae.com/sites/salliemae.newshq.businesswire.com/files/doc_library/file/HowAmericaSaves2015_FINAL.pdf

19. Is ability to delay pleasure connected to life success?
Several studies have shown that young children who were able to delay receiving a reward were more successful when they were older. [Sa+]

http://search.proquest.com/openview/ad2af069fe679833c3d5199c7490308a/1?pq-origsite=gscholar&cbl=1256

20. Are teens interested in learning about saving?
In a US survey, only a third or less of teens said they were interested in learning about saving money. [Sa–]

http://search.proquest.com/docview/218179460?pq-origsite=gscholar

https://takechargetoday.arizona.edu/system/files/Alhabeeb.pdf

21. Is money worth less over time?
Economists have shown that money loses value over time. (This is called inflation.) The money a person has today is worth more than it will be later. [Sa–]

http://www.investopedia.com/ask/answers/042415/what-impact-does-inflation-have-time-value-money.asp

22. Does saving money lead to missing out on important things?
According to finance experts, saving too much money can affect the quality of life and opportunities for enjoyment. [Sa–]

http://money.usnews.com/money/blogs/on-retirement/2013/05/29/the-consequences-of-saving-too-much-for-retirement

http://www.thepracticalsaver.com/can-saving-too-much-money-be-bad/

Chapter 8

■ ■ ■

A Community Future

DECISION. Education: Curriculum. Should the town high school have a standard course of study for all students or allow students some choice of what to study? (p. 85)

DECISION. Education: Leaving age. Should students be required to attend school until age 16 or age 18? (p. 90)

DECISION. Education: Homeschooling? Should a family arriving from a foreign country be permitted to educate their child at home and not send the child to school? (p. 93)

DECISION. Education: Teacher pay. Should all teachers receive the same pay or should teachers with more skill or experience be paid more? (p. 95)

DECISION. Driving. Should teens be permitted to get drivers' licenses at age 16 or age 18? (p. 99)

DECISION. Drinking. Should young people be permitted to drink alcohol at age 18 or age 21? (p. 102)

DECISION. Juvenile v. adult court for teen offenders. Should teens who commit serious crimes be tried in regular adult court or a special court for juveniles? (p. 106)

DECISION. Town sports teams. Should town taxes help to pay the cost of community sports teams? Or should they be paid for entirely by the families who use them? (p. 108)

DECISION. Public transportation. Should town taxes help to pay the cost of buses and trains or should the cost be paid for entirely by the people who use them? (p. 111)

DECISION. Sales tax. Should the town charge a sales tax on everything people buy? Or should the town get the money it needs from a tax on people's earnings? (p. 114)

DECISION. Soda tax. Should an extra tax be charged on soda purchases? (p. 117)

DECISION. Rent control. Should the town limit how much rent a landlord can charge? (p. 121)

DECISION. Elderly care. Should adults be required to care for their elderly parents or should government funds be used to do this? (p. 124)

Only the questions appear in the student edition. Students select a question, respond to the preliminary question about it (How can you make use of this information in your argument?), and then access an answer electronically. These answers and sources are printed for convenience only in this teachers' edition. (See Chapter 11 for an explanation of the symbol in parentheses following each answer.)

DECISION. Education: Curriculum. *Should the town high school have a standard course of study for all students or allow students some choice of what to study?*

Questions about Standard curriculum

1. Are there some skills and knowledge that it is believed all students need to acquire? Code 219d
2. Does a standard course of study eliminate all choice in what students study? 691d
3. Is a standardized course of study helpful to students who change schools? 530d
4. What benefits are gained by learning algebra? 438d
5. What benefits are gained by learning science? 816d
6. What benefits are gained by learning a foreign language? 231d
7. What benefits are gained by studying history? 194d
8. Is it useful to know about what has happened in the past? 358d
9. Is physical education important? 861d
10. How might diversity affect learning? 720d
11. Do students with learning disabilities have different learning needs than average students? 808d
12. Do students who are very able learners have different learning needs than average students? 554d
13. Do employers require that workers are proficient at algebra? 925d

Questions about Curriculum choice

14. Do some schools allow students to choose what to study? 979d
15. Are students more motivated when they have a choice in what to study? 536d
16. Do elective courses give students a chance to study things they are especially interested in? 664d
17. Do elective courses have an effect on school performance? 409d
18. Do elective courses have an effect on test performance? 299d
19. Do students continue studying the subjects they took as electives? 336d
20. How does choosing what to study relate to the real world? 884d
21. Do employers expect their workers to have certain skills? 685d
22. Can allowing course choice improve academic outcomes in traditionally underperforming schools? 789d
23. Do most teens know what career they want to prepare for in college? 128d
24. Are students good decision-makers? 650d
25. Do students work hard in elective courses? 596d

26. What happens when only a few students are interested in an elective? 934d
27. What happens when many students are interested in the same elective? 429d
28. How is student achievement measured if students are studying different things? 176d
29. How do teachers give feedback when students choose to study different things? 422d
30. How is student choice affected by time constraints? 477d

Add questions of your own:

31. _____

32. _____

33. _____

Questions about Standard curriculum

1. Are there some skills and knowledge that it is believed all students need to acquire?
Most nations, including the US, China, and many others, have state or national standards that specify what students should know in key subjects such as language, math, and science. [S+]

http://www.westpoint.edu/cfe/Literature/Turner_10.pdf

2. Does a standard course of study eliminate all choice in what students study?
Schools that have a standardized course of study vary in how much choice they allow students, but most schools allow students to choose some elective courses. [S+]

https://bigfuture.collegeboard.org/get-in/your-high-school-record/how-to-choose-high-school-electives

3. Is a standardized course of study helpful to students who change schools?
A standardized course of study can be helpful to students who change schools if the new school has the same curriculum as the old one. This can make the school change easier for the student. [S+]

http://www.borgenmagazine.com/5-reasons-to-have-a-standardized-curriculum/

4. What benefits are gained by learning algebra?
A study showed that students who take an algebra course score higher on standardized math tests than students who don't. [S+]

http://journals.sagepub.com/doi/abs/10.3102/01623737022003241?journalCode=epaa

5. What benefits are gained by learning science?
Science education specialists claim that studying science can help students develop perseverance, problem-solving skills, and a better understanding of the world. [S+]

http://www.schoolatoz.nsw.edu.au/homework-and-study/other-subjects-and-projects/science/why-science-is-important-in-young-kids-lives

6. What benefits are gained by learning a foreign language?
Many studies have shown that students who learn a foreign language show higher academic performance, cognitive skills (memory, problem solving, attention, intelligence), and more positive attitudes toward that language and the people who speak it. [S+]

https://www.actfl.org/advocacy/what-the-research-shows/studies-supporting

7. What benefits are gained by studying history?
Studies show that learning history can help students develop an ability to assess evidence, conflicting interpretations, and past examples of change. These skills can contribute to good citizenship, identity formation, and understanding of the past. [S+]

https://www.historians.org/about-aha-and-membership/aha-history-and-archives/archives/why-study-history-(1998)

8. Is it useful to know about what has happened in the past?
It has been suggested by many people that knowing what happened in the past helps avoid making the same mistakes in the future. [S+]

https://www.historians.org/publications-and-directories/perspectives-on-history/january-2005/how-do-we-learn-from-history

9. Is physical education important?
Research has shown that physical education improves students' overall physical fitness and motor skills. Students who are physically active also have higher grades, test scores, and attendance rates, and fewer disciplinary problems. [S+]

http://www.veanea.org/home/1000.htm

http://activelivingresearch.org/files/ALR_Brief_ActiveEducation_Summer2009.pdf

10. How might diversity affect learning?
Students are very diverse in terms of culture, language, abilities, and interests. Students may thus have different learning styles and needs. [S–]

http://jespnet.com/journals/Vol_2_No_5_December_2015/11.pdf

11. Do students with learning disabilities have different learning needs than average students?
Students with learning disabilities may have different learning needs than average students. These students may need modifications such as more time for testing, different learning environments, or one-on-one instruction. They also may have different learning goals. [S–]

http://www.ldonline.org/article/8022/

12. Do students who are very able learners have different learning needs than average students?
Students who are very able learners have different learning needs than average students. These students may need modifications such as more challenging assignments, working at a faster pace, or having more choice in what they learn. [S–]

http://www.grandviewlibrary.org/CurriculumAdaptations/General_Gifted.pdf

13. Do employers require that workers are proficient at algebra?
A study showed that only about 5% of entry-level workers will need to be proficient in algebra. [S–]

http://www.nytimes.com/2012/07/29/opinion/sunday/is-algebra-necessary.html

Questions about Curriculum choice

14. Do some schools allow students to choose what to study?
A few schools give students complete choice, but most schools have a combination of required courses and elective courses. All US states have required courses students must take to graduate, but most schools also allow students to choose some courses. [C+]

http://ecs.force.com/mbdata/mbprofall?Rep=HS01

15. Are students more motivated when they have a choice in what to study?
Because students get to choose topics they are interested in and want to explore, this can promote motivation. Research has shown that students show greater motivation in elective classes compared to required classes. [C+]

https://getd.libs.uga.edu/pdfs/ward_jonathan_n_200608_edd.pdf

16. Do elective courses give students a chance to study things they are especially interested in?
Many students develop interests, such as music, at a young age that require years of practice to become proficient. Students cannot expect to leave school as experts in a subject, but electives may allow them to gain knowledge and skills in areas of interest. [C+]

https://www.teachingquality.org/content/why-electives-matter

17. Do elective courses have an effect on school performance?
Taking electives can help students see overlap with their more traditional academic classes. This can lead to a richer learning experience. For example, research shows that students in electives perform better in school and on standardized tests. [C+]

http://www.greatschools.org/gk/articles/choosing-smart-electives/

18. Do elective courses have an effect on test performance?
One study showed that students taking sports or arts electives scored higher on the ACT college entrance test than others. Another study found that students taking a music elective scored higher on the SAT college entrance test than others. [C+]

http://dc.etsu.edu/cgi/viewcontent.cgi?article=3815&context=etd

http://communityunity.cfsites.org/custom.php?pageid=1161

19. Do students continue studying the subjects they took as electives?
Studies show that students are more likely to get a degree or choose a major in a class they took as an elective. [C+]

http://www.miamiherald.com/news/local/community/miami-dade/community-voices/article59407953.html

20. How does choosing what to study relate to the real world?
Students have more responsibility for their own learning when they must choose what to study. They also are expected to develop critical thinking skills more than just facts. These types of skills can prepare students for college and their future careers. [C+]

https://www.theatlantic.com/education/archive/2014/10/what-happens-when-students-control-their-own-education/381828/

21. Do employers expect their workers to have certain skills?
According to a survey, the top five skills employers look for in their workers are leadership, ability to work in a team, written communication skills, problem-solving skills, and verbal communication skills. All of these skills can be learned in a variety of courses. [C+]

http://www.naceweb.org/career-development/trends-and-predictions/job-outlook-2016-attributes-employers-want-to-see-on-new-college-graduates-resumes/

22. Can allowing course choice improve academic outcomes in traditionally underperforming schools?
One study of US schools showed that allowing course choice in urban schools with high percentages of low-income minority students outperformed peers on state assessments, had higher graduation rates, and higher college acceptance and persistence rates. [C+]

https://edpolicy.stanford.edu/sites/default/files/scope-pub-student-centered-research-brief.pdf

23. Do most teens know what career they want to prepare for in college?
Some do but many teens are uncertain about what careers they want to pursue and many change their minds. A Pennsylvania study found that one third of teens had the same career goals at age 14-15 and when asked again at age 17-18. The other two thirds had changed their minds. [C–]

https://edsource.org/2015/survey-most-high-school-students-feel-unprepared-for-college-careers/83752

24. Are students good decision-makers?
Teenagers are generally not good decision-makers. White matter in the brain helps brain cells in communicating, and teenage brains have less white matter in the brain part (the frontal lobes) which controls decision making skills. [C–]

https://www.gjel.com/news/teen-brain-development.html

25. Do students work hard in elective courses?
Students often report looking for easy electives that do not require a lot of work. They also say that some electives are a "waste of time" and expect little of students. [C–]

http://www.ign.com/boards/threads/what-were-the-easiest-classes-for-you-in-high-school.452949991/

26. What happens when only a few students are interested in an elective?
In some cases, if not enough students are interested in an elective, the class may be cancelled due to low enrollment. [C–]

https://www.edgerton.k12.wi.us/cms/lib/WI01919720/Centricity/Domain/156/HSSummerSchoolRegistrationPacket2017.doc.pdf

27. What happens when many students are interested in the same elective?
In some cases, if many students are interested in the same elective, additional sections of that class may be offered. In other cases, not all students may be allowed to take the class. [C–]

http://www.chaminade.org/document.doc?id=775

28. How is student achievement measured if students are studying different things?
Testing is more difficult in less structured environments because it is more difficult to assess which students show greater understanding if they are all doing different things. [C–]

http://www.technofetish.net/mike/hewner-q11.pdf

29. How do teachers give feedback when students choose to study different things?
When each student is studying something different and completing a unique project, it can be difficult for teachers to give effective feedback to each individual student due to time constraints. [C–]

http://www.edweek.org/ew/articles/2016/08/24/do-we-give-students-too-much-choice.html

30. How is student choice affected by time constraints?
Unlimited choice can lead to a great deal of time consuming trial-and-error among students as they continue to explore different topics and problems. Providing guidance can keep students on track. [C–]

http://www.edweek.org/ew/articles/2016/08/24/do-we-give-students-too-much-choice.html

---

DECISION. Education: Leaving age. *Should students be required to attend school until age 16 or age 18?*

Questions about Leaving at 16

1. How much does the government spend on educating a single student each year in a public school? Code 274d

2. Why do students drop out of school? 263d

3. Do students skip school more often if they are unhappy in school and want to drop out? 528d

4. Do all students like school? 974d

5. What jobs are available for individuals without a high school diploma? 729d

6. Are there differences in brain development between 16- and 18-year-olds? 976d

7. Do students who don't complete high school have different life outcomes than those who graduate? 709d

8. Are teens likely to show impulsive behavior? 883d

9. Do students who do not complete high school regret it later in life? 869d

10. Does leaving school without graduating have health outcomes? 864d

Questions about Leaving at 18

11. In some places, are students required by law to stay in school until age 18? 523d

12. Are 18-year-olds emotionally more mature than 16-year-olds? 551d

13. Does requiring students to stay in school until age 18 raise graduation rates? 728d

14. Does the legal school-leaving age affect college enrollment? 608d

15. Does raising the minimum school-leaving age affect economic outcomes? 362d

16. Can requiring students to stay in school longer lead to serious behavior problems? 851d

17. Do teenagers work to contribute to family income? 364d

18. Does raising the minimum school-leaving age to 18 decrease the percentage of students dropping out of school? 292d

Add questions of your own:

19. _____

20. _____

21. _____

Questions about Leaving at 16

1. How much does the government spend on educating a single student each year in a public school?
The US government spends about $12,000 per student enrolled in public school each year. Some countries spend more and some spend less. Switzerland spends about $17,500 per student and Mexico spends about $2,500 per student. [16+]

https://nces.ed.gov/fastfacts/display.asp?id=66

2. Why do students drop out of school?
Research shows that dropping out of school occurs gradually over time. The main reasons students drop out of school are a lack of interest, low parent engagement, low academic performance, and family economic needs. [16+]

http://www.uwaystan.org/blog-entry/09-03-2013/3-reasons-students-dropout-high-school

3. Do students skip school more often if they are unhappy in school and want to drop out?
Research shows that students who miss 20 days of school have a 20% chance of dropping out. [16+]

http://www.huffingtonpost.com/2012/08/29/dropout-signs_n_1837797.html

4. Do all students like school?
In a survey of US students, 75% reported that what they were learning in school was not interesting to them. Less than 2% said they were never bored in school. [16+]

http://www.livescience.com/1308-students-bored-school.html

5. What jobs are available for individuals without a high school diploma?
Without a high school diploma, a person can find a low-paying job in retail, construction, cosmetology, and the restaurant industry. [16+]

http://work.chron.com/careers-available-high-school-diploma-15066.html

6. Are there differences in brain development between 16- and 18-year-olds?
Scientists have found that the part of the brain responsible for weighing risks, making judgments, and controlling impulsive behavior is not fully mature until a person is in their mid-20s. Evidence shows that though 16- and 18-year-olds' brains are still developing, a 16-year-old's brain is generally far less developed than those of teens just a little older. [16–]

http://usatoday30.usatoday.com/news/nation/2005-03-02-teens-cars-main-usat_x.htm

7. Do students who don't complete high school have different life outcomes than those who graduate?
Teens who do not complete high school tend to experience different life outcomes than teens who graduate. Dropouts on average earn less money and are more likely to go to jail, be unmarried, and score lower on happiness ratings. [16–]

http://issues.org/29-2/derek/

8. Are teens likely to show impulsive behavior?
Studies have shown that young people are more likely to engage in impulsive behavior. This means they tend to make decisions for immediate gratification without considering long-term effects. [16–]

http://issues.org/29-2/derek/

9. Do students who do not complete high school regret it later in life?
One study found that 74% of teens who dropped out of high school regretted their decision, saying that if they had to make the decision again, they would have stayed in school. [16–]

http://issues.org/29-2/derek/

10. Does leaving school without graduating have health outcomes?
Teens who leave school at age 16 are more likely to use cigarettes and illegal drugs, become pregnant as teens, and have shorter life expectancies than students required to stay in school until age 18. [16–]

http://issues.org/29-2/derek/

Questions about Leaving at 18

11. In some places, are students required by law to stay in school until age 18?
Not all countries have a minimum school leaving age. In a few countries (such as Bangladesh) the school-leaving age is as young as 10. In most countries it is between 16-18. About half of US states have a minimum school-leaving age of 18. This means that teens must stay in school until age 18, at which point they are no longer legally required to attend school. [18+]

http://issues.org/29-2/derek/

https://www.unicef.org/bangladesh/children_4862.html

12. Are 18-year-olds emotionally more mature than 16-year-olds?
Studies by psychologists have suggested that 18-year-olds are more emotionally mature than 16-year-olds. This means they tend to have better judgement and decision-making skills. [18+]

http://www.apa.org/news/press/releases/2009/10/teen-maturity.aspx

13. Does requiring students to stay in school until age 18 raise graduation rates?
One study found that raising the minimum school-leaving age from 16 to 18 led to a 2.4% increase in graduation rates in the US. This suggests that 55,000 more students would complete high school each year if every US state required school attendance until age 18. [18+]

http://issues.org/29-2/derek/

14. Does the legal school-leaving age affect college enrollment?
One US study found that raising the school-leaving age increased college enrollment by 1.5%. This suggests that if every US state raised the minimum school-leaving age to 18, this would lead to approximately 34,000 more students going to college each year. [18+]

http://issues.org/29-2/derek/

15. Does raising the minimum school-leaving age affect economic outcomes?
One US study found that for each additional year of required schooling, yearly income increases by about 10%. Students were also 3.6% less likely to end up unemployed, 5.5% less likely to end up on welfare, and 8.1% less likely to end up in poverty. [18+]

http://issues.org/29-2/derek/

16. Can requiring students to stay in school longer lead to serious behavior problems?
There is some evidence that requiring students to stay in school can lead to higher rates of violence in schools. [18–]

http://issues.org/29-2/derek/

17. Do teenagers work to contribute to family income?
In many parts of the world, families depend on teenage children contributing to family income in many parts of the world (including Africa, the Middle East, and parts of Asia). However, in many cases teens who work use earnings for their own expenses (clothing, entertainment, and restaurants). [18–]

https://www.bls.gov/opub/mlr/2000/09/art2full.pdf

https://books.google.com/books?id=FXsLabWSG9AC&printsec=frontcover&dq=teen+life+in+africa&hl=en&sa=X&ved=0ahUKEwjz8MeKxczSAhVn44MKHXV3CsMQ6AEIHDAA#v=onepage&q=teen%20life%20in%20africa&f=false

https://books.google.com/books?id=-ewAe5DwteQC&printsec=frontcover&dq=teen+life+in+middle+east&hl=en&sa=X&ved=0ahUKEwj3l6qUxczSAhUMxYMKHXPFDFgQ6AEIHDAA#v=onepage&q=teen%20life%20in%20middle%20east&f=false

https://books.google.com/books?id=7Oz5cvi3z3EC&printsec=frontcover&dq=teen+life+in+asia&hl=en&sa=X&ved=0ahUKEwiJtJLjxMzSAhUM24MKHSUkCD8Q6AEIGjAA#v=onepage&q=income&f=false

18. Does raising the minimum school-leaving age to 18 decrease the percentage of students dropping out of school?
One study found that raising the mandatory school attendance age to 18 was not effective in decreasing dropout rates. [18–]

http://www.aypf.org/documents/renniecenter_25.pdf

DECISION. Education: Homeschooling? *Should a family arriving from a foreign country be permitted to educate their child at home and not send the child to school?*

Questions about Homeschooling

1. How many children are homeschooled? Code 959d
2. Who sets the curriculum for a homeschooled child? 724d
3. Are homeschooling parents qualified to teach their children? 936d
4. How do homeschooled students perform on achievement tests? 369d
5. What can a homeschooled student do for sports and activities? 168d
6. Can homeschooled students do well in college? 416d
7. Is homeschooling legal? 705d

Questions about School

8. Who sets the curriculum for a public school child? 485d
9. Do most schools have specialists to help children if they have specific problems like a learning disability? 604d
10. How many children attend public or private schools in the US? 684d
11. How easily do children learn a second language? 703d
12. Is working with a group in school good for children? 387d
13. What are the requirements to be a public school teacher? 399d
14. How many students are in a typical classroom? 973d

Add questions of your own:

15. _____

16. _____

17. _____

Questions about Homeschooling

1. How many children are homeschooled?
Of all American children ages 5-17 during the 2011-2012 school year almost 2 million were homeschooled. Rates are generally lower elsewhere. [H+]

https://nces.ed.gov/programs/digest/d15/tables/dt15_206.10.asp?current=yes

2. Who sets the curriculum for a homeschooled child?
The family is free to set the curriculum within certain guidelines. [H+]

http://education.findlaw.com/curriculum-standards-school-funding/who-has-educational-authority.html

3. Are homeschooling parents qualified to teach their children?
Homeschooling parents are not required to be certified teachers or to have specific qualifications to teach particular subjects. [H–]

https://www.psychologytoday.com/blog/love-in-time-homeschooling/201007/should-homeschooling-parents-have-college-degrees

4. How do homeschooled students perform on achievement tests?
Research shows that homeschooled students perform well on achievement tests. One study found that homeschooled students performed between 18% and 28% better on an achievement test than public school students. [H+]

https://www.hslda.org/docs/nche/000010/200410250.asp

5. What can a homeschooled student do for sports and activities?
There are many sport teams, programs, and activities at local YMCAs and recreation centers that any children can attend. Many states also allow homeschooled children to play sports for their local public school. [H+]

http://www.learningliftoff.com/can-homeschoolers-play-public-school-sports/#.WPpZT1MrJao

6. Can homeschooled students do well in college?
A study should that homeschool students (66.7%) graduated from college at a higher rate than public school students (57.5%). [H+]

http://www.cbsnews.com/news/can-homeschoolers-do-well-in-college/

7. Is homeschooling legal?
Homeschooling is legal in all 50 US states. Every state has its own laws regarding homeschooling but some laws merely require you to notify your local school district that you are homeschooling your child. [H+]

https://www.hslda.org/laws/

Questions about School

8. Who sets the curriculum for a public school child?
School districts along with city and state governments have education departments that decide what all children need to learn. [S+]

http://education.findlaw.com/curriculum-standards-school-funding/the-roles-of-federal-and-state-governments-in-education.html

9. Do most schools have specialists to help children if they have specific problems like a learning disability?
Almost every public school has a special education teacher on staff full-time. There are federal and state laws that protect and ensure special education services are provided to any child that has a need. [S+]

http://www.ldonline.org/article/6108

10. How many children attend public or private schools in the US?
Of all American children ages 5-17 during the 2011-2012 school year, 97% of children attended public or private schools. [S+]

https://nces.ed.gov/programs/digest/d15/tables/dt15_206.10.asp?current=yes

11. How easily do children learn a second language?
Children exposed to a new language usually learn it very quickly and more easily than teens or adults do. [S+]

https://sites.psu.edu/siowfa14/2014/09/07/learning-a-second-language-is-easier-for-children-but-why/

12. Is working with a group in school good for children?
Group projects can help students develop many skills that are increasingly important in the work world. [S+]

https://www.edutopia.org/blog/deeper-learning-collaboration-key-rebecca-alber

13. What are the requirements to be a public school teacher?
Requirements vary by country, but generally public school teachers must go through teacher training programs and classes and must pass certification exams to become a certified teacher. [S+]

http://www.teachercertificationdegrees.com/

14. How many students are in a typical classroom?
In the US, the typical middle school classroom has an average of 25.5 students. [S–]

https://nces.ed.gov/surveys/sass/tables/sass1112_2013314_t1s_007.asp

---

DECISION. Education: Teacher pay. *Should all teachers receive the same pay or should teachers with more skill or experience be paid more?*

Questions about Same pay

1. Are all teachers currently paid the same salary? Code 532d
2. Why was the idea of equal salaries introduced? 334d
3. How do teacher salaries compare to salaries of similar jobs? 481d
4. Have US teacher salaries increased over time? 640d

Questions about Skill- or experience-based pay

5. How are teachers paid in China? 276d
6. Are teachers in China highly paid overall? 394d
7. Have teacher salaries in China increased over time? 553d
8. Are teachers in favor of skill-based pay? 484d
9. Are all teachers equally effective? 989d
10. Does skill-based pay for teachers affect student achievement? 895d
11. Does money influence people to work harder? 526d
12. Is it difficult to change a teacher pay system? 129d
13. What are some teachers' objections to skill-based pay? 275d
14. Do teachers become more effective with experience? 901d
15. At what point do teachers generally reach their peak effectiveness? 505d
16. How is a teacher's skill measured? 432d
17. Are high test scores an indication of highly-skilled teaching? 323d
18. Have there been negative outcomes of skill-based pay for teachers? 476d
19. How does skill-based pay affect teachers' relationships with one another? 512d
20. Do people with higher salaries like their jobs more? 522d
21. Does skill-based pay create more work for teachers? 943d
22. Do yearly pay raises motivate workers to stay in the job or work harder? 891d

Add questions of your own:

23. _____

24. _____

25. _____

Questions about Same pay

1. Are all teachers currently paid the same salary?
In most US school districts, teachers are paid according to a single salary schedule. This means that teachers in the same district with equal education levels and years of experience receive the same salary. [S+]
http://www.educationworld.com/a_issues/issues/issues374a.shtml

2. Why was the idea of equal salaries introduced?
The idea of equalizing teacher salaries was introduced almost 100 years ago because female, minority, and elementary school teachers were making less money than male, white, and high school teachers. [S+]
http://www.educationworld.com/a_issues/issues/issues374a.shtml

3. How do teacher salaries compare to salaries of similar jobs?
Public school teachers in the US earned 17% less than similar college-educated professionals. [S–]

https://www.washingtonpost.com/news/answer-sheet/wp/2016/08/16/think-teachers-arent-paid-enough-its-worse-than-you-think/?utm_term=.47cce6182c14

4. Have US teacher salaries increased over time?
Teacher salaries in the US have decreased in the past 20 years, but salaries of college graduates in general have gone up. [S–]

https://www.washingtonpost.com/news/answer-sheet/wp/2016/08/16/think-teachers-arent-paid-enough-its-worse-than-you-think/?utm_term=.47cce6182c14

Questions about Skill- or experience-based pay

5. How are teachers paid in China?
Teachers in China receive a base pay plus an additional amount for each year of experience. [E+]

https://www.quora.com/How-much-are-Chinese-teachers-salaries-in-China

6. Are teachers in China highly paid overall?
Teacher pay in China varies greatly by location. Overall, income for teachers is low compared to other professions. [E+]

https://www.quora.com/How-much-are-Chinese-teachers-salaries-in-China

7. Have teacher salaries in China increased over time?
Yes, teacher salaries in China increased substantially between 1993 and 2012. [E+]

https://www.quora.com/How-much-are-Chinese-teachers-salaries-in-China

8. Are teachers in favor of skill-based pay?
According to a survey of US teachers, 40% liked the idea of skill-based pay. This is higher than in previous years. However, teachers report both positive and negative reactions to such plans. [E+/E–]

https://faculty.missouri.edu/~podgurskym/wp-content/uploads/2001/art2001-10.pdf

http://www.cpre.org/images/stories/cpre_pdfs/RB46.pdf

9. Are all teachers equally effective?
There is much evidence to indicate that some teachers do a better job than others as measured by the learning gains their students show. [E+]

http://knowledgecenter.csg.org/kc/content/capitol-research-does-merit-pay-teachers-have-merit-pros-and-cons-new-models-teacher-compensation

10. Does skill-based pay for teachers affect student achievement?
Evidence of a substantial positive impact of performance-based pay on either student achievement or teacher performance is lacking. [E–]

http://www.cpre.org/images/stories/cpre_pdfs/RB46.pdf

11. Does money influence people to work harder?
Some research shows that people faced with rewards such as extra money are actually less motivated. Employees may be more likely to enjoy their job if they focus on the work itself, not the money. [E–]

http://www.rug.nl/gmw/psychology/research/onderzoek_summerschool/firststep/content/papers/4.4.pdf

12. Is it difficult to change a teacher pay system?
Changing a pay system is a time-consuming and expensive process for school boards and teachers unions. Teachers have also shown resistance to changing the pay system. [E–]
http://www.educationworld.com/a_issues/issues/issues374a.shtml

13. What are some teachers' objections to skill-based pay?
Some teachers oppose skill-based pay because it is difficult to evaluate teacher performance, it could decrease teacher morale, and it could cause political problems in schools. [E–]
https://faculty.missouri.edu/~podgurskym/wp-content/uploads/2001/art2001-10.pdf

14. Do teachers become more effective with experience?
Teaching experience is overall positively associated with student achievement gains. [E+]
https://tntp.org/assets/documents/TNTP_FactSheet_TeacherExperience_2012.pdf

15. At what point do teachers generally reach their peak effectiveness?
Some studies have shown peak effectiveness to occur with about five years of teaching experience. [E+/–]
https://tntp.org/assets/documents/TNTP_FactSheet_TeacherExperience_2012.pdf

16. How is a teacher's skill measured?
Several methods are used, but teacher skill is most often measured by the achievement of their students, especially on standardized tests. [E–]
https://faculty.missouri.edu/~podgurskym/wp-content/uploads/2001/art2001-10.pdf

17. Are high test scores an indication of highly-skilled teaching?
Teachers are not the only influence on student test scores. Other factors include previous teachers, family involvement, socioeconomic status, school quality, and the student's intelligence. [E–]
https://faculty.missouri.edu/~podgurskym/wp-content/uploads/2001/art2001-10.pdf

18. Have there been negative outcomes of skill-based pay for teachers?
Skill-based pay for teachers has shown some poor results in England and China. Teachers became focused on student test outcomes. [E–]
https://faculty.missouri.edu/~podgurskym/wp-content/uploads/2001/art2001-10.pdf

19. How does skill-based pay affect teachers' relationships with one another?
Skill-based pay can encourage competition among teachers because they will be competing for higher salaries. [E–]
https://faculty.missouri.edu/~podgurskym/wp-content/uploads/2001/art2001-10.pdf

20. Do people with higher salaries like their jobs more?
Research shows that the relation between salary and job satisfaction is weak. Salary does not have much influence on how much people like their jobs. [E–]
http://www.timothy-judge.com/Judge,%20Piccolo,%20Podsakoff,%20et%20al.%20(JVB%20 2010).pdf

21. Does skill-based pay create more work for teachers?
Teachers in one study complained that the portfolio they had to create for a skill-based pay plan was time-consuming and created too much paperwork. [E–]
http://www.cpre.org/images/stories/cpre_pdfs/RB46.pdf

22. Do yearly pay raises motivate workers to stay in the job or work harder?
The idea that annual pay raises are a useful incentive to keep workers satisfied is now being questioned by many companies. [E–]
https://www.wsj.com/articles/companies-rethink-annual-pay-raises-for-all-employees-1471964521

Chapter 8 ■ A Community Future 99

DECISION. Driving. *Should teens be permitted to get drivers' licenses at age 16 or age 18?*

Questions about Driving at 16

1. Does experience make a difference in driving ability? Code 743d
2. Where do 16-year-olds drive? 548d
3. Are there programs to encourage safe driving among new drivers? 852d
4. Do training programs reduce the number of accidents involving 16-year-olds? 506d
5. How many car accidents involve 16- or 17-year-olds? 996d
6. Are teenagers risky drivers? 324d
7. Do teenage boys have different driving records than teenage girls? 317d
8. Are there differences in brain development between 16- and 18-year-olds? 672d
9. How often do 16-year-olds die in car accidents? 911d
10. Are 16-year-olds more likely to have an accident when peers are in the car? 835d

Questions about Driving at 18

11. At what age is a person allowed to drive? 601d
12. Does teenagers' brain development affect their driving? 955d
13. Do 18-year-olds have fewer car accidents than 16-year-olds? 836d
14. Is there evidence that raising the driving age reduces car accidents? 331d
15. Are 18-year-olds emotionally more mature than 16-year-olds? 677d
16. How might parents be affected by teenagers getting their license at age 18 instead of 16? 606d
17. Does changing the driving age to 18 decrease car accidents? 918d
18. Do more 16- or 18-year-olds report texting while driving? 386d
19. Do teenagers work to contribute to family income? 578d
20. Do most people drive to work? 826d
21. Does everyone have access to public transportation? 531d
22. If teens don't drive until age 18, do they get enough supervised practice? 919d

Add questions of your own:

23. _____

24. _____

25. _____

Questions about Driving at 16

1. Does experience make a difference in driving ability?
Research shows that experience decreases the likelihood of getting into an accident. Teens are 50% more likely to crash in the first month of driving than they are after a year of experience and twice as likely to crash than they are after two years of experience. [16+]

https://www.aaafoundation.org/sites/default/files/2011TeenSafeDriverWeekFS_1.pdf

2. Where do 16-year-olds drive?
Teens become more active in school clubs, social activities, and after-school jobs that often require transportation. They may also drive when not strictly necessary, as a social activity. [16+]

http://www.livestrong.com/article/1006354-reasons-teens-should-drive/

3. Are there programs to encourage safe driving among new drivers?
All US states have graduated driver licensing (GDL) programs to help build safe driving skills among new young drivers. These programs require longer practice periods, limits to driving in high risk conditions (at night), and more adult support as teens gradually build driving skills. [16+]

https://www.cdc.gov/motorvehiclesafety/teen_drivers/teendrivers_factsheet.html

4. Do training programs reduce the number of accidents involving 16-year-olds?
In the US, more comprehensive GDL programs have been found to reduce fatal car crashes by up to 41%. [16+]

https://www.cdc.gov/motorvehiclesafety/teen_drivers/teendrivers_factsheet.html

5. How many car accidents involve 16- or 17-year-olds?
The number of car accidents per mile is three times as high for 16-year-olds as it is for 18–19-year-olds. Sixteen-year-olds have higher accident rates than drivers of any other age. Twenty percent of 16-year-old drivers have an accident within their first year of driving. [16–]

http://www.iihs.org/iihs/topics/t/teenagers/qanda

https://www.dosomething.org/us/facts/11-facts-about-teen-driving

https://www.dosomething.org/us/facts/11-facts-about-teen-driving

6. Are teenagers risky drivers?
Research shows that reckless driving is one of the leading causes of teen accidents. One study that observed teenage drivers leaving high school found that teenagers drove faster than general traffic, and kept less distance from the car in front of them. [16–]

https://www.cdc.gov/motorvehiclesafety/teen_drivers/teendrivers_factsheet.html

https://www.ncbi.nlm.nih.gov/pubmed/15921652

7. Do teenage boys have different driving records than teenage girls?
In one study, teenage boys were found to have the highest rate of high risk driving among high school drivers. They were twice as likely as other drivers to drive 15 mph or more over the speed limit and keep less than a 1 second distance between their car and the car in front of them. [16–]

https://www.ncbi.nlm.nih.gov/pubmed/15921652

8. Are there differences in brain development between 16- and 18-year-olds?
Scientists have found that the part of the brain responsible for weighing risks, making judgments, and controlling impulsive behavior is not fully mature until a person is in their mid-20s. Evidence shows that though 16- and 18-year-olds' brains are still developing, a 16-year-old's brain is generally far less developed than those of teens just a little older. [16–]

http://usatoday30.usatoday.com/news/nation/2005-03-02-teens-cars-main-usat_x.htm

9. How often do 16-year-olds die in car accidents?
Car accidents are the leading cause of death for people under the age of 18. [16–]

https://blog.allstate.com/rethinking-the-minimum-driving-age/

10. Are 16-year-olds more likely to have an accident when peers are in the car?
16–17-year-olds' risk of death per mile increases 44% when just one other teen is in the car. This risk doubles with two teen passengers and quadruples with three or more. [16–]

https://www.aaafoundation.org/sites/default/files/2012TeenDriverRiskAgePassengersFS.pdf

Questions about Driving at 18

11. At what age is a person allowed to drive?
The driving age varies around the world. In most countries it is 18. In Britain it is 17. In most US states, a person can take a test to get a driver's license at age 16. [18+]

https://blog.allstate.com/rethinking-the-minimum-driving-age/

12. Does teenagers' brain development affect their driving?
White matter in the brain helps brain cells in communicating. Adolescent brains have less white matter in the brain part (the frontal lobes) which controls decision making skills. Because of this, teenagers may be more likely to speed, disobey traffic signs, and lose control of their vehicles. [18+]

https://www.gjel.com/news/teen-brain-development.html

13. Do 18-year-olds have fewer car accidents than 16-year-olds?
18–19-year-olds have 3 times fewer car crashes per mile than 16–17-year-olds. The crash risk is highest during the early months of having a license. [18+]

https://www.cdc.gov/MotorVehicleSafety/Teen_Drivers/teendrivers_factsheet.html

14. Is there evidence that raising the driving age reduces car accidents?
Statistics show that in the US, where in most states 16-year-olds can drive with a restricted license, there are 13.9 traffic deaths per 100,000 people. In the UK, where the licensing age is 17, this number is 5.4. In Sweden, where the licensing age is 18, this number is 5.2. [18+]

https://blog.allstate.com/rethinking-the-minimum-driving-age/

15. Are 18-year-olds emotionally more mature than 16-year-olds?
Studies by psychologists have suggested that 18-year-olds are more emotionally mature than 16-year-olds. This means they tend to have better self-control, judgement, and decision-making skills. [18+]

http://www.apa.org/news/press/releases/2009/10/teen-maturity.aspx

16. How might parents be affected by teenagers getting their license at age 18 instead of 16?
If teens don't have their license, parents might have to drive their teen as they become more active in things outside of school (like jobs, clubs, and social events). [18–]

http://www.livestrong.com/article/1006354-reasons-teens-should-drive/

17. Does changing the driving age to 18 decrease car accidents?
A nationwide study in the US showed that making it harder for teenagers to get licenses reduced deadly accidents among 16–17-year-olds. This is because GDL programs restrict things like nighttime driving and number of passengers. Because these restrictions do not apply to 18-year-olds, they have more deadly accidents. [18–]

http://jamanetwork.com/journals/jama/fullarticle/1104325

18. Do more 16- or 18-year-olds report texting while driving?

In one US national survey, 44% of 18–20-year-olds reported texting while driving. In another survey, 26% of US teens age 16–17 reported texting while driving. [18–]

https://www.nhtsa.gov/sites/nhtsa.dot.gov/files/811555.pdf

http://www.pewinternet.org/2009/11/16/teens-and-distracted-driving-major-findings/

19. Do teenagers work to contribute to family income?

In the US, about one third of teens have a job. However, research shows that they are not working for their family's economic necessity but for their own expenses (clothing, entertainment, and restaurants). In some African, Middle Eastern, and Asian countries, teens are expected to contribute to family income. [18–]

https://www.bls.gov/opub/mlr/2000/09/art2full.pdf

https://books.google.com/books?id=FXsLabWSG9AC&printsec=frontcover&dq=teen+life+in+africa&hl=en&sa=X&ved=0ahUKEwjz8MeKxczSAhVn44MKHXV3CsMQ6AEIHDAA#v=onepage&q=teen%20life%20in%20africa&f=false

https://books.google.com/books?id=-ewAe5DwteQC&printsec=frontcover&dq=teen+life+in+middle+east&hl=en&sa=X&ved=0ahUKEwj3l6qUxczSAhUMxYMKHXPFDFgQ6AEIHDAA#v=onepage&q=teen%20life%20in%20middle%20east&f=false

https://books.google.com/books?id=7Oz5cvi3z3EC&printsec=frontcover&dq=teen+life+in+asia&hl=en&sa=X&ved=0ahUKEwiJtJLjxMzSAhUM24MKHSUkCD8Q6AEIGjAA#v=onepage&q=income&f=false

20. Do most people drive to work?

Research shows that approximately 75% of US workers drive themselves to work, whereas approximately 5% use public transportation. [18–]

https://www.rita.dot.gov/bts/sites/rita.dot.gov.bts/files/publications/national_transportation_statistics/html/table_01_41.html

21. Does everyone have access to public transportation?

Some people have easier access to public transportation than others. People living in rural areas are farther away from public transportation than those living in urban areas, and many times these transportation options are not available. [18–]

https://www.transit.dot.gov/sites/fta.dot.gov/files/docs/2015%20NTST.pdf

https://www.fhwa.dot.gov/planning/publications/rural_areas_planning/page03.cfm

22. If teens don't drive until age 18, do they get enough supervised practice?

In order to avoid the restrictions imposed by GDL programs, many teens have delayed getting their license until they turn 18 (when these restrictions no longer apply). Research suggests that by avoiding requirements like adult supervised practice, this may be leading to more accidents among 18-year-olds. [18–]

http://jamanetwork.com/journals/jama/fullarticle/1104325

DECISION. Drinking. *Should young people be permitted to drink alcohol at age 18 or age 21?*

Questions about 18-year-olds drinking

1. Do teens report drinking alcohol? Code 602d

2. At what age is it legal to drink? 620d

3. Are there ever circumstances under which a person not normally allowed legally to drink can do so? 475d

4. When is a person legally considered an adult? 887d
5. If the drinking age was lowered, would teens be more likely to abuse alcohol either as teens or later in life? 600d
6. What is the legal drinking age in countries other than the US? 343d
7. Is there a connection between teen drinking and life success? 611d
8. How does teen drinking affect teens' school performance? 448d
9. Does drinking by older teens have any effect on younger teens? 101d

Questions about 21-year-olds drinking

10. Why was 21 decided on as the legal drinking age in the US? 447d
11. Which groups of people support 21 as the legal drinking age? 742d
12. Was the US law making the drinking age 21 effective? 961d
13. Are 21-year-olds more mature than 18-year-olds? 772d
14. Are there long-term physical effects of drinking alcohol? 455d
15. By what age is brain development completed? 325d
16. Are there short-term physical effects of drinking alcohol? 207d
17. Can alcohol lead to a young person's death? 430d
18. Has the number of alcohol-related deaths for 18–20-year-olds decreased since the drinking age was set at 21? 306d
19. Does the law against drinking below age 21 stop teens from drinking before that age? 738d
20. How are people under age 21 able to drink if it is illegal? 587d

Add questions of your own:

21. _____

22. _____

23. _____

Questions about 18-year-olds drinking

1. Do teens report drinking alcohol?
Teen drinking varies around the world. In some European countries (Austria, Denmark), as many as 80% of 15–16-year-olds report drinking in the past 30 days. In the US, this figure is about 33%. By age 18, it increases to about 65%. [+]

http://www.samhsa.gov/data/sites/default/files/NSDUH-DetTabs2014/NSDUH-DetTabs2014.htm#tab2-15b

http://resources.prev.org/documents/ESPAD.pdf

2. At what age is it legal to drink?
The legal drinking age varies by country. In the US, it is 21. In most countries, it is 18 or 19, but in some it is as young as 10. Some countries have no minimum legal drinking age, and in some it is illegal to drink alcohol at any age. [18+]

http://www.who.int/substance_abuse/publications/global_alcohol_report/msb_gsr_2014_2.pdf?ua=1

3. Are there ever circumstances under which a person not normally allowed legally to drink can do so?
This varies around the world, but in some US states, rules allow people under 21 to drink in special circumstances, such as religious events, medical purposes, or if the person is with a parent or guardian. In Hong Kong, the drinking age is only enforced in public places, so minors can drink in the home. [+]

https://alcoholpolicy.niaaa.nih.gov/state_profiles_of_underage_drinking_laws.html

http://www.scmp.com/lifestyle/health/article/1511128/teenage-binge-drinking-hk-becoming-headache-amid-lack-regulation

4. When is a person legally considered an adult?
The legal age of adulthood varies by country. In all US states (except Nebraska and Alabama where it is 19), a person is legally considered an adult at age 18. The legal rights of adults include voting, marrying, adopting children, joining the armed forces, and holding public office. [18+]

https://hrpo.wustl.edu/wp-content/uploads/2015/01/5-Determining-Legal-Age-to-Consent.pdf

5. If the drinking age was lowered, would teens be more likely to abuse alcohol either as teens or later in life?
It is not likely that lowering the drinking age would lead to increased rates of alcohol abuse. Although some studies show that drinking alcohol earlier in life is linked with abusing alcohol later, there isn't much difference between starting at 18 or 21. Risk is greater if drinking is started in early adolescence, which is under 18. [18+]

https://www.chooseresponsibility.org/frequently_asked_questions/#raised

6. What is the legal drinking age in countries other than the US?
In most countries of the world, including Canada, France, UK, and Australia, the minimum legal drinking age is between 18-19. [18+]

http://drinkingage.procon.org/view.resource.php?resourceID=004294

7. Is there a connection between teen drinking and life success?
While success can mean different things to different people, US children who begin drinking alcohol by age 13 were found 38% more likely to become alcoholics later in life. Alcoholism can affect family relationships, friendships, work performance, and mental health. [–]

http://www.apa.org/monitor/jan08/earlydrinking.aspx

8. How does teen drinking affect teens' school performance?
Studies show that students in US states with a legal drinking age of 18 were 13 times more likely to drop out of high school compared to students in states with a legal drinking age of 21. [–]

https://www.cdc.gov/alcohol/fact-sheets/minimum-legal-drinking-age.htm

9. Does drinking by older teens have any effect on younger teens?
Older teens, including siblings and peers, are role models for younger teens, who try to imitate and follow the older teens. A study showed that older adolescents are often a source of drugs and alcohol for younger adolescents. [18–]

http://www.tandfonline.com/doi/abs/10.3109/10826088609027390

Questions about 21-year-olds drinking

10. Why was 21 decided on as the legal drinking age in the US?
In 1984, President Reagan signed the National Minimum Drinking Age Act to make the drinking age 21. At that time, there was a rise in the number of drunk driving accidents, and groups like MADD (Mothers Against Drunk Driving) hoped to reduce this number by raising the legal drinking age. [21+]

https://www.chooseresponsibility.org/frequently_asked_questions/#raised

11. Which groups of people support 21 as the legal drinking age?
In the US, several groups recommend the legal drinking age be 21, including the American Academy of Pediatrics, Mothers Against Drunk Driving, National Highway Traffic Safety Administration, National Prevention Council, and National Academy of Sciences. [21+]

https://www.cdc.gov/alcohol/fact-sheets/minimum-legal-drinking-age.htm

12. Was the US law making the drinking age 21 effective?
After the law was passed, there was a 16% average decrease in car accidents. The rate of 18–20-year-olds who reported drinking during the previous month also declined from 59% to 40%. Drinking among 21–25-year-olds also declined from 70% to 56%. [21+]

https://www.cdc.gov/alcohol/fact-sheets/minimum-legal-drinking-age.htm

13. Are 21-year-olds more mature than 18-year-olds?
21-year-olds have a greater exposure to the world. Many of them attend college which gives them broader experience. [21+]

http://www.mercurynews.com/2011/05/18/keep-drinking-age-at-21-teens-arent-mature-enough-to-handle-consequences/

14. Are there long-term physical effects of drinking alcohol?
If people drink a lot of alcohol often, they can develop liver disease, kidney damage, malnutrition, or other health conditions. Heavy drinking can also lead to declined thinking and memory abilities. [–]

https://www.chooseresponsibility.org/frequently_asked_questions/#raised

15. By what age is brain development completed?
The prefrontal cortex, which is responsible for abstract thinking and good judgment, is not fully developed until one's early- to mid-20s. [21+]

https://www.chooseresponsibility.org/frequently_asked_questions/#raised

16. Are there short-term physical effects of drinking alcohol?
If large amounts of alcohol are consumed, slower heart and breathing rates may result. The central nervous system can even shut down, causing loss of consciousness, blackout, or even death. Alcohol use can also make a person less in control of their motor skills and worsen their memory. [–]

https://www.chooseresponsibility.org/frequently_asked_questions/#raised

17. Can alcohol lead to a young person's death?
In the US, teen drinking contributes to over 4,300 deaths and 189,000 alcohol-related hospital visits each year. [–]

https://www.cdc.gov/alcohol/fact-sheets/minimum-legal-drinking-age.htm

18. Has the number of alcohol-related deaths for 18–20-year-olds decreased since the drinking age was set at 21?
Many studies show that the overall number of alcohol-related deaths for ages 18–20 has gone down since the national drinking age was set at 21. However, this downward trend began before the law was passed. [21–]

https://www.chooseresponsibility.org/frequently_asked_questions/#raised

19. Does the law against drinking below age 21 stop teens from drinking before that age?
Evidence shows that most 18–20-year-olds ignore the law and drink before the age of 21. [21–]

https://www.chooseresponsibility.org/frequently_asked_questions/#raised

20. How are people under age 21 able to drink if it is illegal?
People drinking illegally under the age of 21 try not to get caught, which often leads to unsafe or irresponsible drinking such as "pre-gaming" and binge drinking. If the drinking age were lowered to 18, these teens wouldn't have to hide their drinking and it could take place in a safer environment. [21–]

https://www.chooseresponsibility.org/frequently_asked_questions/#raised

---

DECISION. Juvenile v. adult court for teen offenders. *Should teens who commit serious crimes be tried in regular adult court or a special court for juveniles?*

Questions about Juvenile offenders and courts

1. How does a juvenile court system differ from a regular one? Code 707d
2. Are punishments for the same crime different in juvenile and adult courts? 821d
3. Would the government save money if they didn't have to pay for a juvenile system? 902d
4. What proportion of violent crimes are committed by juveniles? 897d
5. Do teens sentenced to jail time in juvenile court get jail records? 849d
6. Are teens more likely than adults to repeat their crimes? 762d
7. At what age is the brain fully developed? 855d
8. Do people get smarter as they get older? 756d

Questions about Regular adult court

9. Do all courts give the right to a trial by jury? 652d
10. Are teens at risk of being assaulted in adult prisons? 309d
11. Can people in regular prison get an education there? 172d
12. Do teens in adult prisons spend time with adult prisoners there? 568d

Add questions of your own:

13. _____

14. _____

15. _____

Questions about Juvenile offenders and courts

1. How does a juvenile court system differ from a regular one?
The judges and staff in a juvenile system are specially trained to deal with young people in trouble and know a lot about their problems. [J+]

http://www.americanbar.org/content/dam/aba/migrated/publiced/youthcases_youthcourts.authcheckdam.pdf

2. Are punishments for the same crime different in juvenile and adult courts?
Punishments tend to be less severe and sentences shorter in juvenile court and judges are more likely to give the offender a second chance or to order community service as a punishment, rather than prison. [J+]

http://www.americanbar.org/content/dam/aba/migrated/publiced/youthcases_youthcourts.authcheckdam.pdf

3. Would the government save money if they didn't have to pay for a juvenile system?
Yes, juvenile courts and prisons require more people to run and thus cost more. [J–]

https://www.usnews.com/news/blogs/data-mine/2014/12/09/what-youth-incarceration-costs-taxpayers

4. What proportion of violent crimes are committed by juveniles?
Juveniles were involved in one-quarter of violent crimes in the USA over a 25 year period beginning in the 1990s. [J+]

https://www.ojjdp.gov/ojstatbb/offenders/qa03202.asp?qaDate=19990930

5. Do teens sentenced to jail time in juvenile court get jail records?
They do not if sentences are served in a juvenile detention center; their records are sealed on their release. [J+]

https://www.nap.edu/read/9747/chapter/7#213

6. Are teens more likely than adults to repeat their crimes?
Rates of recidivism vary by age, with younger offenders more likely to repeat. In the US the recidivism rate is 68% for those under age 21, and 16% among those over age 60. [J–]

https://www.ussc.gov/sites/default/files/pdf/research-and-publications/research-publications/2016/recidivism_overview.pdf

7. At what age is the brain fully developed?
The prefrontal cortex, which is responsible for abstract thinking and good judgment, is not fully developed until one's early- to mid-20s. [J+]

https://www.chooseresponsibility.org/frequently_asked_questions/#raised

8. Do people get smarter as they get older?
People do not necessarily get smarter as they get older. But there is evidence that adults think more carefully before they act, compared to teens. [J+]

http://www.americanbar.org/content/dam/aba/migrated/publiced/features/DYJpart2.authcheckdam.pdf

Questions about Regular adult court

9. Do all courts give the right to a trial by jury?
No, only regular courts do. Juvenile courts don't allow trial by jury. A judge hears evidence and rules. [A+]

http://www.nolo.com/legal-encyclopedia/do-juveniles-right-trial-jury.html

10. Are teens at risk of being assaulted in adult prisons?
Yes. Teens in adult jails are 50% more likely to be attacked by another inmate and twice as likely by prison staff, compared to adult prisoners. [A–]

http://www.justicepolicy.org/images/upload/97-02_rep_riskjuvenilesface_jj.pdf

11. Can people in regular prison get an education there?
This varies by prison, but most offer some opportunities for education. The large majority of adult prisoners do not have a high school diploma. In juvenile prisons, all teens attend school regularly and can get credits toward high school graduation. [A–]

http://prisonstudiesproject.org/why-prison-education-programs

12. Do teens in adult prisons spend time with adult prisoners there?
This varies by prison, but in some prisons there are opportunities for them to be together. [A–]

http://www.alternet.org/books/how-teens-cope-prison-after-being-sentenced-adults

---

DECISION. Town sports teams. *Should town taxes help to pay the cost of community sports teams? Or should they be paid for entirely by the families who use them?*

1. What percentage of youth are involved in sports? Code 308d
2. How much daily exercise is needed to stay in good health? 613d
3. What percentage of high school students meet exercise recommendations? 921d
4. What percentage of teens spend their out-of-school time in physical activities? 456d
5. What do teens spend their out-of-school time on? 290d
6. Do students who have free time after school always use it wisely? 412d
7. What do town taxes normally pay for? 639d
8. Do young students continue with a sport once they start to play it? 246d
9. Do young people enjoy playing sports? 735d
10. How can coaching affect a young athlete's enjoyment of a sport? 942d
11. What is the risk of injury in sports? 927d
12. How might sport participation affect a teen's physical development? 142d
13. Do sports increase stress levels? 243d
14. Do sports pose a danger to physical well-being? 279d
15. Is too much competition bad for young athletes? 377d
16. Does it cost money to be on a sports team? 751d
17. What roles do parents play in their children's sports activity? 270d

Add questions of your own:

18. _____

19. _____

20. _____

1. What percentage of youth are involved in sports?
69% of school-age girls and 75% of boys in the US participate in team sports. [T+/F+]
http://www.livestrong.com/article/373329-how-many-youth-participate-in-sports-in-the-u-s/

2. How much daily exercise is needed to stay in good health?
Health experts recommend at least one hour daily of physical activity. This can take any form that the person chooses. [T+/F+]
http://www.apa.org/news/press/releases/stress/2013/exercise.aspx

3. What percentage of high school students meet exercise recommendations?
One four-year study of US high school students found that only 9% fulfilled the exercise recommendations made by The US Centers for Disease Control and Prevention throughout the study period. [T+]
http://www.cbsnews.com/news/teens-dont-get-enough-exercise/

4. What percentage of teens spend their out-of-school time in physical activities?
A US survey found that only 22% of teens choose to spend their out-of-school time in physical activities. [T–]
https://www.chapinhall.org/sites/default/files/publications/Issue_Brief%2005_27_09_Final.pdf

5. What do teens spend their out-of-school time on?
One US study found that 73% of teens spend their out-of-school time on activities like watching TV, listening to music, sleeping, reading, or playing or working on a computer. [T–]
https://www.chapinhall.org/sites/default/files/publications/Issue_Brief%2005_27_09_Final.pdf

6. Do students who have free time after school always use it wisely?
Studies show that youth are most at risk during after-school hours. Juvenile crime rates triple and teens engage in more risky behaviors. Even if they are not getting into trouble, teens are often at home watching TV, playing video games, and eating during this time. [T+]
http://www.afterschoolalliance.org/printPage.cfm?idPage=9AC3841C-B33A-5A21-1C8EE2B59468977F

7. What do town taxes normally pay for?
Town taxes normally pay for things like local public schools, parks, libraries, roads, police, and fire departments. [T–]
https://www.sapling.com/7737352/do-city-taxes-pay

8. Do young students continue with a sport once they start to play it?
About 35% of young athletes quit participating in a sport every year, according to a US survey. By age 15, 70-80% of teens who once played a sport have quit. [T–]
https://www.ncbi.nlm.nih.gov/pmc/articles/PMC3871410/

9. Do young people enjoy playing sports?
One study reported that while "having fun" is the main reason most children play sports, pressure to compete may lead to stress and unhappiness for a child. [T–]

htttps://www.ncbi.nlm.nih.gov/pmc/articles/PMC3871410/

10. How can coaching affect a young athlete's enjoyment of a sport?
Sometimes youth coaches use methods such as verbal criticism, punishments for poor performance, only allowing the best athletes to play, and over-celebrating wins. These practices can be upsetting to young athletes. [T–]

htttps://www.ncbi.nlm.nih.gov/pmc/articles/PMC3871410/

11. What is the risk of injury in sports?
In the US, there are 2.6 million emergency room visits every year for sports-related injuries among those aged 5-24 years. [T–]

htttps://www.ncbi.nlm.nih.gov/pmc/articles/PMC3871410/

12. How might sport participation affect a teen's physical development?
Teenage athletes may experience a decrease in flexibility, coordination, and balance due to their physical development; these changes can increase their risk of injury. [T–]

htttps://www.ncbi.nlm.nih.gov/pmc/articles/PMC3871410/

13. Do sports increase stress levels?
Research indicates that sports settings can induce high levels of competitive stress in many young people, when they do not perform as well as peers. [T–]

htttps://www.psychologytoday.com/blog/coaching-and-parenting-young-athletes/201407/are-youth-sports-too-stressful

14. Do sports pose a danger to physical well-being?
Researchers have found that sports are the leading cause of injury among teens. [T–]

htttps://www.ncbi.nlm.nih.gov/pmc/articles/PMC4210977/

15. Is too much competition bad for young athletes?
Too much competition can lead athletes to focus on winning, which can increase pressure and decrease enjoyment of the sport. A study also found that competition can lead to intense play and increased risk of injury. [T–]

http://www.livestrong.com/article/523284-negatives-of-competitive-sports/

16. Does it cost money to be on a sports team?
Often it does cost money to be on a sports team, to cover expenses such as travel and uniforms. Participating in sports can be a financial hardship for some families. [T+]

htttps://www.ncbi.nlm.nih.gov/pmc/articles/PMC3871410/

17. What roles do parents play in their children's sports activity?
The influence of parents on their children's sports activity varies greatly. It can be a positive source of encouragement and praise for the child's accomplishments. But it can also become a source of anxiety and low self-esteem for the child if the child feels high parental pressure to do well in sports. [T–]

htttps://www.ncbi.nlm.nih.gov/pmc/articles/PMC3661888/

DECISION. Public transportation. *Should town taxes help to pay the cost of buses and trains or should the cost be paid for entirely by the people who use them?*

1. Do towns have enough money to fund public transportation? Code 933d
2. Are people willing to pay more taxes to help fund public transportation? 425d
3. Can using public transportation reduce pollution? 130d
4. How much time do drivers spend due to traffic delays? 844d
5. Can using public transportation save energy? 494d
6. How does public transportation affect community development? 507d
7. Does public transportation reduce the number of accident-related deaths? 199d
8. How many people depend on public transportation to get around? 965d
9. Is public transportation adequate in most big cities? 220d
10. If a government spent less tax money on transportation, would it be more able to fund other services, such as education? 566d
11. Do people who own cars use public transportation? 718d
12. Why might someone with access to a car use public transportation? 885d
13. How does public transportation affect property values? 767d
14. Does the cost of using public transportation affect how much people will use it? 196d
15. Do fewer people drive when public transportation is provided to them at very low or no cost? 315d
16. What negative outcomes can arise if public transportation is provided at very low cost or free of charge? 254d
17. Does increasing public transportation fares affect ridership? 746d
18. What are the fares people pay to ride public transportation used for? 665d
19. How much of public transportation operating costs are covered by user fares? 631d
20. Is car-pooling in private cars a way for people to pay for their own transportation costs? 225d
21. Has car-pooling been successful as a substitute for public transportation? 310d

Add questions of your own:

22. _____

23. _____

24. _____

1. Do towns have enough money to fund public transportation?
Towns need money to fund public transportation systems. They typically ask their voters to fund public transportation projects by approving tax increases. Voters sometimes vote against such tax increases [T–]

https://www.wired.com/2016/11/us-cities-spurned-washington-fund-transit/

2. Are people willing to pay more taxes to help fund public transportation?
During the 2016 US election, 69% of transportation-related funding ballots passed. Voters in many US cities (Los Angeles, San Francisco, Atlanta) approved sales taxes increases to fund public transit operations. [T+]

https://www.wired.com/2016/11/us-cities-spurned-washington-fund-transit/

3. Can using public transportation reduce pollution?
Public transportation can reduce congestion on roadways that causes pollution. Trains and buses produce less pollution than if the same riders traveled in individual cars or even carpooled. [T+]

http://www.uspirgedfund.org/sites/pirg/files/reports/Why-and-How-to-Fund-Public-Transportation.pdf

4. How much time do drivers spend due to traffic delays?
Research has shown that US drivers spend almost 40 hours a year in traffic delays. [T+]

http://www.uspirgedfund.org/sites/pirg/files/reports/Why-and-How-to-Fund-Public-Transportation.pdf

5. Can using public transportation save energy?
Public transportation is more fuel-efficient than driving, and so can save energy. [T+]

http://www.uspirgedfund.org/sites/pirg/files/reports/Why-and-How-to-Fund-Public-Transportation.pdf

6. How does public transportation affect community development?
Increasing public transportation can encourage the development of more walkable communities because people will have less need of cars. [T+]

http://www.uspirgedfund.org/sites/pirg/files/reports/Why-and-How-to-Fund-Public-Transportation.pdf

7. Does public transportation reduce the number of accident-related deaths?
Motor vehicles cause over 40,000 accident-related deaths in the US each year. Public transportation causes less than 300 deaths each year. [T+]

http://www.uspirgedfund.org/sites/pirg/files/reports/Why-and-How-to-Fund-Public-Transportation.pdf

8. How many people depend on public transportation to get around?
40% of all public transportation users are either too poor to own cars, too young or too old to drive, or disabled. Workers around the world depend on public transportation to get to their jobs. 24 million Americans with disabilities depend on public transportation. [T+]

http://www.uspirgedfund.org/sites/pirg/files/reports/Why-and-How-to-Fund-Public-Transportation.pdf

9. Is public transportation adequate in most big cities?
Most often it is not. The Chinese government intends to spend $16 billion in coming years to increase its public transportation system in Beijing in order to combat traffic congestion and pollution. In New York City in 2012, $7.7 billion of state and local tax money went to public transportation. [T+]

http://www.chinadaily.com.cn/china/2012cpc/2012 11/10/content_15910395.htm

https://www.budget.ny.gov/pubs/archive/fy1415archive/eBudget1415/fy1415littlebook/Transportation.pdf

10. If a government spent less tax money on transportation, would it be more able to fund other services, such as education?
Yes, all governments have fixed budgets and what is spent in one way is no longer available to spend in another way.

https://en.wikipedia.org/wiki/Taxation_in_the_United_States [T–]

11. Do people who own cars use public transportation?
Research has shown that approximately one third of public transportation users also have access to cars. [T–]

http://www.uspirgedfund.org/sites/pirg/files/reports/Why-and-How-to-Fund-Public-Transportation.pdf

12. Why might someone with access to a car use public transportation?
Many people who have access to cars choose to take public transportation to avoid traffic and parking issues. Public transportation also provides an alternative when cars are being repaired, when people fly to visit a city, or when there are road closures due to construction or events. [T+]

http://www.uspirgedfund.org/sites/pirg/files/reports/Why-and-How-to-Fund-Public-Transportation.pdf

13. How does public transportation affect property values?
Research has shown that public transportation increases property values. For example, in Washington DC, for every 1,000 feet closer a personal property was to a metro station, its value increased by $70,000. Individual homeowners thus benefit indirectly as well as directly from public transportation [T+]

http://www.uspirgedfund.org/sites/pirg/files/reports/Why-and-How-to-Fund-Public-Transportation.pdf

14. Does the cost of using public transportation affect how much people will use it?
Two experiments that allowed people to ride public transportation for free led to increased ridership. [T+]

http://www.uspirgedfund.org/sites/pirg/files/reports/Why-and-How-to-Fund-Public-Transportation.pdf

15. Do fewer people drive when public transportation is provided to them at very low or no cost?
Experiments with free public transportation have not led to fewer people driving cars. [T–]

http://www.uspirgedfund.org/sites/pirg/files/reports/Why-and-How-to-Fund-Public-Transportation.pdf

http://faculty.wcas.northwestern.edu/~ipsavage/439-manuscript.pdf

16. What negative outcomes can arise if public transportation is provided at very low cost or free of charge?
Experiments with free public transportation have led to increasing numbers of homeless people occupying buses, trains, and ferries. There were also more incidences of graffiti and vandalism near transport stops, which increased maintenance costs. [T–]

http://www.uspirgedfund.org/sites/pirg/files/reports/Why-and-How-to-Fund-Public-Transportation.pdf

17. Does increasing public transportation fares affect ridership?
Research has shown that increasing public transportation fares had led to decreased ridership. This decrease is greater for people with low incomes. [T+]

http://www.uspirgedfund.org/sites/pirg/files/reports/Why-and-How-to-Fund-Public-Transportation.pdf

18. What are the fares people pay to ride public transportation used for?
User fares for public transportation pay for things like employee's salaries, fuel, and other operating costs. Typically, fares do not bring in enough to fully pay costs. [T+]

http://nyc.streetsblog.org/2011/09/07/where-does-your-fare-go-increasingly-to-pay-off-mta-debt/

19. How much of public transportation operating costs are covered by user fares?
The proportion varies. In New York City, user fares cover approximately two-thirds of operating costs. In Miami, user fares cover just 16%. [U–]

http://www.uspirgedfund.org/sites/pirg/files/reports/Why-and-How-to-Fund-Public-Transportation.pdf

20. Is car-pooling in private cars a way for people to pay for their own transportation costs?
Yes, car-pooling can potentially reduce traffic congestion and pollution and is not costly to the government. {T–]

http://www.nytimes.com/interactive/2011/01/29/us/20110129-nat-CARPOOL.html?ref=us

21. Has car-pooling been successful as a substitute for public transportation?
Car-pooling has not become popular. The share of US workers who car-pool to work has dropped by half since 1980, largely because the cost of owning a car became more affordable and workplaces spread out into suburbs. [T–]

http://www.nytimes.com/interactive/2011/01/29/us/20110129-nat-CARPOOL.html?ref=us

---

DECISION. Sales tax. *Should the town charge a sales tax on everything people buy? Or should the town get the money it needs from a tax on people's earnings?*

Questions about Sales tax

1. Who charges sales taxes? Code 214d
2. How is the money gained from sales taxes used? 694d
3. How much sales tax do people pay on things they buy? 930d
4. Is sale tax required or voluntary? 118d
5. Do people who are richer pay more in sales tax than poorer people? 289d
6. Do people pay sales tax on purchases made on the internet? 271d
7. Do people pay sales tax on purchases made from a seller on the street? 318d
8. Are some types of purchases always exempt (excused) from sales tax? 472d

Questions about Income tax

9. Who pays income tax? 939d
10. Is income tax required or voluntary? 288d
11. Do all people pay the same income tax? 303d
12. How much income tax do people pay? 780d
13. Do cities and states also charge income tax? 874d

14. What are local income taxes (those paid to a town, city, or county) used for? 280d

15. Are income tax payments ever refunded? 674d

16. Does income tax reduce income inequality (the income difference between high and low earners)? 421d

17. Are there other taxes on people's wealth besides income tax? 954d

Add questions of your own:

18. _____

19. _____

20. _____

Questions about Sales tax

1. Who charges sales taxes?
National governments, US state governments, and individual cities and towns may all charge sales taxes of varying amounts. Most countries charge some or all of these. These are separate taxes. Thus, if people have to pay an extra sales tax to their town or city, they still have to pay any state and federal taxes. [S+]

http://www.brighthub.com/money/personal-finance/articles/32816.aspx

https://turbotax.intuit.com/tax-tools/tax-tips/Taxes-101/What-are-State-Income-Taxes-/INF14801.html

2. How is the money gained from sales taxes used?
Governments use money from sales taxes to provide many kinds of services. Cities use the money for city services such as buses, while states or countries use it for costs such as highways. Cities and towns use tax money for libraries, parks, police, jails, and museums. [S+]

https://en.wikipedia.org/wiki/Taxation_in_the_United_States

https://www.sapling.com/4869910/what-sales-tax-used

3. How much sales tax do people pay on things they buy?
Sales taxes vary greatly by country and within the US by state and city. Some US states (Alaska, Delaware, Montana, New Hampshire, and Oregon) do not have a sales tax. California has the highest state sales tax at 7.25%. New York state sales tax is 4% and New York City charges an additional 4.5%. In China, the sales tax rate is a constant 17%. Hungary has the highest tax rate — 27%. [S+/–]

http://www.salestaxinstitute.com/resources/rates

https://tradingeconomics.com/china/sales-tax-rate

https://en.wikipedia.org/wiki/List_of_countries_by_tax_rates

4. Is sale tax required or voluntary?
Most local businesses are required to collect sales tax. When purchasing an item in a state with a sales tax, a person is required to pay all sales taxes. [S+/–]

http://www.alllaw.com/articles/tax/article1.asp

5. Do people who are richer pay more in sales tax than poorer people?
Sales tax does not depend on income or wealth. All people pay in sales tax the same percentage of the cost of something they buy. So rich people pay more in sales taxes only if they buy more. [S+/–]

http://www.salestaxinstitute.com/Sales_Tax_FAQs/What_states_impose_sales_use_tax

6. Do people pay sales tax on purchases made on the internet?
People sometimes pay sales tax on purchases made on the internet. For example, if an online store has a physical location in a state that charge sales tax, the buyer must pay a sales tax on the item. If the online store does not have a physical store, they do not always have to charge sales tax. [S–]

http://smallbusiness.findlaw.com/business-taxes/do-you-have-to-pay-sales-tax-on-internet-purchases.html

7. Do people pay sales tax on purchases made from a seller on the street?
People sometimes pay sales tax on purchases made from sellers on the street. Legally, if a person is considered to be a vendor, they must register with the tax department.. However, vendors often ignore this law. [S–]

https://www.tax.ny.gov/pubs_and_bulls/tg_bulletins/st/do_i_need_to_register_for_sales_tax.htm

8. Are some types of purchases always exempt (excused) from sales tax?
Some US states allow tax-exempt or tax-discounted purchase of items that are considered essential items. These may include groceries, medicine, and medical devices. [S+]

http://blog.taxjar.com/non-taxable-items/

Questions about Income tax

9. Who pays income tax?
Income taxes on money that people earn are collected in most places around the world. [I+]

https://en.wikipedia.org/wiki/Income_tax#Around_the_world

10. Is income tax required or voluntary?
Income tax is required and typically deducted from a worker's paycheck. The penalties for failing to report income and pay tax on it are severe. [I+/–]

https://www.irs.com/articles/state-income-tax-vs-federal-income-tax

11. Do all people pay the same income tax?
Income taxes vary by individual as well as by country. Unlike sales tax, the amount a person pays in income tax depends on their income: people who earn more money pay a higher percentage of their earnings in income taxes. People with lower incomes pay a lower percentage. People with very low incomes may pay no tax at all. For example, in the US people in the highest federal tax bracket ($121,505+) pay almost 40% of their income in federal taxes. Those in the lowest tax bracket (less than $9,325) pay 10%. [I+/–]

https://en.wikipedia.org/wiki/Income_tax#Around_the_world

https://taxfoundation.org/2017-tax-brackets/

https://www.irs.com/articles/state-income-tax-vs-federal-income-tax

12. How much income tax do people pay?
The amounts paid in income taxes and the rules surrounding these taxes vary greatly by country. In the US, the maximum percentage (for people with the highest incomes) is 40%, in China it is 45%, and in Sweden it is 60%. [I+/–]

https://en.wikipedia.org/wiki/List_of_countries_by_tax_rates

https://www.irs.com/articles/state-income-tax-vs-federal-income-tax

https://www.irs.com/articles/state-income-tax-vs-federal-income-tax

13. Do cities and states also charge income tax?

Yes, many state and local governments also charge income taxes. These must be paid in addition to federal taxes. In some states, everyone pays the same percentage of their income in taxes, and in others there is no income tax at all.

In some places, such as New York City, residents pay city, state, and federal income taxes. Most cities and states use the same system as the federal tax system, charging workers a varying percentage of their earnings, with higher earning workers paying a higher percentage. [I+/–]

https://en.wikipedia.org/wiki/Income_tax_in_the_United_States

https://www.patriotsoftware.com/payroll/training/blog/what-is-local-income-tax/

14. What are local income taxes (those paid to a town, city, or county) used for?

Local income taxes are typically used for programs like education, parks, and community improvement. [I+]

https://www.patriotsoftware.com/payroll/training/blog/what-is-local-income-tax/

15. Are income tax payments ever refunded?

Most people in the US have their income tax taken out of each paycheck and sent to the government. Sometimes a person pays more than they owe and they receive a refund at the end of the year. [I+]

https://www.irs.com/articles/state-income-tax-vs-federal-income-tax

16. Does income tax reduce income inequality (the income difference between high and low earners)?

Income tax reduces income inequality to some degree since high earners lose a greater percentage of their earnings to taxes than low earners do. [I+/–]

https://en.wikipedia.org/wiki/Income_tax_in_the_United_States

17. Are there other taxes on people's wealth besides income tax?

Yes. In most places people are charged taxes on their homes or other properties they own and on earnings from money they invest. [I+/–]

https://en.wikipedia.org/wiki/Wealth_tax

https://www.libertytax.com/tax-resources/general-tax-information/taxable-nontaxable-income/

DECISION. Soda tax. *Should an extra tax be charged on soda purchases?*

Questions about a soda tax

1. Are many places considering a soda tax? Code 301d
2. How much money would be generated by a soda tax? 796d
3. How much is a soda tax typically? 316d
4. Are there other taxes like a soda tax that have worked? 953d
5. How can drinking less soda improve health? 466d
6. Can drinking soda lead to weight gain? 717d
7. Do sleep problems occur from drinking soda? 516d
8. Does soda have nutritional value? 164d
9. How does soda affect the brain in the long-term? 741d

10. Does drinking soda affect dental health? 922d

11. Can people become addicted to soda? 731d

12. Can the positive health effects of a soda tax be measured? 753d

13. Can avoiding soda help people to lose weight? 823d

14. Would soda taxes prevent obesity? 839d

15. Will soda companies lose money and be in trouble if soda is taxed? 278d

16. Do taxes influence what people buy? 181d

17. Will soda tax money go to lowering the cost of healthy food? 793d

Questions about Leaving soda purchases untaxed

18. Who buys the most soda and benefits most from keeping the price low? 970d

19. Are soda companies doing anything to make soda healthier? 567d

20. How many people work for soda companies? 960d

21. How much soda is sold in the US each year? 156d

22. How much money does the US spend on obesity each year? 838d

23. How does soda affect the brain in the short term? 520d

24. Does drinking soda boost energy? 610d

25. Does drinking soda help digestion? 137d

26. Does soda fulfill the hydration needs of the body? 747d

Add questions of your own:

27. _____

28. _____

29. _____

Questions about a Soda tax

1. Are many places considering a soda tax?
Yes, many US states and several countries are considering some form of a soda tax, and a law imposing such a tax has now been passed in a number of US states. [ST+]

https://en.wikipedia.org/wiki/Sugary_drink_tax#American_localities_with_a_soda_tax

http://www.nejm.org/doi/full/10.1056/NEJMhpr0905723#t=article

2. How much money would be generated by a soda tax?
A 3-cent-per-ounce tax in the US could generate over $24 billion over four years. [ST+]

https://taxfoundation.org/overreaching-obesity-governments-consider-new-taxes-soda-and-candy/

3. How much is a soda tax typically?

Philadelphia and Berkeley are the first two cities to pass a tax on sugary drinks in the US. Berkeley's tax of 1 cent/oz of sugary drink. Philadelphia's tax of 1.5 cents/oz [ST+]

https://en.wikipedia.org/wiki/Sugary_drink_tax#American_localities_with_a_soda_tax

4. Are there other taxes like a soda tax that have worked?

Studies have shown that taxes on tobacco help to reduce demand for tobacco, especially among young smokers. One study showed a 10% increase in cigarette prices would lead to 11.9% fewer teens smoking. [ST+]

https://www.tobaccofreekids.org/research/factsheets/pdf/0146.pdf

5. How can drinking less soda improve health?

Avoiding soda may improve health by lowering the chances of hypertension, asthma, pancreatic cancer, and diabetes. [ST+]

http://inspiyr.com/6-health-benefits-of-not-drinking-soda/

6. Can drinking soda lead to weight gain?

Research suggests that drinking soda may make people want to eat more because it causes a rise in blood sugar. In one study, people who added soda to their regular diet consumed 17% more calories. Consuming more calories leads to weight gain. [ST+]

https://www.ncbi.nlm.nih.gov/pmc/articles/PMC1829363/

https://www.ncbi.nlm.nih.gov/pubmed/10878689

7. Do sleep problems occur from drinking soda?

Research has found that students who consume the caffeine in soda are more likely to have trouble sleeping and to feel tired in the morning. [ST+]

http://www.sciencedirect.com/science/article/pii/S1054139X05002582

8. Does soda have nutritional value?

Soda lacks essential nutrients like vitamins, minerals, antioxidants, or fiber. Soda is said to have "empty" calories because it mainly contains sugar. [ST+]

https://authoritynutrition.com/13-ways-sugary-soda-is-bad-for-you/

9. How does soda affect the brain in the long-term?

Research has shown that drinking sugary beverages is associated with lower brain volume and lower scores on memory tests. Lower brain volume has been linked to higher risk of Alzheimer's disease. [ST+]

https://www.nytimes.com/2017/04/24/well/eat/sugary-drinks-brain-aging.html

10. Does drinking soda affect dental health?

Drinking soda regularly causes plaque to build up on the teeth and can lead to cavities and gum disease. [ST+]

https://wellnessmama.com/379/reasons-to-avoid-soda/

11. Can people become addicted to soda?

Evidence suggests that sugars such as found in soda can lead to reward and craving in ways similar to addictive drugs like cocaine. [ST+]

https://www.ncbi.nlm.nih.gov/pubmed/23719144

12. Can the positive health effects of a soda tax be measured?

One study estimated that a penny-per-ounce tax on sugary drinks could prevent 2.4 million cases of diabetes, 8,000 strokes, and 26,000 premature deaths over a ten year period. [ST+]

https://www.ncbi.nlm.nih.gov/pubmed/22232111

13. Can avoiding soda help people to lose weight?
A study showed that high schoolers who reduced their soda drinking stayed the same weight. Students who made no change gained weight. [ST–]

https://www.ncbi.nlm.nih.gov/pmc/articles/PMC1829363/

14. Would soda taxes prevent obesity?
Soda taxes may reduce soda drinking by as much as 31%, but studies have shown that this may be offset by increased consumption of higher calorie whole milk and other sweetened drinks. [ST–]

http://www.sfgate.com/bayarea/article/S-F-soda-tax-would-drop-consumption-31-percent-5636558.php

http://www.cookcountypublichealth.org/files/pdf/Chaloupka_Report_PRF.pdf

15. Will soda companies lose money and be in trouble if soda is taxed?
Soda companies will probably lose money and be in trouble if soda is taxed because sales will go down. This happens for many products; when cost goes up, sales go down. [ST–]

https://www.nytimes.com/2015/10/04/upshot/soda-industry-struggles-as-consumer-tastes-change.html

https://www.boundless.com/economics/textbooks/boundless-economics-textbook/consumer-choice-and-utility-5/theory-of-consumer-choice-53/impact-of-price-on-consumer-choices-205-12332/

16. Do taxes influence what people buy?
Taxes may influence what people buy, but some studies show that older smokers don't change their smoking when cigarette taxes go up. [ST–]

https://www.ncbi.nlm.nih.gov/pmc/articles/PMC3228562/

17. Will soda tax money go to lowering the cost of healthy food?
There's no way to know for sure what will happen to soda tax money, but tax on unhealthy products like cigarettes and alcohol often gets mixed in with other taxes and is used for different things. [ST–]

http://boston.cbslocal.com/2010/10/01/curious-where-cigarette-tax-money-goes/

Questions about Leaving soda purchases untaxed

18. Who buys the most soda and benefits most from keeping the price low?
About half of Americans drink soda each day. People of lower income on average drink more soda than people of higher income. People in richer neighborhoods in drink less soda. Teens, males, and African Americans drink more soda. [U+]

http://www.dailymail.co.uk/news/article-2033153/Sugar-nation-Half-Americans-drink-soda-daily--poor-people-9-cent-daily-calories-it.html

19. Are soda companies doing anything to make soda healthier?
Coke, Pepsi, and Dr. Pepper have announced that they are planning to reduce the calories Americans get from such beverages by 20% by marketing smaller bottles, bottled water, and diet drinks. [U+]

https://www.nytimes.com/2014/09/24/business/big-soda-companies-agree-on-effort-to-cut-americans-drink-calories.html?_r=0

20. How many people work for soda companies?
Coca-Cola employs about 130,000 people and Pepsi employs 274,000 people worldwide. All these people depend on high soda sales to keep their jobs. [U+]

https://www.reference.com/business-finance/many-employees-coca-cola-403db69dbdcafe64

https://www.edassist.com/~/media/bh/edassist/why-edassist/client-success-stories/pdfs/2015_tuition-program-case-study-cael-pepsico5_nm.ashx

21. How much soda is sold in the US each year?
Americans spend about $65 billion on soda per year. [U–]

http://mentalfloss.com/article/31222/numbers-how-americans-spend-their-money

22. How much money does the US spend on obesity each year?
Obesity costs Americans an estimated $190 billion in medical costs each year. [U–]

https://www.hsph.harvard.edu/obesity-prevention-source/obesity-consequences/economic/

23. How does soda affect the brain in the short term?
When a person consumes sugar, like that found in soda, the reward system in the brain is activated. A chemical called dopamine is released in the brain, which makes people feel pleasure. [U+]

http://www.npr.org/sections/thesalt/2014/01/15/262741403/why-sugar-makes-us-feel-so-good

24. Does drinking soda boost energy?
Most sodas contain caffeine, which gives a short-term energy boost. [U+]

http://bodyfocus.me/html/feel-great/112-want-more-energy-give-up-soda

25. Does drinking soda help digestion?
Some research suggests that drinking carbonated water, as contained in soda, may reduce idigestion problems. [U+]

http://woman.thenest.com/health-benefits-soda-carbonated-water-3526.html

26. Does soda fulfill the hydration needs of the body?
According to the Mayo clinic, if not consumed in excess, soda has the same hydration effects as normal tap water. [U+]

http://woman.thenest.com/health-benefits-soda-carbonated-water-3526.html

---

DECISION. Rent control. *Should the town limit how much rent a landlord can charge?*

1. How does rent control affect the price of renting an apartment or house?
   Code 786d

2. Are rental prices increasing? 699d

3. Can people afford the rising cost of rent? 708d

4. What percentage of a person's income typically goes toward rent? 539d

5. Why do people choose to rent instead of buying a home? 431d

6. Can tenants in rent-controlled apartments be evicted? 702d

7. How common is rent control? 226d

8. How can rent control affect housing availability? 605d

9. How does rent control affect landlords? 829d

10. How does rent control affect the value of all housing? 197d

11. How can rent control affect housing development? 235d

12. How can rent control affect the quality of existing housing? 941d

13. How can rent control affect the rate of homelessness? 267d

14. Are people less likely to move when their apartment is rent-controlled? 395d

15. Can landlords charge other fees instead of increasing rent? 546d
16. Who benefits most from rent control? 420d
17. What do landlords do if they cannot maintain the property they own? 173d
18. Does removing existing rent controls increase housing availability and affordability? 185d
19. What alternatives do people have who cannot find affordable housing? 830d

Add questions of your own:

20. _____
    _____

21. _____
    _____

22. _____
    _____

1. How does rent control affect the price of renting an apartment or house?
Rent control limits the amount that a landlord who owns the property can charge a tenant for rent and/or how much the landlord can raise the rent. This makes it easier for tenants to find affordable housing and to estimate how much their rent will be for years to come. [R+]

http://homeguides.sfgate.com/advantages-disadvantages-rent-controlled-apartment-1869.html

2. Are rental prices increasing?
Rental prices are increasing faster than many other spending categories, especially in US urban areas, where rent increases are often greater than salary increases. Housing costs in other major urban areas around the world are similarly rising rapidly. [R+]

http://fortune.com/2015/10/07/rents-rise-housing/

http://www.mercurynews.com/2017/07/17/bay-area-rent-increases-far-outstrip-wage-gains

https://www.expatistan.com/cost-of-living/beijing?currency=USD

3. Can people afford the rising cost of rent?
A survey showed that rent prices in the US have gone up by about 4% in one decade, but incomes of renters went down by an average of 13%. [R+]

http://www.mercurynews.com/2017/07/17/bay-area-rent-increases-far-outstrip-wage-gains

https://www.bloomberg.com/news/articles/2014-07-17/housings-30-percent-of-income-rule-is-near-useless

4. What percentage of a person's income typically goes toward rent?
A typical rule of thumb is that a person should spend no more than 30% of their income on housing. However, a survey showed that in the US over one-third of people spend more than this 30%, and one-fifth spend more than 50% of their income on housing. [R+]

http://www.governing.com/gov-data/economy-finance/housing-affordability-by-city-income-rental-costs.html

5. Why do people choose to rent instead of buy a home?
Many people choose to rent a home because they cannot afford to buy one. A person may also choose to rent to avoid paying for maintenance or because they do not plan to stay for long. [R+]

https://www.forbes.com/sites/houzz/2015/08/22/10-reasons-to-rent-and-not-buy/#433bfdd2577a

6. Can tenants in rent-controlled apartments be evicted?
People living in rent-regulated apartments are typically protected from being evicted (forced to move out of their apartment) if they are using the space as their residence and otherwise complying with the terms of the lease. [R+]

http://homeguides.sfgate.com/advantages-disadvantages-rent-controlled-apartment-1869.html

7. How common is rent control?
A few large cities have rent control laws, but overall it is not common and in some places it is illegal. [R–]

http://www.urban.org/urban-wire/rent-control-good-policy

8. How can rent control affect housing availability?
Rent control helps to keep prices low, meaning more people want to rent. As a result there may be fewer units available, making it harder for people to find housing to rent. [R–]

http://marketurbanism.com/2016/04/02/rent-control-is-bad-for-both-landlords-and-tenants/

9. How does rent control affect landlords?
Landlords of rent controlled apartments may have trouble meeting their expenses for fuel, utilities, and repairs, and may not be able to maintain apartments in good condition or earn any profit. [R–]

http://www.urban.org/urban-wire/rent-control-good-policy

10. How does rent control affect the value of all housing?
Research has shown that rent controlling some apartments made the value of all housing in the area go down. [R–]

http://econlife.com/2012/11/debating-rent-control/

11. How can rent control affect housing development?
In a rent controlled market, investors may be less willing to put money into housing because there is a limit to how much profit they can make from the rentals. This results in less housing availability. [R–]

http://marketurbanism.com/2016/04/02/rent-control-is-bad-for-both-landlords-and-tenants/

12. How can rent control affect the quality of existing housing?
Rent control may discourage the landlords who own rental housing from updating or repairing their units. Often they can't afford to, and it would cost them money that they could not earn back by raising the rental price. According to one poll, 93% of economists agreed that rent control reduces the quality of housing. [R–]

http://marketurbanism.com/2016/04/02/rent-control-is-bad-for-both-landlords-and-tenants/

https://psmag.com/in-defense-of-rent-control-3cb453119116

13. How can rent control affect the rate of homelessness?
A study showed that cities with rent control had a homelessness rate 164% higher than other cities. [R–]

http://www.csus.edu/indiv/c/chalmersk/econ251fa12/housingregulationscausehomelessness.pdf

14. Are people less likely to move when their apartment is rent-controlled?
A study showed that people living in rent-controlled apartments in New York City stayed three times as long as those who were not. People may stay in their apartments longer even if they do not need the space or the location is no longer convenient because they do not want to risk paying a higher rent elsewhere. [R–]

http://www.nmhc.org/News/The-High-Cost-of-Rent-Control/

124   Part Three   ■   The Decision Topics

15. Can landlords charge other fees instead of increasing rent?
In many towns with rent control, new renters may have to pay high "finder's fees" because it more difficult to find housing. Landlords may also charge new tenants move-in fees ("key money") to make up for their inability to charge more in rent. [R–]

http://www.nmhc.org/News/The-High-Cost-of-Rent-Control/

16. Who benefits most from rent control?
Rent controls can help low-income people find affordable housing, but studies have shown that it is people with higher incomes who tend to benefit most from rent control. They could afford to pay more in rent but because of the rent control they do not have to. [R–]

http://www.nmhc.org/News/The-High-Cost-of-Rent-Control/

17. What do landlords do if they cannot maintain the property they own?
Landlords who cannot meet their expenses may be forced to abandon their properties, further reducing the housing supply.

http://www.nmhc.org/News/The-High-Cost-of-Rent-Control/

18. Does removing existing rent controls increase housing availability and affordability?
Removing rent controls may make housing more available but not necessarily. It may only make it more expensive and less available to those with limited income. [R+]

https://psmag.com/economics/in-defense-of-rent-control

19. What alternatives do people have who cannot find affordable housing?
Public housing, owned by the government rather than private landlords, is available to those with low incomes, but there typically are long waiting lists and no guarantees. [R+]

https://portal.hud.gov/hudportal/HUD?src=/topics/rental_assistance/phprog

---

DECISION. Elderly care. *Should adults be required to care for their elderly parents or should government funds be used to do this?*

Questions about Care by family

1. Are adult children legally responsible to care for their elderly parents?
   Code 375d

2. What percentage of adult sons or daughters report helping to pay for their parents' care? 634d

3. Can adults get a tax credit for helping to pay for their elderly parents' care? 966d

4. How have population trends affected family care of the elderly? 501d

5. How much does a parent on average spend on their child growing up? 928d

6. How near to their parents do adults tend to live? 842d

7. What kind of relationships do elderly parents want with their adult children? 487d

8. How much does it cost to pay for the care of an elderly person in a long-term care facility? 609d

9. How much time on average do grown sons or daughters spend caring for elderly parents? 260d

10. How do elderly parents respond to their adult children's efforts to help them? 426d

11. Do many adults choose not to have children? 454d

12. How can caring for an elderly parent affect a person emotionally? 459d

13. How can caring for an elderly parent affect a person physically? 218d

Questions about Care by government aid

14. What government programs are available to provide care for the elderly? 265d

15. Can an older American be sure they will get Social Security benefits when they retire? 496d

16. Are elderly people required to pay taxes? 638d

17. Must government-run senior care facilities meet quality standards? 967d

18. Do government-run senior care facilities always meet quality standards? 133d

19. Can elderly people afford to stay in their own homes? 100d

20. How many people over 65 live in poverty? 174d

Add questions of your own:

21. _____

22. _____

23. _____

Questions about Care by family

1. Are adult children legally responsible to care for their elderly parents?
In many countries and 20 US states, adult children are legally responsible for providing necessities such as food, clothing, shelter, and medical attention to their elderly parents. [F+]

http://healthland.time.com/2013/07/22/caring-for-aging-parents-should-there-be-a-law/

2. What percentage of adult sons or daughters report helping to pay for their parents' care?
According to a US survey, 36% of adult sons or daughters report helping to pay for their parents' care. The percentage is nearer 50% in countries such as China where there is a cultural norm favoring such care. [F+]

https://www.agingcare.com/articles/state-of-caregiving-2015-report-177710.htm

https://www.chinabusinessreview.com/senior-care-in-china-challenges-and-opportunities/

http://www.bbc.com/news/magazine-35155548

3. Can adults get a tax credit for helping to pay for their elderly parents' care?
If a working adult pays for their elderly parent's care, they are eligible for a tax credit of up to $6,000 in the US, but it is unlikely to be enough to cover the costs. This government assistance to families is less common in other countries. [F+/−]

http://blog.credit.com/2016/02/3-tax-breaks-you-can-get-for-taking-care-of-aging-parents-136398/

4. How have population trends affected family care of the elderly?
Couples having smaller families means there are fewer sons or daughters who can care for them in old age. This problem is especially severe in China due to its one-child policy in effect for several of the past decades. An adult child may have two elderly parents and four elderly grandparents to care for. [F–]

https://www.chinabusinessreview.com/senior-care-in-china-challenges-and-opportunities/

5. How much does a parent on average spend on their child growing up?
The average cost to raise a child from birth to age 18 ranges from $145,000-$450,000 in the US, depending on a family's income and geographic location. This cost includes housing, food, transportation, clothing, healthcare, and education, but does not include the cost of college. [F+]

http://money.cnn.com/2014/08/18/pf/child-cost/

6. How near to their parents do adults tend to live?
In the US, 20% of adults live more than two hours away from their parents, and 80% live within two hours. In China, much migration from rural to urban areas has greatly reduced the tradition of cross-generation homes. [F+/–]

https://www.nytimes.com/interactive/2015/12/24/upshot/24up-family.html

7. What kind of relationships do elderly parents want with their adult children?
A US study based on interviews with elderly parents showed that they want to be independent, but also hope their children will be available to help when they need it. [F+]

http://journals.sagepub.com/doi/abs/10.1177/0164027504264677

8. How much does it cost to pay for the care of an elderly person in a long-term care facility?
The average cost for one year at a private long-term care facility in the US is around $50,000. Such facilities are not always available, especially in less developed countries. [F–]

https://web.stanford.edu/class/e297c/poverty_prejudice/soc_sec/elderly.htm

9. How much time on average do grown sons or daughters spend caring for elderly parents?
Adult children in the US who care for their elderly parents spend on average 20 hours a week taking them to medical appointments and providing cooking and household help. [F–]

http://www.griswoldhomecare.com/blog/should-you-take-care-of-your-aging-parents/

10. How do elderly parents respond to their adult children's efforts to help them?
Many elderly parents report ignoring or resisting their children's attempts to provide assistance. Many also withhold information from their adult children in an attempt to limit their involvement. [F–]

http://journals.sagepub.com/doi/abs/10.1177/0164027504264677

11. Do many adults choose not to have children?
In 2014, about 15% of US adult women ages 40-44 did not have children. Childbearing has similarly declined in other developed countries. [F–]

http://www.pewsocialtrends.org/2015/05/07/childlessness/

12. How can caring for an elderly parent affect a person emotionally?
Research has shown that adults who care for an elderly parent are more likely to suffer from depression and stress. Many also feel burdened by providing care or feel guilty for spending less time with their own spouse and children. They may also disagree with siblings about what assistance to provide and how to provide it. [F–]

http://www.huffingtonpost.com/glenn-d-braunstein-md/caregivers-aging-parents_b_3071979.html

http://www.griswoldhomecare.com/blog/should-you-take-care-of-your-aging-parents/

13. How can caring for an elderly parent affect a person physically?
One US poll showed that persons providing care for an elderly person report having twice as many chronic health conditions (such as high blood pressure) as the average American. [F–]

http://www.griswoldhomecare.com/blog/should-you-take-care-of-your-aging-parents/

Questions about Care by government aid

14. What government programs are available to provide care for the elderly?
In the US, many senior citizens rely on the government Medicare program, available to help pay for healthcare for people over age 65. Medicare is limited, however, in covering assistance needed at home. Other countries have similar programs, such as the National Health Service in the United Kingdom. [G+/–]

https://www.medicare.gov/

https://web.stanford.edu/class/e297c/poverty_prejudice/soc_sec/elderly.htm

https://hubpages.com/politics/US-Medicare-Vs-UK-NHS

15. Can an older American be sure they will get Social Security benefits when they retire?
Yes, if they have contributed when they were working. Everyone who has contributed is entitled, no matter how much money they already have. Other countries vary greatly in the retirement income their government provides. [G+]

https://www.ssa.gov/pubs/EN-05-10035.pdf

16. Are elderly people required to pay taxes?
Americans above 65 years of age are still required to file income tax returns if their gross income surpasses a fixed amount. If a person is living on Social Security alone, they do not have to file a tax return. [G+]

https://turbotax.intuit.com/tax-tools/tax-tips/Taxes-101/When-Does-a-Senior-Citizen-on-Social-Security-Stop-Filing-Taxes-/INF14328.html

17. Must government-run senior care facilities meet quality standards?
Government-run senior care facilities must follow certain rules and standards, aimed at ensuring they maintain high quality. Caring for the elderly in a family home does not require such regulation. [G+]

https://yougov.co.uk/news/2012/05/25/your-views-who-should-be-responsible-caring-elderl/

18. Do government-run senior care facilities always meet quality standards?
The quality of government-run senior care facilities varies, with ones of higher quality costing more. [G–]

https://yougov.co.uk/news/2012/05/25/your-views-who-should-be-responsible-caring-elderl/

19. Can elderly people afford to stay in their own homes?
There exist government and private programs to assist with housing expense, such as tax exemptions and reverse mortgages. These, however, do not provide for care needed in the home, nor does Medicare. [G+/–]

https://portal.hud.gov/hudportal/HUD?src=/program_offices/housing/sfh/hecm/rmtopten

https://www.medicare.gov/

https://reverse.org/what-is-a-reverse-mortgage/

20. How many people over 65 live in poverty?
This varies by country. In the US, between 10-15% of people over age 65 live in poverty. [Sa–]

http://kff.org/medicare/issue-brief/poverty-among-seniors-an-updated-analysis-of-national-and-state-level-poverty-rates-under-the-official-and-supplemental-poverty-measures/

Chapter 9

■ ■ ■

A National Future

DECISION. Voting rights. Should everyone be allowed to vote or should voters be required to show they have studied the candidates and issues? (p. 130)

DECISION. Voting age. Should the age one is eligible to vote be 16 or 18? (p. 132)

DECISION. National service. Should high school graduates be required to do some community or military or international service (such as the Peace Corps)? (p. 135)

DECISION. Health insurance. Should individuals be required to have health insurance they pay a monthly fee for? (p. 138)

DECISION. National curriculum. Should all schools in a country have the same required school curriculum or should this be left up to local communities? (p. 142)

DECISION. Animal research. Should animals be used in research to test new medical procedures, drugs or other products? (p. 145)

DECISION. Social security tax. Should people be required to pay a social security tax from each paycheck that will provide money when they retire, or should people save on their own for their retirement? (p. 148)

DECISION. Drugs. Is use of illegal drugs best reduced by educating people about its dangers or by making drugs less available? (p. 152)

DECISION. Tobacco. Is smoking best reduced by educating people about its dangers or by charging a very high tax on purchase of cigarettes? (p. 156)

DECISION. Capital punishment. Should the death sentence be used to punish serious crimes such as murder? (p. 159)

DECISION. Abortion. Should it be against the law for a woman to undergo a medical procedure to end a pregnancy? (p. 162)

DECISION. Euthanasia. Should it be allowed to help someone who wants to end their life? (p. 167)

Only the questions appear in the student edition. Students select a question, respond to the preliminary question about it (How might you make use of this information in your argument?), and then access an answer electronically. These answers and sources are printed for convenience only in this teachers' edition. (See Chapter 11 for an explanation of the symbol in parentheses following each answer.)

DECISION. Voting rights. *Should everyone be allowed to vote or should voters be required to show they have studied the candidates and issues?*

1. How many countries allow their citizens to vote? Code 592d
2. Do any countries require their citizens to vote? 189d
3. Does the US Constitution guarantee the right to vote? 576d
4. What are grounds for losing the right to vote in the US? 969d
5. Must a person be a citizen to vote in a national election in the US? 202d
6. Are people informed about politics? 827d
7. Does everyone vote when they are allowed to? 886d
8. Do ballot issues being voted on often affect many people? 663d
9. Are voters likely to vote on an issue without understanding what it is about? 251d
10. How can poorly informed voters become more informed? 515d
11. Is it possible for citizens to be informed on every candidate and issue on a ballot? 221d
12. In what ways has voting been restricted in the past? 212d
13. How many people would likely fail a knowledge test about the US political system? 569d

Add questions of your own:

14. _____

15. _____

16. _____

1. How many countries allow their citizens to vote?
Almost all countries allow their citizens to vote. However, in a few countries there are limits as to who can vote (for example, women cannot vote in Saudi Arabia). [E+]

https://mic.com/articles/18646/this-is-what-makes-america-amazing-9-countries-where-you-still-cannot-vote#.YQhBYpBdL

2. Do any countries require their citizens to vote?
Voting in elections is mandatory for citizens in 22 countries. For example, in Australia if a person does not vote they can be fined $20. [E+]

http://www.pbs.org/newshour/rundown/22-countries-voting-mandatory/

3. Does the US Constitution guarantee the right to vote?
There is no passage in the US Constitution that explicitly guarantees the right to vote. However, there are amendments that prohibit taking away someone's vote because of their race or gender. [E–]

https://www.nytimes.com/2016/04/25/opinion/should-everybody-vote.html?_r=0

4. What are grounds for losing the right to vote in the US?
Being convicted of a felony is grounds for losing the right to vote in the US in some states but not others. [E+/–]

http://felonvoting.procon.org

5. Must a person be a citizen to vote in a national election in the US?
Yes, only citizens can vote in the US. Residents, whether living in the US legally or illegally, are not allowed to vote. [E–]

http://law.justia.com/constitution/us/amendment-14/92-voter-qualifications.html

6. Are people informed about politics?
Many polls have shown that many US citizens know little about how the American political system works. 70% do not know what the Constitution is, 58% do not know the three branches of government, and 29% do not know who the current Vice President is. [E–]

http://dailycaller.com/2014/02/12/should-all-citizens-be-allowed-to-vote/

7. Does everyone vote when they are allowed to?
People do not always vote even when their country allows them to. In the 2016 US Presidential election, 55% of the voting-age population voted. [E–]

http://www.pewresearch.org/fact-tank/2017/05/15/u-s-voter-turnout-trails-most-developed-countries/

8. Do ballot issues being voted on often affect many people?
Many ballot issues often affect citizens of the country and around the world. For example, people must choose between matters of national security, whether to go to war with another country, and how to deal with the country's debt. [E+]

http://dailycaller.com/2014/02/12/should-all-citizens-be-allowed-to-vote/

9. Are voters likely to vote on an issue without understanding what it is about?
Yes, studies have shown that many voters make choices with little understanding of what they are voting for and what the issues are surrounding the vote. [S+]

https://www.washingtonpost.com/news/volokh-conspiracy/wp/2016/11/08/time-to-take-political-ignorance-seriously/?utm_term=.7df4510e592c

10. How can poorly informed voters become more informed?
A study showed that poorly informed voters can behave like well-informed voters when they study and make use of available information shortcuts. [S+]

http://www.jstor.org/stable/2944882?seq=1#page_scan_tab_contents

11. Is it possible for citizens to be informed on every candidate and issue on a ballot?
There is so much legislation passed at every level of government that it would not be possible for a citizen to be informed on every candidate and issue. [S–]

http://wdet.org/posts/2016/02/02/82385-people-vote-on-what-they-care-about-whether-theyre-informed-or-not/

12. In what ways has voting been restricted in the past?
In the US before 1965, many people who wanted to vote had to take literacy and comprehension tests to show they were qualified to vote. However, the tests were found to discriminate, with higher success rates for one race over another. This kept many minorities from voting. [S–]

http://www.crmvet.org/info/lithome.htm

13. How many people would likely fail a knowledge test about the US political system?
In one US study, 38% of voters could not pass a basic US citizenship test. [S–]

http://caffertyfile.blogs.cnn.com/2011/04/12/should-basic-citizenship-test-be-part-of-voter-registration/

DECISION. Voting age. *Should the age one is eligible to vote be 16 or 18?*

Questions about Voting at 16

1. Are 16-year-olds ever regarded as adults? 373d
2. Do teens contribute to society by paying taxes? 995d
3. Do teens under the age of 18 participate in politics? 140d
4. Are people more likely to continue to vote if they first vote at an early age? 693d
5. Do political issues affect people younger than 18? 573d
6. In what ways do teens under the age of 18 contribute to society? 236d
7. Do the majority of young people participate in politics? 795d
8. Are young people more or less likely to vote than older adults? 339d
9. Are teenagers knowledgeable about current events? 356d
10. Are there differences in brain development between 16- and 18-year-olds? 987d
11. Do students take a class in government in high school? 139d

Questions about Voting at 18

12. At what age do teens become eligible to vote? 152d
13. When is a person legally considered an adult? 460d
14. At what age do most students graduate from high school? 406d
15. Are 18-year-olds emotionally more mature than 16-year-olds? 391d
16. Are younger teens more or less likely to vote than older teens? 106d

Add questions of your own:

17. _____

18. _____

19. _____

Questions about Voting at 16

1. Are 16-year-olds ever regarded as adults?
16-year-olds are often considered adults if they are being tried for an offense in a court of law. About 250,000 US teens under 18 are tried, sentenced, or incarcerated as adults every year. [16+]

http://www.youthrights.org/issues/voting-age/top-ten-reasons-to-lower-the-voting-age/

2. Do teens contribute to society by paying taxes?
In 2011, US teens under 18 paid over $730 million in income tax. Teens are also required to pay sales tax. [16+]

http://www.youthrights.org/issues/voting-age/top-ten-reasons-to-lower-the-voting-age/
http://www.alllaw.com/articles/tax/article1.asp

3. Do teens under the age of 18 participate in politics?
Some teens under the age of 18 engage in the political process even though they can't vote. Some have managed political campaigns, formed political groups at school, advocated their rights in government, and used social media to express opinions. [16+]

http://www.youthrights.org/issues/voting-age/top-ten-reasons-to-lower-the-voting-age/

4. Are people more likely to continue to vote if they first vote at an early age?
Research has shown that people who vote in one election are more likely to vote in the next election. Beginning to vote at an early age may thus begin a habit. [16+]

http://www.youthrights.org/issues/voting-age/top-ten-reasons-to-lower-the-voting-age/

5. Do political issues affect people younger than 18?
Many political issues affect young people more than any other age group. Some of these are the environment, education, and poverty. [16+]

http://www.youthrights.org/issues/voting-age/top-ten-reasons-to-lower-the-voting-age/

6. In what ways do teens under the age of 18 contribute to society?
Many teens under the age of 18 actively contribute to society by working and volunteering in their communities. Many also help care for their family members and financially contribute to their families. [16+]

http://www.youthrights.org/issues/voting-age/top-ten-reasons-to-lower-the-voting-age/

7. Do the majority of young people participate in politics?
According to a US survey, almost 90% of young people ages 18-24 are registered to vote. However, less than 30% consistently follow political news and less than one quarter have volunteered for a political campaign. [16–]

https://www.hamilton.edu/news/polls/political-attitudes-of-young-americans

8. Are young people more or less likely to vote than older adults?
Young people are less likely to vote than any other age group. In the 2016 US presidential election, about 45% of US citizens under 30 eligible to vote in fact voted. This percentage is compared to about 55% of people age 30-44, 65% of people age 45-59, and 70% of people age 60 or older. [16–]

http://www.electproject.org/home/voter-turnout/demographics

9. Are teenagers knowledgeable about current events?
Research has shown that there is an increasing gap in political knowledge between the young and the old. One study showed that 60% of teenagers between age 12-17 pay little attention to daily news. [16–]

http://uk.reuters.com/article/life-usa-news-teenagers-dc-idUKN1036737320070710

10. Are there differences in brain development between 16- and 18-year-olds?
Scientists have found that the part of the brain responsible for weighing risks, making judgments, and controlling impulsive behavior is not fully mature until a person is in their mid-20s. Evidence shows that though 16- and 18-year-olds' brains are still developing, a 16-year-old's brain is generally less developed than those of teens just a little older. [16–]

http://usatoday30.usatoday.com/news/nation/2005-03-02-teens-cars-main-usat_x.htm

11. Do students take a class in government in high school?
Most US high schools require students to pass a course in government to graduate. Students may not have taken this course by age 16 depending on their school's requirements. [16–]

http://www.newsmax.com/FastFeatures/lower-voting-age-pros-and-cons/2015/07/18/id/657834/

Questions about Voting at 18

12. At what age do teens become eligible to vote?
The current eligible voting age in most countries, including the US, is 18. In a few countries in South America and Europe (such as Brazil and Austria), it is 16 or 17. [18+]

http://www.economist.com/news/leaders/21716030-young-voters-are-becoming-disillusioned-elections-catch-them-early-and-teach-them-value

http://www.latimes.com/opinion/op-ed/la-oe-steinberg-lower-voting-age-20141104-story.html

13. When is a person legally considered an adult?
The legal age of adulthood varies by country. In all US states (except Nebraska and Alabama where it is 19), a person is legally considered an adult at age 18. The legal rights of adults include voting, marrying, adopting children, joining the armed forces, and holding public office. [18+]

https://hrpo.wustl.edu/wp-content/uploads/2015/01/5-Determining-Legal-Age-to-Consent.pdf

14. At what age do most students graduate from high school?
Most US students complete high school at age 18. Some drop out earlier and may finish later with a GED. [18+]

http://www.economist.com/news/leaders/21716030-young-voters-are-becoming-disillusioned-elections-catch-them-early-and-teach-them-value

15. Are 18-year-olds emotionally more mature than 16-year-olds?
Studies by psychologists have suggested that 18-year-olds are more emotionally mature than 16-year-olds. This means they tend to have better self-control, judgement, and decision-making skills. [18+]

http://www.apa.org/news/press/releases/2009/10/teen-maturity.aspx

16. Are younger teens more or less likely to vote than older teens?
When 16-year-olds were allowed to vote in Scotland, 75% of those who registered voted, compared to only 54% of 18-year-olds. In Austria, voter turnout is higher for citizens under 18 than it is for 19- to 25-year-olds. [18–]

http://www.economist.com/news/leaders/21716030-young-voters-are-becoming-disillusioned-elections-catch-them-early-and-teach-them-value

---

DECISION. National service. *Should high school graduates be required to do some community or military or international service (such as the Peace Corps)?*

1. Are there benefits of participating in service work? Code 116d
2. Does service increase well-being? 524d
3. Does service affect citizenship? 495d
4. If it is not required, do young people choose to do some type of service? 503d
5. Can students earn scholarships from doing service? 259d
6. Can doing service help a person later find paid employment? 689d
7. Are there enough volunteers to serve in the military? 758d
8. What benefits are available for young people who join the military? 114d
9. What pay do enlistees in the military receive? 417d
10. Is it possible to receive college credit for service in the military? 245d
11. What opportunities are available for high school graduates in the Peace Corps? 404d
12. Can anyone serve in the Peace Corps? 777d
13. Do enlistees in the Peace Corps receive a salary? 397d
14. Is it possible to receive college credit for service in the Peace Corps? 730d
15. What pay do community service workers receive? 393d
16. Is it possible to receive college credit for community service? 371d
17. Is attending college expensive? 121d
18. Do most families have enough saved to pay for college? 763d
19. Do most teens know what career they want to prepare for? 112d
20. What do young people typically do after graduating from high school? 877d
21. Is doing service more beneficial for some people than others? 559d
22. Do young people who do service continue to do so later in life? 541d
23. If teens do something else first, do they go to college later? 538d
24. Does pre-college service lower lifetime earnings? 583d

Add questions of your own:

25. _____

26. _____

27. _____

1. Are there benefits of participating in service work?
Doing unpaid or low-paid service often allows someone to meet people they would not otherwise meet and better understand people different from themselves. [S+]

https://www.scholarships.com/resources/public-service-and-volunteering/benefits-of-volunteerism-in-high-school/

2. Does service increase well-being?
One study found that people who volunteer to help others report better health and more happiness than those who do not. [S+]

http://eprints.lse.ac.uk/24592/

3. Does service affect citizenship?
Research has shown that young people who do community service are also more likely to vote. [S+]

http://www.unce.unr.edu/publications/files/cd/2003/FS0323.pdf

4. If it is not required, do young people choose to do some type of service?
About one fourth of young people do some type of service work during their teens. [S+/–]

www.bls.gov/news.release/volun.t01.htm

5. Can students earn scholarships by doing service?
Scholarships based on a record of community service are one of the most common types of scholarships awarded to college applicants. [S+]

https://www.scholarships.com/resources/public-service-and-volunteering/benefits-of-volunteerism-in-high-school/

6. Can doing service help a person later find paid employment?
Service jobs can help a person acquire skills such as problem solving, teamwork, and the ability to follow instruction. These are skills many employers look for when hiring workers. [S+]

www.teenlife.com/blogs/why-community-service-work-beneficial-teenagers

7. Are there enough volunteers to serve in the military?
The number of US citizens who are able to serve in the military is decreasing. As of 2015, the Army was its smallest size in over 75 years. This puts the country at some risk. [S+]

http://www.politico.eu/article/the-militarys-real-problem-fewer-americans-are-joining/

8. What benefits are available for young people who join the military?
People who serve in the military receive tangible benefits such as education tuition assistance, special training, and healthcare. There are also intangible benefits such as the pride and honor of serving one's country. [S+]

http://www.military.com/join-armed-forces/military-benefits-overview.html

9. What pay do enlistees in the military receive?
An enlisted member of the military at the lowest rank will receive a monthly salary of $1592. This rate rises with time spent in the military and an increase of rank to as high as $7806 a month. [S+]

http://www.militaryrates.com/military-pay-charts-e1_e5_2017

10. Is it possible to receive college credit for service in the military?
It is possible to receive college credit for one's military service. A decision as to what credit will be awarded is made by the college or university and is based on a person's training and experience. [S+]

http://www.military.com/education/timesaving-programs/college-credit-for-military-experience.html

11. What opportunities are available for high school graduates in the Peace Corps?
For a high school graduate without a college degree, there are positions available, but each of them requires significant relevant experience in place of a college degree. [S+]

https://www.peacecorps.gov/stories/do-i-need-a-college-degree-to-serve-in-the-peace-corps-part-1/

12. Can anyone serve in the Peace Corps?
There are competitive education and skill requirements that people who want to serve in the Peace Corps must meet. Less than 25% of applicants are selected to serve. [S–]

https://www.peacecorps.gov/stories/how-competitive-is-the-peace-corps/

13. Do enlistees in the Peace Corps receive a salary?
No. Peace Corps workers receive a living allowance and healthcare, The amount varies, depending on the standard and cost of living where they are serving. [S+]

http://files.peacecorps.gov/documents/MS-221-Policy.pdf

14. Is it possible to receive college credit for service in the Peace Corps?
It is possible to receive credit and other benefits for graduate school through Master's International and Fellows/USA program. The programs vary depending on the university. [S+]

http://www.rollins.edu/career-life-planning/documents/webinar-peace-corps-handouts.pdf

15. What pay do community service workers receive?
The typical community service worker in the US can earn up to $35,000 a year. This varies depending on location. [S+]

http://www.careerbuilder.com/insights/community-service-worker

16. Is it possible to receive college credit for community service?
Some colleges do offer credit for community service work. [S+]

http://www.mycollegeadvice.org/blog/2013/12/20/credits-for-volunteering

17. Is attending college expensive?
Yes and getting more so in the US. A few community colleges offer free courses but most charge tuition from $10,000 to more than $30,000 per year. [S+/–]

https://www.nytimes.com/2015/09/13/magazine/is-college-tuition-too-high.html?_r=0

18. Do most families have enough saved to pay for college?
In 2015, only 45% of US parents with children under age 18 saved for college. More than half of the parents said they don't have enough money to save for college. [S+/–]

https://salliemae.newshq.businesswire.com/sites/salliemae.newshq.businesswire.com/files/doc_library/file/HowAmericaSaves2015_FINAL.pdf

138   Part Three ■ The Decision Topics

19. Do most teens know what career they want to prepare for?
Some do but many teens are uncertain about what careers they want to pursue and many change their minds. A Pennsylvania study found that one third of teens had the same career goals at age 14-15 and when asked again at age 17-18. The other two thirds had changed their minds. [S+]

https://edsource.org/2015/survey-most-high-school-students-feel-unprepared-for-college-careers/83752

20. What do young people typically do after graduating from high school?
In 2016, about 70% of US high school graduates went on to college or university. [S–]

https://www.bls.gov/news.release/hsgec.nr0.htm

21. Is doing service more beneficial for some people than others?
One study suggests that doing service is not beneficial until age 40. The study found that young people had good emotional health regardless of whether they did service. However, after 40 mental health and well-being was significantly higher for those who did service. [S–]

http://www.telegraph.co.uk/science/2016/08/09/volunteering-is-not-beneficial-until-you-hit-40-study-finds/

22. Do young people who do service continue to do so later in life?
One study found that requiring community service in high school can reduce volunteering later in life. [S–]

http://www.edweek.org/ew/articles/2013/08/21/01volunteer_ep.h33.html

23. If teens do something else first, do they go to college later?
Some do but others don't, especially if they have good job opportunities. A study by the National Center for Education Statistics found that students who postponed college for one year were less likely to get a college degree than those who went right to college. [S–]

https://nces.ed.gov/pubs90/90346_1.pdf

24. Does pre-college service lower lifetime earnings?
Service work prior to college can reduce a person's lifetime savings because they spend fewer years in the paid work force.

https://cew.georgetown.edu/wp-content/uploads/2014/11/collegepayoff-complete.pdf

---

DECISION. Health insurance. *Should individuals be required to have health insurance they pay a monthly fee for?*

1. What are some countries that provide a national healthcare system paid for by mandatory taxes? Code 191d
2. Does the US provide a universal healthcare program for all Americans? 353d
3. Does China provide healthcare for all its citizens? 890d
4. Is healthcare expensive? 223d
5. Are employers in the US required to provide health insurance for their employees? 991d
6. Does health insurance only cover emergency care? 945d
7. Can health insurance save a person money? 781d
8. Can people get health insurance through their jobs? 653d
9. How much does health insurance cost? 304d

10. Is it easy to get health insurance? 790d

11. Is health insurance less expensive when everyone participates in it? 704d

12. If given the option, do healthy people buy health insurance? 929d

13. Is health insurance available for those who cannot afford it? 131d

14. Does health insurance always make healthcare affordable? 975d

15. If a person has not obtained health insurance, can they still receive emergency care? 833d

16. When health insurance is required, is there a penalty if a person does not have it? 411d

17. Do people choose to pay the penalty for not having health insurance instead of buying a plan? 157d

18. Are people generally satisfied with the health insurance plan they choose? 754d

19. What are the differences in likely healthcare needs for different age groups? 802d

20. What is Medicare? 822d

21. Do people understand how health insurance works? 710d

22. Are there possible advantages to having alternative healthcare plans and providers to choose from? 986d

Add questions of your own:

23. _____

24. _____

25. _____

1. What are some countries that provide a national healthcare system paid for by mandatory taxes?
A number of countries provide universal healthcare to their citizens, including Canada, England, Australia, Brazil, Korea, and Russia. [H+]

https://www.theatlantic.com/international/archive/2012/06/heres-a-map-of-the-countries-that-provide-universal-health-care-americas-still-not-on-it/259153/

2. Does the US provide a universal healthcare program for all Americans?
It does not at this time, but it requires that all individuals purchase their own health insurance to cover their care. [H+/–]

https://www.healthcare.gov

3. Does China provide healthcare for all its citizens?
The Chinese government is working to provide healthcare for all its citizens, but adequate healthcare is still not available for everyone, particularly in rural areas. [H+]

http://www.albertoforchielli.com/2015/11/13/the-chinese-healthcare-system-how-it-works-and-future-trends/

4. Is healthcare expensive?

Yes, most nations spend a great deal on healthcare. China spent an estimated 5.4 percent of its gross domestic product (GDP) on healthcare of its citizens in 2013. In the US it is now nearing 20%. [H+]

http://www.albertoforchielli.com/2015/11/13/the-chinese-healthcare-system-how-it-works-and-future-trends/

http://www.healthsystemtracker.org/chart-collection/health-healthcare-system-overview/?_sf_s=of+the+healthcare#item-u-s-fewer-physician-consultations-per-capita-comparable-countries

5 Are employers in the US required to provide health insurance for their employees?

As of 2015 in the US, employers with over 50 full-time employees must provide health insurance to their employees. [H+]

https://www.zanebenefits.com/blog/bid/289948/does-my-employer-have-to-provide-health-insurance

6. Does health insurance only cover emergency care?

Health insurance covers costs related to maintaining a person's health, as well as treating accidents and illnesses. This usually includes preventive care such as checkups and vaccinations. Health plans vary greatly, however, in what conditions and treatments they cover. H+/–]

https://www.healthcare.gov/why-coverage-is-important/coverage-protects-you/

7. Can health insurance save a person money?

Health insurance can save a person a lot of money if they have a serious illness or accident. Without insurance, healthcare can be very costly; a hospital stay in the US, for example, can average $30,000, and cancer treatment can cost over $100,000. Insurance helps to cover these costs. [H+]

https://www.healthcare.gov/why-coverage-is-important/protection-from-high-medical-costs/

8. Can people get health insurance through their jobs?

Many US employers offer health insurance to their employees, depending on the size of their employer's business, but many others must arrange their own health insurance. [H–]

http://www.health.com/health/article/0,,20455928,00.html

9. How much does health insurance cost?

In countries such as the US that do not have a universal care plan, health insurance plans can be very expensive, often more than $10,000 per year. [H–]

https://www.healthcare.gov/choose-a-plan/your-total-costs/

10. Is it easy to get health insurance?

Choosing a health insurance company and plan can be difficult and can require a lot of research. There are many options, each with a different price and coverage. People often compare several options before choosing a plan. [H–]

http://guides.wsj.com/health/health-costs/how-to-buy-an-individual-health-insurance-plan/

11. Is health insurance less expensive when everyone participates in it?

When more people are paying into health insurance, the per-person cost of insurance goes down. [H+]

http://www.health.com/health/article/0,,20455928,00.html

12. If given the option, do healthy people buy health insurance?

When health insurance is not required, many healthy people choose not to buy it because they do not believe they need it. This makes costs higher for people who do buy health insurance. [H+]

http://www.health.com/health/article/0,,20455928,00.html

13. Is health insurance available for those who cannot afford it?
Some people who cannot afford to buy health insurance qualify for a US program called Medicaid, a government program for low-income individuals and families. Others do not have incomes low enough to qualify for Medicaid. [H+/–]

http://www.health.com/health/article/0,,20455928,00.html

14. Does health insurance always make healthcare affordable?
Even with health insurance, all costs may not be paid and needed care remains too expensive. [H–]

https://www.healthcare.gov/choose-a-plan/your-total-costs/

15. If a person has not obtained health insurance, can they still receive emergency care?
Yes, emergency care is available at hospital emergency rooms and in some places urgent care centers. The patient is expected to pay for the service, but if they cannot, the service provider covers the cost. [H+]

https://www.healthcare.gov/using-marketplace-coverage/getting-emergency-care/

16. When health insurance is required, is there a penalty if a person does not have it?
In the US, if a person can afford health insurance but does not buy it, they must pay a fee. This is either 2.5% of a person's monthly income, or $695, whichever is higher. [H–]

https://www.healthcare.gov/fees/fee-for-not-being-covered/

17. Do people choose to pay the penalty for not having health insurance instead of buying a plan?
Some people choose to pay a penalty for not having health insurance because it is less expensive than buying a plan. In 2014, 7.5 million Americans paid an average of $200 each in fees for not having health insurance. [H–]

http://www.commonwealthfund.org/publications/issue-briefs/2015/may/problem-of-underinsurance

https://www.nytimes.com/2016/01/04/us/many-see-irs-fines-as-more-affordable-than-insurance.html

18. Are people generally satisfied with the health insurance plan they choose?
About two-thirds of Americans say that their health insurance is excellent or good. Only 10% say it is poor. This is a higher percentage of satisfaction than people report in most nations having a single national care system. [H+]

http://www.gallup.com/poll/186740/americans-own-healthcare-ratings-little-changed-aca.aspx

19. What are the differences in likely healthcare needs for different age groups?'
After infancy, medical costs remain low during childhood, adolescence, and early adulthood. They then begin to increase, sharply by age 60 and become highest at age 80 and above. [H–]

http://www.healthcostinstitute.org/files/Age-Curve-Study_0.pdf

20. What is Medicare?
Medicare is a US medical healthcare system provided free of charge to all Americans age 65 and over. Some over 65 supplement Medicare with their own private insurance that they purchase. [H–]

https://www.medicare2017.org

21. Do people understand how health insurance works?
A survey showed that only 4% of Americans could define important features of health insurance plans like deductible, copay, coinsurance, and out-of-pocket maximum. [H–]

http://www.cnbc.com/2016/11/04/many-americans-dont-know-much-about-health-insurance--and-it-will-cost-them.html

22. Are there possible advantages to having alternative healthcare plans and providers to choose from?
A choice of providers may encourage alternative providers to compete with lower costs. [H+/–]

http://www.healthsystemtracker.org/chart-collection/health-healthcare-system-overview/?_sf_s=of+the+healthcare#item-u-s-fewer-physician-consultations-per-capita-comparable-countries

---

DECISION. National curriculum. *Should all schools in a country have the same required school curriculum or should this be left up to local communities?*

Questions about National curriculum

1. What countries have a required national curriculum? Code 867d
2. What is a typical national high school curriculum in countries that have one? 326d
3. What is a typical required high school curriculum in US states? 949d
4. Do colleges and universities have a required curriculum? 993d
5. How many required high school math courses do students typically take? 224d
6. How many required high school science courses do students typically take? 858d
7. Do students still have some choice even when a school has a standard required curriculum? 107d
8. Does a standard curriculum help students who change schools? 403d
9. How can a national government improve its country's educational system if it does not have a national curriculum? 649d
10. Who determines what the standardized curriculum will include? 151d
11. Does a national curriculum serve the needs of schools in different kinds of communities? 812d
12. What knowledge or skills do employers say are needed for students to be effective when they enter the workplace? 444d

Questions about Local curriculum

13. Are students very different from one another when they first enter school? 740d
14. Do all high school students expect to attend college? 486d
15. Do most teens know what career they want to prepare for in college? 374d
16. Do students vary in their confidence that their education has provided them what they need to be prepared for their adult lives? 479d
17. Do students learn more about their communities if its schools develop a local curriculum? 737d

18. If local schools determine their own curriculum, can different schools be compared? 354d

19. What are some of the challenges to developing a local curriculum? 361d

Add questions of your own:

20. _____

21. _____

22. _____

Questions about National curriculum

1. What countries have a required national curriculum?
Many countries have a national curriculum, including England, Japan, and France. The US does not have a required national curriculum but many states follow common guidelines. China has a three-level curriculum model consisting of curricula developed at the national level, regional level and school level. [N+]

http://www.mempowered.com/children/international-curricula

https://www.oecd.org/china/Education-in-China-a-snapshot.pdf

2. What is a typical national high school curriculum in countries that have one?
For countries that have a national curriculum, typically courses include language, math, science, history, geography, and civics. Most countries also agree that art, physical education, and health should be taught. [N+/–]

http://www.mempowered.com/children/international-curricula

3. What is a typical required high school curriculum in US states?
A typical US high school curriculum requires students to take courses in language arts, social studies, math, science, and electives. [N+/–]

http://heav.org/typical-course-of-study-high-school-program/

4. Do colleges and universities have a required curriculum?
At one time, many colleges and universities had a core curriculum for all students, but only a few now have specific required courses. Instead, most colleges allow students to choose among several courses to satisfy their requirements. [N–]

https://www.forbes.com/sites/georgeleef/2013/11/07/the-terrible-erosion-of-the-college-curriculum/#30190dd15ebb

5. How many required high school math courses do students typically take?
Students typically take 3-4 years of required math courses in high school. [N+/–]

http://ecs.force.com/mbdata/mbprofall?Rep=HS01

6. How many required high school science courses do students typically take?
High school science requirements vary more than math requirement, with some schools requiring as little as one year of general science. However, 3-4 years of science are required for admission to many colleges. [N+/–]

http://ecs.force.com/mbdata/mbprofall?Rep=HS01

7. Do students still have some choice even when a school has a standard required curriculum?
Within a standardized curriculum, teachers often can still choose activities and resources geared toward their students' needs and interests. [N+]

http://www.ascd.org/publications/books/107040/chapters/Success-for-all-Students-in-Inclusion-Classes.aspx

8. Does a standard curriculum help students who change schools?
A standardized curriculum across schools makes it easier for students to transfer from one school to another without disrupting their learning. [N+]

http://www.borgenmagazine.com/5-reasons-to-have-a-standardized-curriculum/

9. How can a national government improve its country's educational system if it does not have a national curriculum?
A large portion of education in the US is paid for by the federal government. In order for a school district to get federal funding, it must meet various standards set by the federal government. [N+]

http://education.findlaw.com/curriculum-standards-school-funding/the-roles-of-federal-and-state-governments-in-education.html

10. Who determines what the standardized curriculum will include?
This varies by country. In the case of the Common Core State Standards that the US developed and recommends to states, education leaders worked with teachers and other education experts and received input from the public. [N+/–]

http://www.corestandards.org/about-the-standards/frequently-asked-questions/

11. Does a national curriculum serve the needs of schools in different kinds of communities?
Not necessarily. Research suggests that teachers in rural areas in the US view national standards as not addressing issues most relevant to the local community. [N–]

http://jrre.vmhost.psu.edu/wp-content/uploads/2014/02/16-3_4.pdf

12. What knowledge or skills do employers say are needed for students to be effective when they enter the workplace?
Employers report seeking workers who are quick learners and easily learn what they need to know and work well with others. They are less concerned about specific knowledge. [N–]

http://www.naceweb.org/career-readiness/competencies/career-readiness-defined/
https://www.livecareer.com/quintessential/job-skills-values

Questions about Local curriculum

13. Are students very different from one another when they first enter school?
Today's society is very diverse in terms of culture and language, meaning that different students bring different abilities, motivations, and learning styles into the classroom from an early age. [L+]

http://jespnet.com/journals/Vol_2_No_5_December_2015/11.pdf

14. Do all high school students expect to attend college?
This varies greatly across and within nations, but even in nations where a high percentage go to college, a quarter to a third do not plan to go to college. [N–]

*http://www.youthtruthsurvey.org/college-and-career-readiness/
?gclid=EAIaIQobChMI7rXtu_6p1QIVl4-zCh3GYQlMEAMYAiAAEgKW_PD_BwE*

15. Do most teens know what career they want to prepare for in college?
Some do but many teens are uncertain about what careers they want to pursue and many change their minds. A Pennsylvania study found that one third of teens had the same career goals at age 14-15 and when asked again at age 17-18. The other two thirds had changed their minds. [L+]

https://edsource.org/2015/survey-most-high-school-students-feel-unprepared-for-college-careers/83752

16. Do students vary in their confidence that their education has provided them what they need to be prepared for their adult lives?
Yes, there is great variability in students' beliefs that their schooling has prepared them well for what they wish to do as adults, with over half believing they are unprepared. [L+]

http://www.youthtruthsurvey.org/college-and-career-readiness/?gclid=EAIaIQobChMI7rXtu_6p1QIVl4-zCh3GYQlMEAMYAiAAEgKW_PD_BwE

17. Do students learn more about their communities if its schools develop a local curriculum?
Research has suggested that after implementing a local curriculum, students gained more knowledge and skills related to their community. Closer relationships also developed between the communities and schools and students participate more in the community. [L+]

http://www.aare.edu.au/publications-database.php/4288/local-based-curriculum-development-a-case-study-of-watsamankit-elementary-school-thailand

http://theschoolsproject.org/curriculum-localization/

18. If local schools determine their own curriculum, can different schools be compared?
If local schools set the curriculum, there would exist a lack of consistency across schools, with students living in different, even nearby communities learning quite different things. [L–]

http://www.teach-nology.com/poll/10.php

19. What are some of the challenges to developing a local curriculum?
A major challenge in creating a local curriculum is the staff's skill in creating it. When principals and teachers are unprepared for the curriculum to change, they may feel unequipped to do it, and an attempt to localize the curriculum has not been successful. [L–]

http://theschoolsproject.org/curriculum-localization/

DECISION. Animal research. *Should animals be used in research to test new medical procedures, drugs or other products?*

Questions about Animal use in research

1. Why have animals been used in research? Code 211d
2. How many animals are involved in research each year in the US? 683d
3. Has animal testing led to cures for any human diseases? 144d
4. How similar are humans and animals in terms of diseases they get? 656d
5. Can medical testing of animals be of any benefit to animals? 440d
6. Are there types of research that can be performed with animals but not humans? 188d

7. Are animals used for other reasons than testing medical treatments? 646d
8. Can researchers use as many animals as they wish in their research? 908d
9. How are animals treated in research laboratories? 332d

Questions about Alternatives to research with animals

10. Can information be gained from studying human cells in a laboratory? 594d
11. Can computers be used to predict how humans will respond to a treatment? 998d
12. Can statistics be used to analyze how people react to different events? 964d
13. Can bodies of humans who have recently died be used for research? 915d
14. Can synthetic versions of human organs be used in research? 900d
15. Can models made from human tissue be used to test new drugs? 894d

Add questions of your own:

16. _____
17. _____
18. _____

Questions about Animal use in research

1. Why have animals been used in research?
Animal organs often resemble human organs, so medicines may work in similar ways. [A+]
http://www.theaps.org/mm/SciencePolicy/AnimalResearch/Publications/animals/quest1.html

2. How many animals are involved in research each year in the US?
The US Department of Agriculture reports that use of animals in research was at its highest of over two million per year in the early 1990s and fell to a low of below a million in 2016. [A–]
https://www.navs.org/what-we-do/keep-you-informed/science-corner/animals-used-in-research/?gclid=EAIaIQobChMIr7i1p2q1QIVWVcNCh3Iug62EAAYASAAEgLSp_D_BwE#.WXpDs-mRC0s

3. Has animal testing led to cures for any human diseases?
Animal testing has led to treatments and cures for many human diseases. For example, research with dogs led to treatments for diabetes, research with armadillos led to leprosy vaccines, and research with monkeys have led to treatments for hepatitis, polio, and AIDS. [A+]
http://self.gutenberg.org/articles/eng/Animal_experimentation

4. How similar are humans and animals in terms of diseases they get?
Many of the diseases that humans get—such as cancer, malaria, asthma, arthritis, and heart failure—are also found in animals. [A+]
http://self.gutenberg.org/articles/eng/Animal_experimentation

5. Can medical testing of animals be of any benefit to animals?
Many of the medications that are given to sick animals (such as pets and zoo animals) were discovered as a result of medical research for human purposes that involved those animals. [A+]

https://www.nap.edu/read/10089/chapter/7

6. Are there types of research that can be performed with animals but not humans?
Many studies of living bodies are so complicated and uncertain in their effects that they could not be carried out with humans. [A+]

http://www.theaps.org/mm/SciencePolicy/AnimalResearch/Publications/animals/quest1.html

7. Are animals used for other reasons than testing medical treatments?
Animals may be used to test reactions to new cosmetics or other products for the human body. [A+]

http://self.gutenberg.org/articles/eng/Animal_experimentation

8. Can researchers use as many animals as they wish in their research?
Regulations exist that require that scientists use as few animals as possible to conduct their research. [A+]

http://self.gutenberg.org/articles/eng/Animal_experimentation

9. How are animals treated in research laboratories?
There are laws in place to help ensure that distress and pain in animals is kept to a minimum. However, the daily treatment of animals is not known because the testing places cannot be monitored at all times and records are not shared. [A–]

http://self.gutenberg.org/articles/eng/Animal_experimentation

Questions about Alternatives to animal research

10. Can information be gained from studying human cells in a laboratory?
Studies of human cells under a microscope provide valuable information and can avoid the need for surgery. For example, examining human tissue can determine whether a person has cancer. [ALT+]

https://www.ncbi.nlm.nih.gov/books/NBK13237/

11. Can computers be used to predict how humans will respond to a treatment?
Computer models are frequently used to study how the human body functions and how it is likely to respond to different events. [ALT+]

https://www.nigms.nih.gov/Education/Pages/modelorg_factsheet.aspx

12. Can statistics be used to analyze how people react to different events?
Statisticians have helped link cigarette smoke to lung cancer and diet to heart disease by studying large numbers of people over periods of time. [ALT+]

https://www.ncbi.nlm.nih.gov/pmc/articles/PMC3809994/

https://www.hsph.harvard.edu/nutritionsource/salt-and-sodium/sodium-health-risks-and-disease/

13. Can bodies of humans who have recently died be used for research?
Examining human bodies soon after death can help to better understand causes and effects of diseases and medicines. [ALT+]

http://www.cnn.com/2010/HEALTH/10/28/body.after.you.die/

14. Can synthetic versions of human organs be used in research?
Studies involving the effect of sunscreen on a material like human skin produced quick results, compared to the length of time required for animal testing. [ALT+]

https://www.ncbi.nlm.nih.gov/pmc/articles/PMC2699641/

15. Can models made from human tissue be used to test new drugs?
Recently developed models made from human cells were designed to mimic more closely how the human body works and can be used to test how humans react to drugs. [ALT+]

http://www.neavs.org/alternatives/in-testing

DECISION. Social security tax. *Should people be required to pay a social security tax from each paycheck that will provide money when they retire, or should people save on their own for their retirement?*

Questions about Social Security

1. What is social security tax? Code 825d
2. Is the Social Security benefit that is paid to older people the same as a pension? 817d
3. How much must American workers and employers pay to the Social Security fund? 488d
4. Do all countries have a Social Security program? 700d
5. Can an older person be sure they will get Social Security benefits? 408d
6. At what age can you begin to get Social Security benefits? 415d
7. Does a person need to be retired to get Social Security benefits? 889d
8. Do all older persons get the same Social Security benefit? 697d
9. What happens if an older person has never worked or contributed to the Social Security system? 229d
10. Does the Social Security program cost the government a lot? 669d
11. Is the money that is subtracted from workers' paychecks kept safe for them until their old age? 192d
12. Do all workers contribute the same percentage of their salary to the Social Security program? 846d
13. If instead of contributing to the Social Security program workers had this money to use as they wanted to, would they be better off financially? 871d
14. Is it possible for the US Social Security program to run out of money? 926d
15. If the Social Security program runs out of money, what will happen? 736d
16. Is the US Social Security program likely to run out of money? 227d

Questions about Saving

17. Do programs exist to help workers save? 714d
18. Do programs exist to help people learn how to manage their money well? 619d
19. Can people be helped to think more about their future selves in old age? 295d
20. Must older people leave their homes if they run out of money? 198d
21. Do grown children often help to support their parents? 593d

22. How many people over 65 live in poverty? 350d

23. How much do working people save from their incomes? 873d

24. Do people plan for their old age? 179d

25. Do all employers give their employees a pension when they retire? 184d

26. Is it easy to predict how much money you will need in old age? 621d

27. Are programs that help people learn to save money effective? 117d

Add questions of your own:

28. _____

29. _____

30. _____

Questions about Social Security

1. What is social security tax?
The social security program in the US was begun by President Roosevelt in 1935. Workers and employers each contribute a percentage of the worker's pay to fund the program. After workers reach about age 67, it provides them a monthly allowance for the rest of their lives. [SS+]

https://www.ssa.gov/policy/docs/ssb/v70n3/v70n3p1.html

2. Is the Social Security benefit that is paid to older people the same as a pension?
No. Some, but not all, employers pay a pension to their own employees when the employee retires. Social Security is a US government program that all employers and employees are required to contribute to. [SS+]

https://www.avvo.com/legal-guides/ugc/pensions-vs-social-security

3. How much must American workers and employers pay to the Social Security fund?
In the US, workers pay 6.2% of every paycheck and the employer pays another 6.2%. In some countries, the required contributions for similar programs are higher. One of the highest is in Italy, where the employer contributes 33% of every paycheck and the worker contributes 9%. In a few countries, such as Armenia, only the employee contributes, not the employer. [SS+]

https://www.ssa.gov/policy/docs/progdesc/ssptw/

4. Do all countries have a Social Security program?
No. Most countries provide some kinds of help to their older citizens, but in some countries (such as Turkey, Greece, and India) it is paid for at least partly by the government's general funds that come from many types of taxes. A few countries that have a Social Security program similar to the one in the US are Brazil, Germany, Kenya, Singapore, and Sweden. China has a program similar to that in the US, but its enforcement has been more lax than in the US and reforms are underway. [SS+/−]

https://www.ssa.gov/policy/docs/progdesc/ssptw/2016-2017/europe/index.html

http://www.clb.org.hk/content/china's-social-security-system

5. Can an older person be sure they will get Social Security benefits?
Yes, everyone should receive the stated benefit if they have contributed when they were employed, no matter how much money they already have. [SS+]

htttps://www.ssa.gov/pubs/EN-05-10035.pdf

6. At what age can you begin to get Social Security benefits?
The age varies by country and ranges from as young as 50 to about 65 or 66. In the US, you must be 66 or 67 to get full benefits. You can retire beginning at age 62 but your benefit will be lowered. [SS+]

htttps://www.ssa.gov/planners/retire/1943.html

7. Does a person need to be retired to get Social Security benefits?
No, in most countries if you have reached the required age, you can get benefits and continue to work. Some exceptions are Germany, Greece, and Spain, where you must be retired. [SS+]

htttps://www.ssa.gov/pubs/EN-05-10035.pdf
htttps://www.ssa.gov/policy/docs/progdesc/ssptw/2016-2017/europe/index.html

8. Do all older persons get the same Social Security benefit?
No. The average benefit in 2016 in the US is $1360 per month, but some people get much less and some much more. In most countries it varies depending on how much you contributed while employed. In a few countries, such as Armenia, it depends only on number of years you worked). [SS+/–]

htttps://www.ssa.gov/policy/docs/statcomps/supplement/2015/supplement15.pdf

9. What happens if an older person has never worked or contributed to the Social Security system?
Most countries, including the US, help such people, but they must show they are in need, and they do not get as big a benefit as workers do. [SS+]

http://www.seniorcorps.org/social-security/can-i-collect-social-security-benefits-if-i-never-worked/

10. Does the Social Security program cost the government a lot?
Yes. In the US, 25% of government spending, or $888 billion, in 2015 went to Social Security benefits. [SS–]

https://www.cbpp.org/research/federal-budget/policy-basics-where-do-our-federal-tax-dollars-go

11. Is the money that is subtracted from workers' paychecks kept safe for them until their old age?
No. The money is used for benefits to today's older people. When today's workers are old, new younger workers will contribute the money for benefits to today's workers. [SS–]

https://www.ssa.gov/policy/docs/chartbooks/fast_facts/2015/fast_facts15.pdf

12. Do all workers contribute the same percentage of their salary to the Social Security program?
No, workers who earn more than $118,500 per year contribute only 6.2% of $118,500. So, a worker who earns $118,500 per year and one who earns $518,500 per year contribute the same amount: 6.2% of $118,500. [SS+/–]

http://nchra.shrm.org/news/2016/10/2017-wages-subject-social-security-fica-rise-127200

13. If instead of contributing to the Social Security program workers had this money to use as they wanted to, would they be better off financially?
This depends what they do with the money. Some claim they could invest the money themselves and would end up with a larger amount in their old age than they will receive from Social Security. [SS–]

https://usatoday30.usatoday.com/money/perfi/columnist/krantz/2011-04-27-opting-out-of-social-security_n.htm

14. Is it possible for the US Social Security program to run out of money?

Yes. It needs to bring in enough money from the contributions of current working people to pay the older people who currently receive Social Security benefits. In countries where old age benefits come from general government funds, this is less likely to happen, because the government can use money from other taxes, such as sales tax, to pay for the benefits to old people. [SS–]

http://www.investmentnews.com/article/20161222/FREE/161229967/social-security-program-to-run-out-of-money-in-calendar-year-2029

15. If the Social Security program runs out of money, what will happen?

Most likely, people will still get benefits, but changes will need to be made. Some possibilities are:
   a) Give benefits only to older people who need them and not to those who have enough money to take care of themselves.
   b) Increase age at which people can start to receive benefits (currently age 66 or 67 in US).
   c) Increase the percentage of their pay that workers and employers must contribute.
   d) Use money from other government sources, such as sales tax. [SS–]

https://www.ssa.gov/policy/docs/ssb/v70n3/v70n3p111.html

16. Is the US Social Security program likely to run out of money?

There are different views, but most agree the system will not have enough money to keep paying the level of benefits old people receive today. One estimate is that this will happen in 2029. [SS–]

http://www.investmentnews.com/article/20161222/FREE/161229967/social-security-program-to-run-out-of-money-in-calendar-year-2029

Questions about Saving

17. Do programs exist to help workers save?

Yes. Individual Retirement Accounts (IRAs) are now widely available. An individual can choose to invest money in such an account and keep control of it, taking it out if needed or saving it for old age. [Sa+]

https://www.wellsfargo.com/help/faqs/investing-ira/

18. Do programs exist to help people learn how to manage their money well?

Classes exist in the US and other countries to teach financial skills and money management to children and adults. They are part of the curriculum in about half of US states. In parts of China all schools have them. [Sa+]

http://money.usnews.com/money/personal-finance/articles/2016-03-22/your-guide-to-inexpensive-online-money-management-classes

http://www.businessinsider.com/high-schools-teaching-personal-finance-2015-4

19. Can people be helped to think more about their future selves in old age?

One study says yes. After seeing computer-generated photos of themselves as older people, young people were more willing to save or invest, rather than spend, $1000 they were told they would receive. [Sa+]

https://www.ncbi.nlm.nih.gov/pmc/articles/PMC3949005/

20. Must older people leave their homes if they run out of money?

If people own their homes, reverse mortgages are available to help people stay in their homes. These allow home owners to receive a monthly payment from a lender. The lender will be paid back when the house is sold after the owner has died. [Sa+]

https://reverse.org/what-is-a-reverse-mortgage/

152   Part Three ■ The Decision Topics

21. Do grown children often help to support their parents?
According to a US survey, 36% of adult sons or daughters report helping to pay for their parents' care. The percentage is nearer 50% in countries such as China where there is a cultural norm favoring such care. [Sa+/–]

https://www.agingcare.com/articles/state-of-caregiving-2015-report-177710.htm

https://www.chinabusinessreview.com/senior-care-in-china-challenges-and-opportunities/

http://www.bbc.com/news/magazine-35155548

22. How many people over 65 live in poverty?
This varies by country. In the US, between 10-15% of people over age 65 live in poverty. [Sa–]

http://kff.org/medicare/issue-brief/poverty-among-seniors-an-updated-analysis-of-national-and-state-level-poverty-rates-under-the-official-and-supplemental-poverty-measures/

23. How much do working people save from their incomes?
There is great variation in savings, even among people with similar lifetime incomes; many people save none of their income and others save a great deal. [Sa+/–]

http://www.financialsamurai.com/the-average-savings-rates-by-income-wealth-class/

24. Do people plan for their old age?
Only some people plan for their old age. One study showed that one third of people 50 and over had not thought about their retirement needs. Other studies have shown that most workers do not know much about the pensions or benefits they will have in old age; many don't know much about financial matters such as interest rates and inflation. [Sa–]

http://time.com/money/4258451/retirement-savings-survey/

http://www.dartmouth.edu/~alusardi/Papers/Literacy_Information_Education.pdf

25. Do all employers give their employees a pension when they retire?
No. One third or more of private companies do not provide their workers pensions. [Sa–]

http://employment-law.freeadvice.com/employment-law/pensions_benefits/all030303.htm

26. Is it easy to predict how much money you will need in old age?
No. To decide how much they need to save for old age, people need to predict many factors, such as how long they are likely to live, their health, how much interest their savings will gain, and how inflation and interest rates will affect prices. [Sa–]

http://www.investopedia.com/university/retirement/retirement2.asp

27. Are programs that help people learn to save money effective?
People can be taught financial skills and money management. However, studies have shown that classes for workers on money matters have only a small effect on their savings plans and savings behavior. [Sa–]

https://thebillfold.com/the-problem-with-financial-literacy-is-that-it-doesn-t-work-ce79d2800d56

DECISION. Drugs. *Is use of illegal drugs best reduced by educating people about its dangers or by making drugs less available?*

Questions about Educating against drug use

1. What are the dangers of using illegal drugs? Code 589d

2. How common is drug use around the world? 319d

3. How often do people die as a result of drug use? 870d

4. How often are people admitted to hospitals as a result of drug use? 561d
5. Are high school students given information regarding the dangers of drug use? 648d
6. Are elementary school students given information regarding the dangers of drug use? 436d
7. Has educating parents of teens been effective in reducing drug use? 775d
8. Is there a relation between school activity and drug use? 542d
9. Do programs exist to help people lower or end drug use? 182d
10. How much money is spent on drug treatment and prevention? 545d
11. Do people stop drug use permanently after attending a treatment program? 944d
12. Can drug education programs be effective in preventing drug use? 675d
13. How do teens react to drug education programs? 813d
14. Have drug education programs been proven effective in reducing drug use? 774d
15. How many US schools have effective prevention programs? 803d

Questions about Lowering drug availability

16. Is it easy to obtain illegal drugs? 625d
17. How much is spent on purchase of illegal drugs? 668d
18. Is illegal drug use related to age? 215d
19. Who sells illegal drugs? 388d
20. Is drug production and sale a good business? 984d
21. Is drug availability related to teens' drug use? 799d
22. Does increased drug availability increase use? 544d
23. How does the price of illegal drugs affect drug use? 504d
24. How can drugs become less available? 811d

Add questions of your own:

25. _____

26. _____

27. _____

Questions about Educating against drug use

1. What are the dangers of using illegal drugs?
The dangers of using illegal drugs include addiction, physical and mental health problems, job loss, and relationship problems. [E+]

http://luxury.rehabs.com/drug-addiction/dangers-of-drug-addiction/

2. How common is drug use around the world?
Drug use is common around the world. It is estimated that in 2012, between 162 million and 324 million people, corresponding to between 3.5 per cent and 7.0 per cent of the world population aged 15-64, had used an illicit drug. [E+]

http://www.unodc.org/documents/wdr2014/World_Drug_Report_2014_web.pdf

3. How often do people die as a result of drug use?
In the US about 570,000 people die each year as a result of drug use. 22,000 of these deaths are related to illegal drugs. [E+]

https://teens.drugabuse.gov/national-drug-alcohol-facts-week/drug-facts-chat-day-drug-use

4. How often are people admitted to hospitals as a result of drug use?
About 2.1 million people each year in the US are admitted to a hospital as a result of drug abuse. 21.2% of these are related to illegal drug use. [E+]

https://www.drugabuse.gov/publications/drugfacts/drug-related-hospital-emergency-room-visits

5. Are high school students given information regarding the dangers of drug use?
US law requires that all schools receiving federal funding provide drug education and prevention programs. [E+]

http://www.educationworld.com/a_curr/school_climate/drug_prevention_program_isnt_working.shtml

6. Are elementary school students given information regarding the dangers of drug use?
US law requires that all schools receiving federal funding provide drug education and prevention programs. [E+]

http://www.educationworld.com/a_curr/school_climate/drug_prevention_program_isnt_working.shtml

7. Has educating parents of teens been effective in reducing drug use?
Some family-based prevention programs focused on parenting skills, communication, and creating family rules about drug use have been shown effective in reducing teen drug use. [E+]

https://www.ncbi.nlm.nih.gov/pmc/articles/PMC2916744/

8. Is there a relation between school activity and drug use?
Studies show that students who are engaged and involved in schools and communities are less likely to use drugs. [E+]

https://www.ncbi.nlm.nih.gov/pmc/articles/PMC2916744/

9. Do programs exist to help people lower or end drug use?
There are a variety of programs to help people with drug use. These are usually long-term programs that can involve therapy, medication, or a combination of the two. [E+]

https://www.drugabuse.gov/publications/principles-drug-addiction-treatment-research-based-guide-third-edition/frequently-asked-questions/what-drug-addiction-treatment

10. How much money is spent on drug treatment and prevention?
Drug prevention efforts exist around the world, but the amount spent is small compared to the total cost of drug use. About $500 billion is spent in the US each year due to drug use. Only about 2% of this is spent on treatment and prevention programs. [E–]

http://www.cnn.com/2009/HEALTH/05/28/addiction.costs/

https://medium.com/foggy-bottom/fighting-global-drug-addiction-c75face18f7b

11. Do people stop drug use permanently after attending a treatment program?
People do not always permanently stop drug use after attending a treatment program. Drug addiction is usually a long-term disorder and people frequently start using again. [E–]

https://www.drugabuse.gov/publications/principles-drug-addiction-treatment-research-based-guide-third-edition/frequently-asked-questions/what-drug-addiction-treatment

12. Can drug education programs be effective in preventing drug use?
Programs vary in effectiveness. Studies show that the most effective programs are interactive, focus on drug resistance and social skills, and take place over multiple years. Young people who participate in such programs have lower rates of drug use than those who do not participate. [E+]

https://www.ncbi.nlm.nih.gov/pmc/articles/PMC2916744/

13. How do teens react to drug education programs?
Many early prevention attempts focused on lecturing teens and scaring them into not using drugs. These programs did not show much effectiveness. [E–]

https://www.ncbi.nlm.nih.gov/pmc/articles/PMC2916744/

14. Have drug education programs been proven effective in reducing drug use?
Not all drug education programs currently in use have been supported by research. A review of several studies showed that teens enrolled in the DARE program were just as likely to use drugs as those not enrolled in the program. [E]

https://www.scientificamerican.com/article/why-just-say-no-doesnt-work/

15. How many US schools have effective prevention programs?
Studies have shown that only 35% of public schools and 13% of private schools in the US have drug prevention programs that have proven to be effective. [E–]

http://www.educationworld.com/a_curr/school_climate/drug_prevention_program_isnt_working.shtml

Questions about Lowering drug availability

16. Is it easy to obtain illegal drugs?
It can be easy to obtain illegal drugs. Teens commonly obtain illegal drugs at school, at home, online, and by using false IDs. [LA+]

https://www.teenrehabcenter.org/resources/how-do-teens-get-drugs/

17. How much is spent on purchase of illegal drugs?
Drugs are used around the world, but the US continues to be the largest market for purchase of illegal drugs. Americans spend about $100 billion a year on illegal drugs. Much of this expenditure makes its way back to other countries to support drug production. [LA+]

https://obamawhitehouse.archives.gov/blog/2014/03/07/how-much-do-americans-really-spend-drugs-each-year

http://www.pbs.org/wgbh/pages/frontline/shows/drugs/special/math.html

156   Part Three   ■   The Decision Topics

18. Is illegal drug use related to age?
According to US data, drug use increases most during the teenage years and declines through adulthood. If people use drugs early in life, they are more like to use and abuse them later in life. [LA+]

https://www.ncbi.nlm.nih.gov/pmc/articles/PMC2916744/

19. Who sells illegal drugs?
A study showed that many illegal drug dealers had tough childhoods and have been drug users themselves since an early age. More than half did not complete high school, and two thirds have served a prison sentence. They thus have limited job opportunities. [LA+]

https://www.jrf.org.uk/report/understanding-drug-selling-local-communities

20. Is drug production and sale a good business?
Yes, drug production and sale is an extremely lucrative, high-yield business. Illegal drugs are inexpensive to produce and the market prices are very high compared to costs. [LA+]

http://www.pbs.org/wgbh/pages/frontline/shows/drugs/special/math.html

21. Is drug availability related to teens' drug use?
Research shows that teens use substances in social settings during their early teen years, most often with drugs that are readily available. Some become regular users or progress to other illegal drugs. [LA+]

https://www.ncbi.nlm.nih.gov/pmc/articles/PMC2916744/

22. Does increased drug availability increase use?
When illegal drugs are available to people, they are more likely to use them. Recently, for example, heroin has become more accessible and the number of new users has gone up. [LA+]

https://www.ncjrs.gov/ondcppubs/publications/policy/99ndcs/iv-g.html

23. How does the price of illegal drugs affect drug use?
When a product becomes less available, its price typically goes up. Estimates are that a 10% increase in the price of illegal drugs would lead to about a 6% decrease in use. [LA+]

https://www.nap.edu/read/10021/chapter/7#142

24. How can drugs become less available?
To make drugs less available, drug enforcement must increase internationally, with more inspections in airports and in cities. Also necessary is agreement among countries that reducing the drug supply is an important priority. [LA–]

https://www.ncjrs.gov/ondcppubs/publications/policy/99ndcs/iv-g.html

---

DECISION. Tobacco. *Is smoking best reduced by educating people about its dangers or by charging a very high tax on purchase of cigarettes?*

Questions about Educating on tobacco

1. Does smoking cigarettes involve drug use? Code 760d
2. What are the effects of the nicotine in cigarettes on the body? 441d
3. Is smoking a cause of death? 143d
4. Are more educated people less likely to smoke? 580d
5. Are people aware of the dangers of smoking? 340d
6. At what age do people start smoking? 321d

7. Are young people more susceptible to start smoking than adults? 676d
8. What is the relation between educational achievement and smoking? 994d
9. Has educating people about dangers of tobacco use eliminated smoking? 819d
10. Are any education efforts effective to reduce or prevent smoking? 917d
11. Are education efforts to reduce or prevent smoking adequate? 632d

Questions about Taxing cigarette sales

12. Do people pay a tax when they buy cigarettes? 297d
13. What happens to tax money from cigarette sales? 103d
14. How does cigarette tax affect cigarette sales? 599d
15. Is there evidence that raising cost of cigarettes reduces smoking? 312d
16. Is it difficult to raise taxes on cigarettes? 186d
17. Who controls the prices of cigarettes? 782d
18. Are there ways people avoid high cigarette taxes? 832d
19. Do cigarette taxes affect some groups of people more than others? 848d

Add questions of your own:

20. _____
_____
21. _____
_____
22. _____
_____

Questions about Educating on tobacco

1. Does smoking cigarettes involve drug use?
Yes, the main active ingredient in tobacco smoked in cigarettes is nicotine, and nicotine is a drug that is addictive. [E+]

https://www.ucanquit2.org/NicotineEffects

2. What are the effects of the nicotine in cigarettes on the body?
Nicotine boosts the brain's "reward center," releasing chemicals that cause a pleasant feeling. Adrenaline is then released, increasing heart rate and blood pressure, and making breathing rapid and shallow. As nicotine use continues, these effects can damage your heart, arteries, and lungs, increasing the risk for heart attack, stroke, and chronic lung disease. [E+]

https://www.ucanquit2.org/NicotineEffects

3. Is smoking a cause of death?
Cigarette smoking is responsible for more than 480,000 deaths per year in the United States, including more than 41,000 deaths resulting from secondhand smoke exposure. This is about one in five deaths annually, or 1,300 deaths every day. On average, smokers die 10 years earlier than nonsmokers. [E+]

www.cdc.gov/tobacco/data_statistics/fact_sheets/fast_facts/index.htm

4. Are more educated people less likely to smoke?
Yes, the relation between education and smoking is strong. People with less than a high school education are more likely to smoke and less likely to attempt to quit smoking, compared to individuals with more education. [E+]

https://academic.oup.com/ije/article/37/3/615/742307/Educational-attainment-and-cigarette-smoking-a

5. Are people aware of the dangers of smoking?
Knowledge about the health risks of smoking is high, even among smokers. In one study, lung and heart damage was identified as a risk by over 90% of smokers and cancer by over 70%. [E–]

https://www.ncbi.nlm.nih.gov

6. At what age do people start smoking?
Almost all smokers begin as children or teens. 88% of US adult smokers report that they started smoking by age 18. [E+]

https://www.ncbi.nlm.nih.gov/books/NBK99239/

7. Are young people more susceptible to start smoking than adults?
There are many social, biological, and environmental factors that influence young people to smoke. Teens are especially vulnerable to social influences from peers and media. School policies, peers, and expectations about the future measured at ages 13 to 15 predict smoking at ages 26 to 29. [E+]

https://www.ncbi.nlm.nih.gov/books/NBK99239/

https://news.yale.edu/2014/05/20/why-don-t-highly-educated-smoke

8. What is the relation between educational achievement and smoking?
Research shows that teens who have lower academic achievement are more likely to begin to use tobacco and to become regular users. [E+]

https://www.ncbi.nlm.nih.gov/books/NBK99239/

9. Has educating people about dangers of tobacco use eliminated smoking?
Although there are many programs intended to reduce or eliminate smoking in young people, generation after generation continues to smoke. [E–]

https://www.ncbi.nlm.nih.gov/books/NBK99239/

10. Are any education efforts effective to reduce or prevent smoking?
Some studies report effectiveness. Students who have participated in proven-effective prevention programs showed lower rates of smoking than students who did not participate. [E+]

https://www.ncbi.nlm.nih.gov/pmc/articles/PMC2916744/

11. Are education efforts to reduce or prevent smoking adequate?
No, the US spends less than two cents of every cigarette tax revenue dollar on efforts to reduce smoking.

https://www.tobaccofreekids.org/what_we_do/state_local/prevention_cessation/

Questions about Taxing cigarette sales

12. Do people pay a tax when they buy cigarettes?
Cigarettes are widely taxed but the rates vary widely among different countries and among different states within the US. The US is ranked 36th out of the 50 most populous countries in terms of the percent of cigarette pack costs from taxes. Taxes make up about 40% of the cost of a pack of cigarettes in the US and in China, compared to 82% in England, which has the highest cigarette taxes. [T+/–]

https://en.wikipedia.org/wiki/Cigarette_taxes_in_the_United_States#State_cigarette_tax_rates

http://global.tobaccofreekids.org/files/pdfs/en/China_tobacco_taxes_summary_en.pdf

13. What happens to tax money from cigarette sales?
One study found that the US spent less than 3% of its tobacco revenues on anti-smoking programs. The rest of the money was used for general expenses or programs other than tobacco control. [T–]

http://health.usnews.com/health-news/news/articles/2012/05/24/states-use-only-fraction-of-tobacco-revenues-to-fight-smoking-study-finds

14. How does cigarette tax affect cigarette sales?
There is a strong relation between increasing costs and decreasing consumption of most products, including cigarettes. In the US, in every state that raised its cigarette tax, sales sharply decreased. [T+]

https://www.tobaccofreekids.org/research/factsheets/pdf/0146.pdf

15. Is there evidence that raising cost of cigarettes reduces smoking?
Raising cigarette prices has been shown to reduce smoking, especially among young people. When US prices went up in the 1980s it was estimated to cause 2 million adults to quit smoking and prevent 600,000 teenagers from starting to smoke. A general estimate is that for every 10% increase in the price of cigarettes, the rate of smoking decreases by 3-5%. [T+]

https://www.tobaccofreekids.org/research/factsheets/pdf/0146.pdf

16. Is it difficult to raise taxes on cigarettes?
Cigarette taxes are a special kind of tax, called an excise tax. In many countries, these taxes are complicated and involve many loopholes. Sometimes the tobacco companies take advantage of these loopholes to avoid the full amount of taxes, making it hard for the government to raise prices. [T–]

http://apps.who.int/iris/bitstream/10665/112841/1/WHO_NMH_PND_14.2_eng.pdf

17. Who controls the prices of cigarettes?
US cigarette prices are mostly set by the tobacco companies. The government can affect prices by increasing the taxes on cigarette sales, rather than the cigarette price itself. [T–]

https://www.tobaccofreekids.org/research/factsheets/pdf/0146.pdf

18. Are there ways people avoid high cigarette taxes?
In the US, where cigarette taxes vary by state, many people simply go to lower-tax states to purchase their cigarettes. [T–]

https://www.tobaccofreekids.org/research/factsheets/pdf/0146.pdf

19. Do cigarette taxes affect some groups of people more than others?
Because smoking is more common among people who are less wealthy and less educated, cigarette taxes are more costly to people with lower incomes and to young people. [T–]

https://priceonomics.com/how-cigarettes-tax-the-poor/

DECISION. Capital punishment. *Should the death sentence be used to punish serious crimes such as murder?*

1. How many countries practice capital punishment? Code 815d
2. What is the most common punishment for intentional (1st degree) murder? 570d
3. Does capital punishment lower murder rates? 242d
4. Does capital punishment ever discourage someone from committing a serious crime? 508d

5. Are fewer serious crimes committed in places that have the death penalty? 859d

6. Can capital punishment increase murder rates? 518d

7. Does a publicized death sentence lower crime rates? 169d

8. Does capital punishment affect how safe police are on the job? 281d

9. Does capital punishment affect how safe police feel on the job? 330d

10. How many people support the death penalty? 990d

11. Do people agree with how often the death penalty is used? 946d

12. Is the death penalty costly to carry out? 125d

13. How much does it cost to maintain a death row prisoner awaiting a death sentence? 666d

14. How much does the drug used in lethal injection cost? 464d

15. Are juveniles subject to the death penalty? 860d

16. Are mentally disabled people subject to the death penalty? 847d

17. Are innocent people ever sentenced to death? 725d

18. Do criminals sentenced to death always receive a fair trial? 458d

19. Are people sometimes sentenced to death for non-serious crimes? 904d

20. Are people who commit a serious crime such as murder likely to commit another crime after being released from prison? 171d

Add questions of your own:

21. _____

22. _____

23. _____

1. How many countries practice capital punishment?
Worldwide, 58 nations practice capital punishment, and 95 nations do not allow it. [CP+/–]

http://www.telegraph.co.uk/travel/maps-and-graphics/countries-that-still-have-the-death-penalty/

2. What is the most common punishment for intentional (1st degree) murder?
In most countries, people convicted of intentional murder are charged with a life sentence in prison. They may or may not be eligible for parole after serving a number of years in prison. [CP–]

https://fullfact.org/crime/how-long-do-murderers-serve-prison/

3. Does capital punishment lower murder rates?
Findings are mixed, but several studies have shown that murder rates are not significantly lower in US states that allow capital punishment. [CP–]

https://www.dartmouth.edu/~chance/teaching_aids/books_articles/JLpaper.pdf

4. Does capital punishment ever discourage someone from committing a serious crime?
There are cases where the death penalty has prevented murder. One example is a Los Angeles case where the suspects reported that they did not use weapons in their robbery because they did not to be charged with murder and sentenced to death. [CP+]

https://www.dartmouth.edu/~chance/teaching_aids/books_articles/JLpaper.pdf

5. Are fewer serious crimes committed in places that have the death penalty?
In the US, murder is more common in states with the death penalty than states without it. [CP–]

https://www.dartmouth.edu/~chance/teaching_aids/books_articles/JLpaper.pdf

6. Can capital punishment increase murder rates?
A comparison was made of murder rates in 10 pairs of neighboring states with different capital punishment laws. In 8 of the 10 pairs, murder rates were higher in the state with capital punishment. [CP–]

https://math.dartmouth.edu/~lamperti/my%20DP%20paper,%20current%20edit.htm#_edn6

7. Does a publicized death sentence lower crime rates?
A study showed that in the 60 days following five highly publicized executions, murder rates were higher than usual. [CP–]

https://www.dartmouth.edu/~chance/teaching_aids/books_articles/JLpaper.pdf

8. Does capital punishment affect how safe police are on the job?
Research has shown that police and prison guards working in US states with the death penalty are no safer than those who work in states without it. [CP–]

https://www.dartmouth.edu/~chance/teaching_aids/books_articles/JLpaper.pdf

9. Does capital punishment affect how safe police feel on the job?
A survey showed that police working in states with the death penalty believe it makes them safer. [CP+]

https://www.dartmouth.edu/~chance/teaching_aids/books_articles/JLpaper.pdf

10. How many people support the death penalty?
This varies around the world. In a US survey, 60% of respondents favor the death penalty for a person convicted of murder. [CP+]

http://www.gallup.com/poll/1606/death-penalty.aspx

11. Do people agree with how often the death penalty is used?
Two-thirds of US survey respondents agreed that the death penalty is either used the right amount or should be used more. [CP+]

http://www.gallup.com/poll/1606/death-penalty.aspx

12. Is the death penalty costly to carry out?
Yes, the death penalty is significantly more costly to carry out than a prison sentence. Estimates vary but the cost is at least twice as much as a prison sentence. [CP–]

https://deathpenaltyinfo.org/news/past/16/2017

13. How much does it cost to maintain a death row prisoner awaiting a death sentence?
Death row prisoners cost taxpayers $90,000 more per year than other prisoners. [CP–]

https://deathpenaltyinfo.org/costs-death-penalty

14. How much does the drug used in lethal injection cost?
The cost for the lethal injection drug is less than $100. [CP+]

http://www.prodeathpenalty.com/methods.htm

15. Are juveniles subject to the death penalty?
In 2005, the US Supreme Court struck down the death penalty for juveniles. The US was one of the last countries that allowed the death penalty for offenders under 18. [CP+]

https://deathpenaltyinfo.org/50-Facts

16. Are mentally disabled people subject to the death penalty?
In 2002, the US Supreme Court struck down the death penalty for people with intellectual disabilities. [CP+]

https://deathpenaltyinfo.org/50-Facts

17. Are innocent people ever sentenced to death?
It is estimated that one in every 25 people sentenced to death in the US are wrongly accused and are in fact innocent. [CP–]

http://www.newsweek.com/one-25-executed-us-innocent-study-claims-248889

18. Do criminals sentenced to death always receive a fair trial?
In many countries, accused criminals sentenced to death did not receive a fair trial according to international standards. In some cases torture was used to get the person to confess. [CP–]

https://www.amnesty.org/en/latest/news/2016/04/death-penalty-2015-facts-and-figures/

19. Are people sometimes sentenced to death for non-serious crimes?
There are cases where people have been sentenced to death for offences that did not meet the "most serious crimes" threshold. In 12 countries in Asia and the Middle East, people were sentenced to death for drug-related and economic crimes, adultery, and violating religious beliefs. [CP–]

https://www.amnesty.org/en/latest/news/2016/04/death-penalty-2015-facts-and-figures/

20. Are people who commit a serious crime such as murder likely to commit another crime after being released from prison?
One study showed that 71% of violent criminals are arrested for a new crime within 5 years of being released from prison; 33% were arrested for another violent offense. [CP+]

http://www.cbsnews.com/news/once-a-criminal-always-a-criminal/

DECISION. Abortion. *Should it be against the law for a woman to undergo a medical procedure to end a pregnancy?*

Questions about Abortion

1. What is the difference between an abortion and a miscarriage? Code 769d
2. How is an abortion performed? 240d
3. Where and when in a pregnancy is abortion legally allowed? 680d
4. Is it easy to find an abortion provider? 658d
5. Are abortions safe? 291d
6. How common is abortion? 348d
7. Is it possible an abortion fails to end a pregnancy? 398d
8. Do teens have abortions? 145d
9. What is the age range of women having abortions? 768d

10. How much does an abortion cost? 999d

11. What are the most common reasons women have abortions? 401d

12. Is abortion often used as an alternative to contraceptive use? 498d

13. How many abortions are related to rape? 190d

14. Does having an abortion affect a woman's physical health? 232d

15. Can having an abortion affect a woman's mental health? 558d

16. Do women regret abortions? 574d

17. When is a fetus considered a person? 216d

Questions about Alternatives to abortion

18. What are alternatives to abortion? 535d

19. If a woman doesn't have an abortion and gives birth, must she raise the child or provide for its needs? 136d

20. How much does it cost to care for a child in the first three years of its life? 636d

21. How common is adoption? 673d

22. Can a woman be paid for giving her baby up in adoption? 285d

23. Once a baby is adopted, can the birth mother change her mind and reclaim the baby? 344d

24. Must the birth father agree to an adoption? 445d

25. Does a birth mother have the right to keep her identity secret? 262d

26. Can an adopted child search for its birth mother? 982d

Add questions of your own:

27. _____

28. _____

29. _____

Questions about Abortion

1. What is the difference between an abortion and a miscarriage?
Abortion is a medical process used to end a pregnancy through medication or surgery. Miscarriage is when a pregnancy ends spontaneously through an accident, injury, or natural causes. [A+]

http://www.medic8.com/healthguide/abortion/what-is-abortion.html

2. How is an abortion performed?

Many different methods may be used to perform an abortion depending on the stage of pregnancy. In early pregnancy, a combination of drugs is usually effective. After 16-20 weeks, a surgical procedure is necessary, involving a suction tube inserted into the uterus to remove the fetus. [A+]

https://www.lifesitenews.com/ldn/abortiontypes/

http://www.womenonwaves.org/en/page/702/how-to-do-an-abortion-with-pills--misoprostol--cytotec

http://americanpregnancy.org/unplanned-pregnancy/surgical-abortions/

3. Where and when in a pregnancy is abortion legally allowed?

Laws about whether and when abortions can be performed vary greatly from one country to another and from one state to another within the US. In a few countries (such as Northern Ireland, Poland, Iran) abortion is illegal except in special circumstances (such as rape, threat to the mother's life) and in a few (such as the Dominican Republic and Chile) it is illegal under any circumstances. Most countries allow abortions up to somewhere between 10 and 26 weeks of pregnancy. Some countries restrict circumstances permitting abortion while others have no restrictions [A+]

http://www.pewresearch.org/fact-tank/2015/10/06/how-abortion-is-regulated-around-the-world/

4. Is it easy to find an abortion provider?

Depending on the legal status of abortion in the country a woman lives in, it is generally possible to find an abortion provider without great difficulty, but a woman may have to travel some distance to do so. [A+]

http://www.abortion.com

5. Are abortions safe?

Abortions are generally safe if performed early and under medically high-quality conditions. A woman's risk of dying from having an abortion is 0.6 in 100,000, while the risk of dying from giving birth is around 14 times higher (8.8 in 100,000). [A+]

http://www.reuters.com/article/us-medical-abortions-are-safe-study-idUSBRE8BJ1CW20121220

http://abortion.procon.org

6. How common is abortion?

Approximately 56 million abortions occur each year throughout the world. In the US, the frequency of abortions per 1,000 women has declined from 29.3 in 1980 to 14.6 in 2014, possibly due to increased availability of contraceptives. In 2013, 664,435 reported abortions were performed in the US. [A+]

https://www.guttmacher.org/fact-sheet/induced-abortion-worldwide

https://www.cdc.gov/reproductivehealth/data_stats/abortion.htm

7. Is it possible an abortion fails to end a pregnancy?

About 2 in every 1,000 abortions fail and need to be repeated to end the pregnancy. [A–]

https://www.mariestopes.org.uk/women/abortion/surgical-abortion-explained/what-are-failure-rates-and-risks-abortion

8. Do teens have abortions?

Rates vary greatly by country. About 1 million teens become pregnant in the US each year. About one third of these pregnancies end in abortion. [A+]

http://www.choicespregnancy.org/facts-and-statistics-about-teenage-abortion

9. What is the age range of women having abortions?
A US study reports that most abortions are from women in their 20s. 26% are from women in their 30s and 13% are from women under age 20. Less than 5% are from women over 40. [A+]

http://kff.org/womens-health-policy/state-indicator/distribution-of-abortions-by-age/?currentTimeframe=0&sortModel=%7B%22colId%22:%22Location%22,%22sort%22:%22asc%22%7D

10. How much does an abortion cost?
Abortion costs vary around the world. In some countries (China, England, France) abortion is free. In some countries it can be very expensive. In the US the average cost is about $470. [A+]

http://consciencemag.org/2013/09/16/abortion-costs-around-the-world/

11. What are the most common reasons women have abortions?
The most common reasons women give for having abortions are that having a child would interfere with their education, work, or ability to care for other family members; that they could not afford a child; or that they did not want to be a single mother or were experiencing relationship problems. [A+]

https://www.guttmacher.org/sites/default/files/pdfs/journals/3711005.pdf

12. Is abortion often used as an alternative to contraceptive use?
Fifty-one percent of abortion patients in 2008 were using a contraceptive method in the month they became pregnant. [A+/–]

https://www.guttmacher.org/fact-sheet/induced-abortion-united-states?gclid=EAIaIQobChMIoLfElqSs1QIVmUoNCh2VOgONEAAYAyAAEgJyEPD_BwE

13. How many abortions are related to rape?
In the US, about 32,000 abortions each year are related to rape — about 5% of all abortions. [A+]

https://www.ncbi.nlm.nih.gov/pubmed/8765248

14. Does having an abortion affect a woman's physical health?
Having an abortion may affect the mother's physical health at least temporarily. Frequent side effects include abdominal pain, nausea, vomiting, diarrhea, and bleeding. More serious complications occur in about 1-2% of abortions. [A+]

http://americanpregnancy.org/unplanned-pregnancy/abortion-side-effects/

15. Can having an abortion affect a woman's mental health?
Researchers have reported that the risk of mental health problems is no greater if women have a first-trimester abortion than if they carry the pregnancy to term. [A+]

https://www.guttmacher.org/fact-sheet/induced-abortion-united-states?gclid=EAIaIQobChMIoLfElqSs1QIVmUoNCh2VOgONEAAYAyAAEgJyEPD_BwE

16. Do women regret abortions?
One study reports that 95% of women who have had abortions do not regret their decision. [A+]

http://time.com/3956781/women-abortion-regret-reproductive-health/

17. When is a fetus considered a person?
The time at which a fetus becomes a person is judged differently by philosophers, religious traditions, politicians, and doctors. Some believe the fetus is a person at conception, others at the point it could survive outside the womb (20-24 weeks), and others not until birth. [A+/–]

http://www.livestrong.com/article/256004-when-does-the-fetus-become-a-baby/

Questions about Alternatives to abortion

18. What are alternatives to abortion?
Alternatives to abortion include parenting the child, finding a family member to raise the baby, or placing the baby for adoption. [A–]

http://www.womensource.org/free-pregnancy-services/pregnancy-options/

19. If a woman doesn't have an abortion and gives birth, must she raise the child or provide for its needs?
If a woman chooses to give birth to a child, she is not required to raise the child or provide for its needs herself. After the baby is born, she may choose to place the baby for adoption or foster care. [A–]

http://www.acog.org/Patients/FAQs/Pregnancy-Choices-Raising-the-Baby-Adoption-and-Abortion

20. How much does it cost to care for a child in the first three years of its life?
The average cost of caring for a child is between $12,800-$14,970 per year in the US. This would equal between $38,400-$44,910 for the first three years of its life. [A+/–]

http://www.huffingtonpost.com/2014/08/18/cost-of-raising-a-child_n_5688179.html

21. How common is adoption?
About 250,000 adoptions take place each year worldwide. About 135,000 adoptions take place each year in the US. [A–]

http://archive.boston.com/news/world/articles/2007/07/08/child_adoptions_worldwide/
http://www.pbs.org/pov/offandrunning/fact-sheet/

22. Can a woman be paid for giving her baby up in adoption?
A woman cannot legally be paid for the adoption itself, but she can receive money to help cover pregnancy-related expenses and living expenses during the pregnancy. [A–]

http://www.americanadoptions.com/pregnant/get_paid_for_adoption

23. Once a baby is adopted, can the birth mother change her mind and reclaim the baby?
The birth mother (and father) can change their minds about an adoption at any point before their parental rights have been legally ended. The time varies depending on many factors, but is usually between one and 30 days. [A–]

http://www.childadoptionlaws.com/adoption_laws_faq.htm

24. Must the birth father agree to an adoption?
If the birth father is known he typically must agree to the adoption. There are circumstances in which the birth mother can pursue adoption on her own, such as if the birth father is unknown or in prison. [A–]

http://www.americanadoptions.com/pregnant/birth_father_isnt_supportive

25. Does a birth mother have the right to keep her identity secret?
A birth mother can choose to have a closed or confidential adoption, which keeps her identity secret. She has no contact with the adoptive family during or after the adoption. [A–]

http://www.americanadoptions.com/pregnant/can_i_keep_this_a_secret

26. Can an adopted child search for its birth mother?
An adopted child may choose to search for its birth mother. Today there are websites and social media that can assist with this process. [A–]

htttps://www.adopted.com/

Chapter 9 ■ A National Future   167

DECISION. Euthanasia. *Should it be allowed to help someone who wants to end their life?*

1. What is euthanasia? Code 467d
2. What is the difference between passive and active euthanasia? 857d
3. What is the most common reason a person seeks euthanasia? 414d
4. What are other reasons a person may seek euthanasia? 932d
5. Can a person be charged with a crime of trying to end their life? 241d
6. Can a person be charged with a crime of assisting someone to end that person's life? 958d
7. When someone tries to assist someone to end that person's life, is it always successful? 671d
8. Are many diseases incurable? 351d
9. Is most pain treatable? 951d
10. Can depression be treated? 734d
11. Do people sometimes change their minds about wishing to die? 465d
12. Are doctors in favor of allowing doctor-assisted suicide? 346d
13. How many people annually are successful in ending their own life? 381d
14. How many people annually are successful in assisting someone to end that person's life? 489d
15. What say do family members have regarding a person who seeks euthanasia? 378d
16. If a person is unable to make their own decisions and has made no advance directive, what rights do family members have to make decisions on the person's behalf? 773d
17. At what point in people's lives is their care most costly? 779d

Add questions of your own:

18. _____

19. _____

20. _____

1. What is euthanasia?
Euthanasia is generally defined as deliberate, painless inducement of a quick death. [+/–]
https://en.wikipedia.org/wiki/Euthanasia

2. What is the difference between passive and active euthanasia?
Passive euthanasia entails the withholding of food or common treatments, such as antibiotics, necessary for continuance of life. Active euthanasia entails deliberate administration of a lethal substance that causes death. It may or may not be assisted by another person. [+/–]

http://www.life.org.nz/euthanasia/abouteuthanasia/methods-of-euthanasia/

3. What is the most common reason a person seeks euthanasia?
The most frequent reason a person seeks euthanasia is for physical and/or mental discomfort not easily relieved and caused by a condition not believed to be curable, to the point that the person's quality of life is greatly diminished. [+/–]

http://euthanasia.procon.org/view.answers.php?questionID=000199

4. What are other reasons a person may seek euthanasia?
Reasons a person may seek euthanasia include severe depression, not wanting to be a burden to family members, and economic hardship. [+]

http://euthanasia.procon.org/view.answers.php?questionID=000199

5. Can a person be charged with a crime of trying to end their life?
Suicide is not illegal in the US or many other countries. In some countries, however, a person who attempts or follows through with suicide can be charged with a crime. If the person dies, the government may take their property and their family may be responsible for related expenses. [+/–]

http://mentalhealthdaily.com/2014/07/24/is-suicide-illegal-suicide-laws-by-country/

6. Can a person be charged with a crime of assisting someone to end that person's life?
In many countries, such as China, a person can be charged with a crime if they assist someone else in ending their life. In other countries, such as Belgium, assisted suicide is legal. In the US, assisted suicide is legal in only six of 50 states. [+/–]

http://mentalhealthdaily.com/2014/07/24/is-suicide-illegal-suicide-laws-by-country/

http://euthanasia.procon.org/view.resource.php?resourceID=000132

7. When someone tries to assist someone to end that person's life, is it always successful?
Complications occur in 7% of assisted suicide cases, and problems with completion (longer-than-expected time to death or awakening of the patient) occur in 16% of cases. [+/–]

http://www.life.org.nz/euthanasia/euthanasiakeyissues/complications-and-euthanasia/

8. Are many diseases incurable?
Yes, a number of different diseases have no known cures and lead predictably to decline and eventual death. The period of time until death cannot be predicted exactly, however, and there are cases of unexpected apparent recovery. [+]

http://listverse.com/2007/10/04/top-10-incurable-diseases/

9. Is most pain treatable?
Most pain is treatable. There are many methods that can be used to treat pain, including medication, exercise, counseling, and surgery. [–]

http://www.webmd.com/pain-management/how_is_pain_treated#1

10. Can depression be treated?
Depression can be treated, even if it is severe. Treatments include medication, counseling, and lifestyle changes.

https://www.helpguide.org/articles/depression/depression-treatment.htm

11. Do people sometimes change their minds about wishing to die?
Research has shown that most people who attempt suicide and are unsuccessful change their minds about wishing to die and do not make further attempts. Five years later, only 4% have followed through in ending their own life. [–]

https://www.nrlc.org/archive/news/1999/NRL999/termill.html

12. Are doctors in favor of allowing doctor-assisted suicide?
In one US study, doctors were about evenly split on the issue. [+/–]

http://www.medscape.com/viewarticle/731485_2

13. How many people annually are successful in ending their own life?
In the US, more then 44,000 people die each year by suicide. [+/–]

https://afsp.org/about-suicide/suicide-statistics/

14. How many people annually are successful in assisting someone to end that person's life?
In US states where assisted suicide is legal, between 50-150 people are successful. In other European countries, the numbers are lower (less than 30). [+/–]

https://www.theguardian.com/news/datablog/2014/jul/18/how-many-people-choose-assisted-suicide-where-it-is-legal

15. What say do family members have regarding a person who seeks euthanasia?
It is rare for a person to request assisted suicide without discussing it with their family first. However, there is not a clear legal role for the family in cases where a person wants to end their own life. [–]

https://quod.lib.umich.edu/m/mfr/4919087.0001.103/--physician-assisted-suicide-family-issues?rgn=main;view=fulltext

16. If a person is unable to make their own decisions and has made no advance directive, what rights do family members have to make decisions on the person's behalf?
First the spouse, then adult children, and then parents are most often the ones given authority to make decisions for an incapacitated family member. [+/–]

http://euthanasia.procon.org/view.answers.php?questionID=000175

17. At what point in people's lives is their care most costly?
Medical and personal care is often very costly. In the US, however, only 13% of the $1.6 trillion spent in 2011 on healthcare was devoted to care of individuals in their last year of life. Rather than age, health condition was found the more important determiner of cost. [+/–]

https://www.ncbi.nlm.nih.gov/pmc/articles/PMC4638261/

Chapter 10

■ ■ ■

A World Future

DECISION. Aid to other nations. Should a powerful nation intervene to help another nation in trouble or focus only on its own problems? (p. 172)

DECISION. United Nations. Should the United Nations be made more powerful or less powerful than it is now? (p. 173)

DECISION. Space exploration. Should nations cooperate or compete in exploring outer space? (p. 176)

DECISION. Immigration. Should a nation allow people from other countries to come live in their country based on what they can contribute or how bad life is where they come from? (p. 179)

DECISION. Population control. Should countries whose population is growing too rapidly to feed their people try to reduce growth by educating people about the benefits of smaller family size or by a government policy that restricts family size? (p. 182)

DECISION. Organ sales. Should paying or receiving money for a body organ such as a kidney be allowed? (p. 186)

DECISION. Weapons of mass destruction. Some countries are believed to have or be developing weapons powerful enough to destroy all humanity. Should efforts be made to stop them by using persuasion or by using force? (p. 188)

DECISION. Charity. Your family wants to make a donation to help children. Should they give money to a family they know whose parent has just lost their job or should they send it to a community in Africa where children are starving? (p. 192)

Only the questions appear in the student edition. Students select a question, respond to the preliminary question about it (How might you make use of this information in your argument?), and then access an answer electronically. These answers and sources are printed for convenience only in this teachers' edition. (See Chapter 11 for an explanation of the symbol in parentheses following each answer.)

DECISION. Aid to other nations. *Should a powerful nation intervene to help another nation in trouble or focus only on its own problems?*

1. Do most wealthy nations assist other countries? Code 138d
2. Do most government officials and politicians agree about whether their government should take action in places far from home? 878d
3. Can a wealthy nation afford to help other nations? 160d
4. Is poverty a serious problem in a wealthy country such as the USA? 657d
5. How much money did it cost for a US soldier to serve in Afghanistan? 328d
6. What was the role of the United States in World War II? 618d
7. How has the United States prevented violence in other countries? 888d
8. What happened during the 1990s in Rwanda? 166d
9. What happened in 2011 in Egypt? 183d
10. Was the US effort to help South Vietnam become a democracy successful? 765d
11. Are the citizens of Syria safe? 210d

Add questions of your own:

12. _____

13. _____

14. _____

1. Do most wealthy nations assist other countries?
Most wealthy countries spend some money helping another country but how much they spend differs greatly by country. [A+]

https://www.theguardian.com/global-development-professionals-network/2015/sep/09/foreign-aid-which-countries-are-the-most-generous

2. Do most government officials and politicians agree about whether their government should take action in places far from home?
Most often they do not and there are different viewpoints on what to do and whether to do anything at all. [A–]

https://www.devex.com/news/where-they-stand-democrats-and-republicans-on-u-s-foreign-aid-79096

3. Can a wealthy nation afford to help other nations?
Views differ. Even wealthy countries have many problems within their own country. In 2015 the US was over $18 trillion in debt—that is about $54,000 for every person (including children) in the USA. [A–]

http://solutions.heritage.org/the-economy/federal-spending-budget-and-debt/

4. Is poverty a serious problem in a wealthy country such as the US?
Yes. In 2015, 43.1 million people (13.5% of the population) lived in poverty in the US. This means they did not have enough money to feed, house, and cloth themselves and their families adequately. [A–]

htttps://www.census.gov/library/publications/2016/demo/p60-256.html

5. How much money did it cost for a US solider to serve in Afghanistan?
It costs the US somewhere between $850,000 and 2.1 million per year for each American soldier serving in Afghanistan. [A–]

http://security.blogs.cnn.com/2012/02/28/one-soldier-one-year-850000-and-rising/

6. What was the role of the United States in World War II?
In World War II, the Nazis in Germany killed 6 million Jews and other groups of people. The United States' intervention in the war is a major reason the war ended and the killing stopped. [A+]

http://www.history.com/topics/world-war-ii/american-response-to-the-holocaust

7. How has the United States prevented violence in other countries?
After World War II, the US spent about $182 billion (in 2014 dollars) helping European countries rebuild; this may have helped to prevent future violence. [A+]

https://www.usnews.com/opinion/blogs/world-report/2014/06/06/the-lessons-from-us-aid-after-world-war-ii

8. What happened during the 1990s in Rwanda?
During the 1990s, the US decided not to get involved in a civil war in the African country of Rwanda where the Hutus killed an estimated 500,000–1,000,000 Tutsis. [A+]

http://www.history.com/this-day-in-history/civil-war-erupts-in-rwanda

9. What happened in 2011 in Egypt?
In 2011, the United States decided not to intervene in Egypt, where Egyptian people wanted to overthrow dictator president Hosni Mubarak. The people eventually overthrew Mubarak and elected a new president without any outside help. [A–]

https://www.theatlantic.com/international/archive/2015/10/middle-east-egypt-us-policy/409537/

10. Was the US effort to help South Vietnam become a democracy successful?
It was not. South Vietnam and North Vietnam are today a single country that does not have a democratic government. [A–]

http://thevietnamwar.info/vietnam-still-communist-country/

11. Are the citizens of Syria safe?
They are not. Citizens of Syria who object to the Syrian government's policies are in danger of being harmed and often killed. [A+]

https://www.nytimes.com/interactive/2015/09/14/world/middleeast/syria-war-deaths.html

---

DECISION. United Nations. *Should the United Nations be made more powerful or less powerful than it is now?*

1. What is the United Nations? Code 282d
2. Why was the United Nations founded? 952d
3. Can any nation gain admission to the United Nations? 881d

4. How is the work of the United Nations funded? 104d

5. Does the United Nations have other goals than peace-keeping? 110d

6. What are some other global issues that have been considered by the United Nations? 810d

7. How is the United Nations involved in promoting and protecting world-wide human rights? 384d

8. What can the United Nations do in the case of human rights violations around the world? 750d

9. What has the United Nations done in recent years with regard to world health? 770d

10. Does the United Nations attempt to settle disputes between member nations? 818d

11. Has the United Nations successfully mediated international conflicts? 805d

12. Has the United Nations experienced failures in the roles it has played in international conflicts? 912d

13. Has the United Nations faced serious criticisms? 109d

14. What does the United Nations seek to do in the future? 457d

Add questions of your own:

15. _____

16. _____

17. _____

1. What is the United Nations?
The United Nations is an international organization founded in 1945 to promote international cooperation among nations and preserve world peace. There were an initial 51 member nations and there are now 193. [+]

www.un.org

2. Why was the United Nations founded?
The United Nations was founded after World War II in the hope of helping to avoid further world-wide wars and conflicts. It replaced an earlier organization having a similar goal, the League of Nations. [+]

www.un.org

3. Can any nation gain admission to the United Nations?
Admission as a member nation must be approved by a two thirds majority vote. In disputes between nations, the UN must decide whether a nation should be recognized as legitimate. For example, North Korea claims to be the sole legitimate government of Korea, but both North Korea and South Korea are members of the UN. [+/–]

www.un.org

4. How is the work of the United Nations funded?
Each member nation is assessed dues based on its ability to pay, measured by gross national income. The two-year budget for 2012–13 was $5.512 billion in total. Top contributors in 2016 were the US (22%), Japan (10%), China (8%), and Germany (6%). [+/–]

https://www.un.org/en/hq/dm/pdfs/oppba/Regular%20Budget.pdf

http://wikipedia.org/wiki/United_Nations

5. Does the United Nations have other goals than peace-keeping?
In the decades after its founding, the United Nations began to spend less on peace-keeping and more on economic and social development of less developed nations. [+]

http://wikipedia.org/wiki/United_Nations

6. What are some other global issues that have been considered by the United Nations?
The United Nations has considered issues such as climate change, sustainable development, human rights, disarmament, terrorism, humanitarian and health emergencies, gender equality, governance, and food production. [+]

www.un.org

7. How is the United Nations involved in promoting and protecting world-wide human rights?
A series of international human rights treaties have been adopted since 1945. The *High Commissioner for Human Rights* of the UN comments regularly on human rights situations around the world and has the authority to investigate situations and issue reports on them. The peacekeeping budget of $8.27 billion is calculated separately. [+]

www.un.org

http://wikipedia.org/wiki/United_Nations

8. What can the United Nations do in the case of human rights violations around the world?
The UN Charter gives the Security Council the authority to investigate and mediate human rights violations. The Security Council may issue a ceasefire directive, dispatch military observers or a peacekeeping force. It can also propose economic sanctions, arms embargos, financial penalties and severance of diplomatic relations. [+]

www.un.org

9. What has the United Nations done in recent years with regard to world health?
The Global Health Crises Task Force of the United Nations was formed in 2016. It has focused on what is needed for effective action on health crises. It has examined to what extent earlier recommendations were being implemented, identified obstacles to implementation and considered mechanisms to assess the preparedness of the UN system to address health emergencies. The UN General Assembly presented a briefing on health issues in May 2017. [+]

www.un.org

10. Does the United Nations attempt to settle disputes between member nations?
An *International Court of Justice* of the United Nations seeks to settles legal disputes submitted to it by member nations, in accordance with international law. It is composed of 15 judges, each from a different nation, who serve terms of nine years. Member nations may or may not abide by the decisions of the Court of Justice. [+/–]

www.un.org

11. Has the United Nations successfully mediated international conflicts?
Yes, for example the UN negotiated an end to the Salvadoran Civil War and launched successful peacekeeping missions in Sierra Leone and Namibia. [+]

http://www.telegraph.co.uk/news/worldnews/europe/bosnia/11729436/Srebrenica-20-years-on-What-have-been-the-successes-and-failures-of-UN-peacekeeping-missions.html

12. Has the United Nations experienced failures in the roles it has played in international conflicts?

Yes, its efforts in conflicts in Sri Lanka, Somalia and Bosnia were widely criticized as failures. Also criticized has been the UN indecision in failing to intervene in the genocide in Rwanda. In connection with Sri Lanka the UN Secretary General Ban Ki-moon blamed member countries for not providing the UN with support to meet the tasks set by themselves. [–]

http://www.telegraph.co.uk/news/worldnews/europe/bosnia/11729436/Srebrenica-20-years-on-What-have-been-the-successes-and-failures-of-UN-peacekeeping-missions.html

http://www.firstpost.com/world/un-failed-during-final-days-of-lankan-ethnic-war-ban-ki-moon-1133061.html

https://en.wikipedia.org/wiki/United_Nations_Assistance_Mission_for_Rwanda

13. Has the United Nations faced serious criticisms?

American and European critics of the UN condemned the organization for perceived mismanagement and corruption. The UN attempted reform efforts in 1997 in the face of threats from the US to withhold its UN dues. [–]

https://news.google.com/newspapers?nid=1309&dat=19980116&id=TvxOAAAAIBAJ&sjid=-BQEAAAAIBAJ&pg=4023,6546189

14. What does the United Nations seek to do in the future?

In a 2015 resolution adopted by the UN as the 2030 Agenda for Sustainable Development, the UN pledged to between now and 2030, "end poverty and hunger everywhere" and "combat inequalities within and among countries." [+]

http://www.un.org/en/ga/search/view_doc.asp?symbol=A/RES/70/1&Lang=E

DECISION. Space exploration. *Should nations cooperate or compete in exploring outer space?*

1. What is NASA? Code 690d
2. Are efforts made to promote the value to a nation of investing in space exploration? 910d
3. Do citizens favor spending government money on space exploration? 149d
4. Does space exploration have benefits that make it worth the very high cost? 527d
5. How costly is space exploration? 154d
6. Have nations competed to be the first in space? 681d
7. When was a man-made object first sent into space and what nation did it? 158d
8. When did the first walk in space by a human occur? 662d
9. When did a human first land on the moon? 581d
10. Have national leaders promoted efforts to be first in space? 584d
11. Are efforts continuing to compete in space exploration? 392d
12. Does China have a space program? 534d
13. Have there been initiatives for nations to join together in space exploration? 590d

14. What is the International Space Station (ISS) Program? 269d

15. Is it certain that nations will cooperate in space exploration? 957d

Add questions of your own:

16. _____

17. _____

18. _____

1. What is NASA?
NASA is the National Aeronautics and Space Administration, an agency of the US government that heads the US program in aerospace research. It was established in 1958 by President Eisenhower and continues to govern US space activities. [comp+]

https://www.nasa.gov/about/org_index.html

2. Are efforts made to promote the value to a nation of investing in space exploration?
Yes, NASA for example has prepared and circulated material promoting American space exploration. [comp+]

https://www.youtube.com/watch?v=kp4pJGLGdDs

3. Do citizens favor spending government money on space exploration?
In a 2003 poll, 71% of US citizens agreed that space exploration was "a good investment." [comp+]

http://www.pollingreport.com/space2.htm

4. Does space exploration have benefits that make it worth the very high cost?
Opinions differ, but a case has been made that the US space program creates new technologies that advance the national economy. [comp+]

http://freakonomics.com/2008/01/11/is-space-exploration-worth-the-cost-a-freakonomics-quorum/

5. How costly is space exploration?
Space exploration is extremely expensive. It is estimated that the US spent $196.5 billion on its space shuttle program over a 30-year period beginning in 1971. [comp–]

https://www.space.com/11358-nasa-space-shuttle-program-cost-30-years.html

6. Have nations competed to be the first in space?
Yes, the most well-known case is the competition between the US and the Soviet Union in the mid-20th century to be the first to achieve space goals. The Soviet Union was first more often than the US. [comp+]

http://www.historyshotsinfoart.com/space/timeline.cfm

7. When was a man-made object first sent into space and what nation did it?
The Soviet Union launched Sputnik 1 in 1957. It was a 58 cm metal sphere that circled the earth. It remained in orbit about 3 months and circled the earth over 1000 times. [comp+]

http://www.russianspaceweb.com/sputnik_mission.html

8. When did the first walk in space by a human occur?
The first space walk was made in 1965 by Soviet cosmonaut Alexey Leonov. He spent 12 minutes outside his spacecraft. [comp+]

https://www.jsc.nasa.gov/history/walking/EVAChron.pdf

9. When did a human first land on the moon?
The American Apollo 11 mission in 1969 was the first to land a human on the moon. [comp+]

https://www.space.com/10469-neil-armstrong-explains-famous-apollo-11-moonwalk.html

10. Have national leaders promoted efforts to be first in space?
Yes, US President Kennedy became concerned about the perceived Soviet lead and in a 1961 speech pledged as a national goal that "before this decade is out, [of] landing a man on the Moon and returning him safely to the Earth." USSR Premier Khrushchev did not publicly confirm or deny the Soviets were pursuing a "Moon race." But they did pursue such a program in secret over the next nine years. [comp+]

https://en.wikipedia.org/wiki/Space_Race#Kennedy_directs_the_Race_toward_the_Moon

11. Are efforts continuing to compete in space exploration?
Yes, in 2017 the US legislature proposed creating a Space Corp to oversee competition in space exploration. Its purpose would be to defend American interests in space and to ensure the US can "fight and win wars" in space. [comp+]

https://www.nytimes.com/2017/07/26/us/politics/congress-budget-space-corps-pentagon-opposition.html

12. Does China have a space program?
Yes, China has one of the major current programs to explore space. China announced it conducted 21 successful space missions in 2016, and 19 the year before that. This puts China in a close second behind the US, which saw 22 successful launches, and ahead of Russia, which conducted 16. [comp+]

https://www.theatlantic.com/science/archive/2017/01/china-space/497846/

13. Have there been initiatives for nations to join together in space exploration?
Yes. In a 1963 speech before the United Nations US President Kennedy proposed that the US and the Soviet Union join forces in their efforts to reach the Moon and thus avoid "duplication, of research, construction, and expenditure." Russian Premier Khrushchev initially rejected Kennedy's proposal but was reported to later be more favorable. Kennedy's death occurred shortly thereafter and the proposal did not go forward. [coop+]

http://www.spacedaily.com/news/russia-97h.html

14. What is the International Space Station (ISS) Program?
The International Space Station Program was created in 1998 in an agreement between 15 nations. Its purpose is to establish cooperation in design and operation of a permanent inhabited space station for peaceful purposes. The US and Russia are members but China is not. Complex ageements have been made among participating nations regarding shared use and costs. [coop+]

https://www.space.com/8034-international-space-station-fly-2028-nasa-partners.html

15. Is it certain that nations will cooperate in space exploration?
No. The future of the International Space Station Program is not assured beyond 2020. [coop–]

https://www.space.com/8034-international-space-station-fly-2028-nasa-partners.html

DECISION. Immigration. *Should a nation allow people from other countries to come live in their country based on what they can contribute or how bad life is where they come from?*

1. What nation admits the largest number of people from other places to come to live in their country? Code 853d
2. How many legal immigrants arrive in the US each year? 739d
3. What countries do immigrants to the US come from? 450d
4. Do American citizens favor allowing people from other countries to come to the US to live? 745d
5. Do immigrants to the US speak English or learn to speak it quickly after they arrive? 385d
6. Are immigrants to the US well-educated? 716d
7. What kinds of work do immigrants do in the US? 247d
8. What contributions can immigrants make to the US? 222d
9. Does immigrant work in unskilled jobs benefit the US? 294d
10. Can anyone who wishes decide to immigrate to the US? 820d
11. How does someone enter the US as a refugee or asylum seeker? 461d
12. What countries do US refugees to the US come from? 357d
13. How bad were conditions in Rwanda during and after the 1990s civil war? 617d
14. What are conditions like in Syria in 2017? 502d
15. How have Somali refugees adjusted to life in the US? 533d

Add questions of your own:

16. _____
17. _____
18. _____

1. What nation admits the largest number of people from other places to come to live in their country?
The US admits a larger number of immigrants to live in the US permanently than does any other nation. [C+/N+]

https://en.wikipedia.org/wiki/Immigration_to_the_United_States

2. How many legal immigrants arrive in the US each year?

About one million immigrants legally arrive to live in the US each year. An estimated one-and-a-half million enter illegally intending to remain. About 13% of the US population were born elsewhere and immigrated to the US. [C+/N+]

http://www.migrationpolicy.org/article/frequently-requested-statistics-immigrants-and-immigration-united-states-1/#1c

https://en.wikipedia.org/wiki/Immigration_to_the_United_States

3. What countries do immigrants to the US come from?

The countries that the largest number of immigrants to the US come from are Mexico, China, Philippines, and India. But each year 50,000 or more immigrants arrive from each of 78 different countries. [C+/N+]

http://www.migrationpolicy.org/article/frequently-requested-statistics-immigrants-and-immigration-united-states-1/#1c

https://en.wikipedia.org/wiki/Immigration_to_the_United_States

4. Do American citizens favor allowing people from other countries to come to the US to live?

A 2009 survey found that 52% of Americans believed immigration of foreigners to the US was a good thing overall for the US. [C+/N+]

http://www.gallup.com/poll/122057/americans-return-tougher-immigration-stance.aspx

5. Do immigrants to the US speak English or learn to speak it quickly after they arrive?

An estimated 50% of foreign-born US residents are classified as "Limited English Proficient." [C–/N–]

http://www.migrationpolicy.org/article/frequently-requested-statistics-immigrants-and-immigration-united-states-1/#1c

6. Are immigrants to the US well-educated?

About one quarter of immigrants to the US above age 25 have college degrees or higher, about the same percentage as native-born Americans. About one third of immigrants lack a high school diploma, compared to 11% of native-born Americans. Immigrants are especially highly represented in scientific fields, where more than half of science Ph.d. holders in the US are foreign born. [C+/N+]

http://www.migrationpolicy.org/article/frequently-requested-statistics-immigrants-and-immigration-united-states-1/#1c

http://www.nber.org/digest/nov16/w22623.html

7. What kinds of work do immigrants do in the US?

Immigrants to the US work in quite varied jobs. About a quarter hold well-paying professional jobs (compared to about a third of native-born Americans). About a quarter of immigrants work in less well-paying jobs such as construction (about the same proportion as native-born Americans). [C+/N+]

http://www.migrationpolicy.org/article/frequently-requested-statistics-immigrants-and-immigration-united-states-1/#1c

8. What contributions can immigrants make to the US?

Immigrants to the US have high rates of invention and innovation. They create businesses at higher rates than natives. They have started more than half (44 of 87) of America's startup companies valued at $1 billion or more. [C+/N+]

http://www.sciencedirect.com/science/article/pii/S0094119009000679

http://www.nber.org/papers/w22385

http://nfap.com/wp-content/uploads/2016/03/Immigrants-and-Billion-Dollar-Startups.NFAP-Policy-Brief.March-2016.pdf

9. Does immigrant work in unskilled jobs benefit the US?

Immigrant work in unskilled jobs can benefit the US because immigrants may do types of work that natives are unwilling to do, raising overall economic productivity. [C+/N+]

https://en.wikipedia.org/wiki/Immigration_to_the_United_States

http://legacy.iza.org/en/webcontent/publications/papers/viewAbstract?dp_id=10492

10. Can anyone who wishes decide to immigrate to the US?

No, if anyone could enter and stay, there would be far too many people entering the US to be able to find housing and jobs. To immigrate legally to the US, someone must have one of three reasons: 1) to unite with family members already in the US; 2) to have an invitation of employment in the US; 3) to flee danger or extreme hardship in one's home country. [C–/N–]

http://www.migrationpolicy.org/article/legal-immigration-united-states/

11. How does someone enter the US as a refugee or asylum seeker?

Refugees apply to the US for residence from their home country. Asylum seekers come to the US and then request the right to stay. In either case, they must prove a well-founded fear of being in serious danger in their home country. The number of persons who may be admitted to the US as refugees each year is established by the president in consultation with Congress. [N+]

http://www.migrationpolicy.org/article/refugees-and-asylees-united-states-1/

12. What countries do US refugees to the US come from?

The countries US refugees come from varies as conditions change in those countries. Between 1991 and 2008, the US admitted almost 50,000 refugees from **Iraq**, where prolonged conditions of war made life there very difficult and dangerous. In 2016, there were about 6 million citizens of **Syria** in need of refugee status due to continuing civil war dating back to 2011. The US has accepted only about 16,000 Syrians; Turkey, Lebanon, Jordan, and Germany have accepted one to three million each. The US did little to rescue citizens from **Rwanda** when civil war in the 1990s led two million to flee to refugee camps. The US has accepted more refugees from **Somalia** (about 250,000), where civil war broke out in the 1990s. [N+/–]

http://www.migrationpolicy.org/article/refugees-and-asylees-united-states-1/

https://en.wikipedia.org/wiki/Refugees_of_the_Syrian_Civil_War

https://en.wikipedia.org/wiki/Somali_diaspora#Global_distribution

https://en.wikipedia.org/wiki/Rwandan_genocide#Refugee_crisis.2C_insurgency.2C_and_two_Congo_Wars

13. How bad were conditions in Rwanda during and after the 1990s civil war?

Rwandan government estimated the number of victims as over a million. Thousands of widows were subjected to rape and of about 400,000 orphans 85,000 of them were forced to become heads of families. Arrests overwhelmed the Rwandan prison system, leading to what was described as cruel, inhuman, or degrading treatment. [N+]

https://en.wikipedia.org/wiki/Rwandan_genocide#Refugee_crisis.2C_insurgency.2C_and_two_Congo_Wars

14. What are conditions like in Syria in 2017?

Since 2013, the Syrian civil war has killed a reported 470,000. Half the population have been killed or forced to flee their homes. Bombs are destroying crowded cities and food and medical care are in short supply. Harsh winters and hot summers make life even more difficult. Families are struggling to survive inside Syria, or risking their lives to travel in hope of being taken in elsewhere. [N+]

https://www.mercycorps.org/articles/iraq-jordan-lebanon-syria-turkey/quick-facts-what-you-need-know-about-syria-crisis

15. How have Somali refugees adjusted to life in the US?

The largest number of Somali immigrants in the US have settled in Minnesota. They have adjusted well and contribute to their local communities. Their children are educated in local schools. They have opened many Somali owned stores and restaurants that reflect Somali culture and traditions. [N+/C+]

http://www.startribune.com/inside-little-mogadishu-no-one-is-an-outcast/414876214

DECISION. Population control. *Should countries whose population is growing too rapidly to feed their people try to reduce growth by educating people about the benefits of smaller family size or by a government policy that restricts family size?*

Questions about a Government solution

1. The government of what large nation experimented with enforcing a one-child family size to reduce rapid population growth? Code 389d
2. Did China have a need to reduce its population growth? 931d
3. Did people in China agree with the one-child policy and accept it? 591d
4. Was China's one-child policy strictly enforced throughout the country? 366d
5. If a couple wanted to have more than one child, could they go outside China to do so? 748d
6. What happened if a Chinese family had twins? 167d
7. Was China's one-child policy successful in reducing population growth? 615d
8. Has China's one-child policy affected gender balance? 296d
9. Will the one-child policy cause hardship for couples in their old age? 801d
10. Do only children face difficulties not encountered by children who grow up with brothers or sisters? 572d
11. Will relaxation of the one-child policy lead to a new surge of population growth in China? 776d

Questions about an Education solution

12. In what nation do women now have the largest number of children? 623d
13. How do the people of Niger make a living? 719d
14. What is Niger's most urgent problem? 866d
15. How important is it to reduce population growth in Niger? 314d
16. Do the people of Niger have access to contraceptives that would make it possible for them to practice birth control? 490d
17. Do couples in Niger want to reduce population growth in their country by limiting the size of their families? 633d
18. Are there reasons people of Niger don't practice birth control even if birth control methods are available? 876d

19. Do the people of Niger obtain adequate education? 313d

20. Do leaders of the nation of Niger hope to limit its population growth? 588d

21. Is the government of Niger devoting funds to encourage birth control among its people? 233d

22. Are organizations outside Niger attempting to influence the people of Niger to reduce the country's population growth? 108d

Add questions of your own:

23. _____

_____

24. _____

_____

25. _____

_____

Questions about a Government solution

1. The government of what large nation experimented with enforcing a one-child family size to reduce rapid population growth?
China introduced a one-child policy in 1979. The policy limited couples to having one child. If they had more, they were subject to fines and termination of the pregnancy. The policy was gradually relaxed and was changed to a two-child policy in 2016. [G+/−]

https://en.wikipedia.org/wiki/One-child_policy

http://www.chinadaily.com.cn/china/2007-07/11/content_5432238.htm

2. Did China have a need to reduce its population growth?
The population of China grew from around 540 million in 1949 to 940 million in 1976. Less than half of China's land is suitable for humans to live on, limiting possibilities for expansion of residential areas. In the 1970s, China's ability to provide for its rapidly growing population was in serious question. Agricultural improvements appeared unable to sufficiently increase food supply to keep up with the expanding demand of so many people. Creating enough jobs and housing for young people was also in doubt, as were sufficient medical care and social services. [G+]

http://www.fmprc.gov.cn/ce/celt/eng/zt/zfbps/t125241.htm

3. Did people in China agree with the one-child policy and accept it?
76% of Chinese people supported the one-child policy in a 2008 survey. [G+]

http://www.pewglobal.org/2008/07/22/the-chinese-celebrate-their-roaring-economy-as-they-struggle-with-its-costs/

4. Was China's one-child policy strictly enforced throughout the country?
China's one-child policy was not evenly enforced across all parts of the country. It was more strictly enforced in cities than in rural areas. Couples could avoid the policy by paying the required fines. After 2007, about half of couples were allowed to have a second child if their first child was a daughter. [G−]

https://web.archive.org/web/20120330215041/http://www.unescap.org/esid/psis/population/database/chinadata/intro.htm

5. If a couple wanted to have more than one child, could they go outside China to do so?
A Chinese couple can go to another country to have a child. However, if they return to China and do not register the child, they cannot obtain birth certificates or proper documentation for the child. The child thus cannot enter school or receive healthcare. Some Chinese parents and children have applied for and been granted residence in the US on the grounds that the one-child policy is a form of political persecution. [G+/–]

https://en.wikipedia.org/wiki/One-child_policy

6. What happened if a Chinese family had twins?
The one-child policy is a "one birth" policy; parents are permitted to give birth one time even it results in multiple children. [G+]

https://en.wikipedia.org/wiki/One-child_policy

7. Was China's one-child policy successful in reducing population growth?
The birth rate in China fell from more than five births per woman in the early 1970s to 1.5 in 2010. The Chinese government claims 400 million births were prevented by the policy. This figure has been questioned, however, because other factors such as economic growth contributes to population decline. China's population continues to grow, but at a slower rate than previously. [G+/–]

http://www.fmprc.gov.cn/ce/celt/eng/zt/zfbps/t125241.htm

http://archive.boston.com/news/world/asia/articles/2011/10/27/chinas_touting_of_1_child_rules_draws_challenges/

http://dragonreport.com/Dragon_Report/Challenges_files/Wang_pp115-129.pdf

8. Has China's one-child policy affected gender balance?
The balance of male to female births is normally about 105 maies to 100 females. An imbalance of 117 to 100 was reached in China by 2013, reflecting the preference of many couples that their only child be a boy. Estimates are that there will be 30 million more men than women in China in 2020. [G–]

http://www.jstor.org/stable/2938438?origin=crossref&seq=1#page_scan_tab_contents

9. Will the one-child policy cause hardship for couples in their old age?
The Chinese culture has a tradition of relying heavily on their children for support in old age. Without an improved public pension system, many Chinese may enter old age without pensions and with inadequate family support. China will lose 67 million working-age people by 2030, while simultaneously doubling the number of elderly. [G–]

http://www.chinadaily.com.cn/china/2014-12/16/content_19093408.htm

10. Do only children face difficulties not encountered by children who grow up with brothers or sisters?
A review of studies finds few consistent differences in the personalities of only children and children who have siblings. [G+]

http://journals.sagepub.com/doi/abs/10.1177/0022022197282003?journalCode=jcca

http://www.jstor.org/stable/352302?origin=crossref&seq=1#page_scan_tab_contents

11. Will relaxation of the one-child policy lead to a new surge of population growth in China?
It is unlikely that Chinese couples will return to having larger families. Less than half the expected number of couples applied to have a second child in 2014 when the one-child policy was relaxed to a two-child policy. Young Chinese couples report a desire to have fewer children for economic reasons and women's increased desire to have professional careers. [G+]

http://www.chinadaily.com.cn/china/2014-12/16/content_19093408.htm

http://www.cbc.ca/news/world/5-things-to-know-about-china-s-1-child-policy-1.3294335

Questions about an Education solution

12. In what nation do women now have the largest number of children?
Niger, a large country of 19 million people in the Sahara desert in Africa, is believed to have the highest fertility rate in the world — an average of 7.1 children per woman. [E+/G+]

http://www.bbc.com/news/world-africa-13943662

13. How do the people of Niger make a living?
The large majority of people in Niger are farmers who grow crops to feed themselves. [E+/G+]

https://en.wikipedia.org/wiki/Niger

14. What is Niger's most urgent problem?
Niger faces the increasing challenge of feeding its rapidly growing population. Only about 15% of Niger's land is fit for farming. The dry climate adds to the challenge, with frequent drought and resulting emergency food shortages. [E+/G+]

http://www.bbc.com/news/world-africa-13943662

https://en.wikipedia.org/wiki/Niger

15. How important is it to reduce population growth in Niger?
Niger's growth rate is the highest in the world and a source of concern worldwide. At the current rate of growth, it is predicted that there will be 56 million people in Niger by 2050, up from 1.7 million in 1960. If so, the demands on the economy, social services and the environment will become unmanageable. [E+/G+]

http://www.irinnews.org/report/75801/niger-population-explosion-threatens-development-gains

16. Do the people of Niger have access to contraceptives that would make it possible for them to practice birth control?
Birth control supplies are not easily available to many people in Niger. However, efforts are being made to make them more available. The United Nations Population Fund (UNFPA) sends large quantities of contraceptives to Niger in an effort to encourage their use and reduce pregnancies. [E+]

https://www.economist.com/news/middle-east-and-africa/21612239-runaway-birth-rates-are-disaster-population-explosion

17. Do couples in Niger want to reduce population growth in their country by limiting the size of their families?
Only a minority of couples in Niger want to have smaller-sized families. In a survey of how many children they would like to have, the women of Niger on average said 9 and the men 12. Only 20% of women said they wished they had means to control births. [E–]

http://www.irinnews.org/report/75801/niger-population-explosion-threatens-development-gains

18. Are there reasons people of Niger don't practice birth control even if birth control methods are available?
A large family is a traditional value in the culture of Niger. Children are a status symbol. Children also are a source of labor in producing enough food. Parents also believe children will care for them in their old age. [E–/G–]

http://www.dw.com/en/niger-sleepwalking-into-huge-population-growth/a-19084486

19. Do the people of Niger obtain adequate education?
Most of the people of Niger live in rural areas and do not have access to schools. In 2015, less than 30% of the population could read or write — one of the lowest literacy rates in the world. Much of the population does not have access to schools. Children must often work to help with farming. Girls rarely attend school for more than a few years. [E–]

https://en.wikipedia.org/wiki/Niger

20. Do leaders of the nation of Niger hope to limit its population growth?
Niger officials have stated they hope to increase the percentage of women limiting births to 20%. They also hope to raise the marriage age from 15 to 18, reducing the number of years a woman will produce children. [E+/G+]

http://www.irinnews.org/report/75801/niger-population-explosion-threatens-development-gains

21. Is the government of Niger devoting funds to encourage birth control among its people?
The government of Niger claims support birth control but allocates only a tiny proportion of its budget to this effort. [G–]

http://www.irinnews.org/report/75801/niger-population-explosion-threatens-development-gains

22. Are organizations outside Niger attempting to influence the people of Niger to reduce the country's population growth?
The United Nations Population Fund (UNFPA) attempts to teach women of Niger about birth control methods and to discourage rumors that these methods are unsafe. It also runs a "school for husbands" which teaches men, who traditionally object to women's use of birth control, about family planning.

http://www.irinnews.org/report/75801/niger-population-explosion-threatens-development-gains

---

DECISION. Organ sales. *Should paying or receiving money for a body organ such as a kidney be allowed?*

Questions about Kidney donation

1. What is a kidney and why do people have to have one? Code 651d
2. Do people needing a new kidney to replace a failed one die because they can't get a kidney donation in time? 134d
3. Do many people agree to donate a kidney to someone who needs one? 603d
4. Do enough people volunteer to donate their kidneys for there to be enough kidneys to go around to those who need them? 981d
5. Have methods been tried to increase organ donation? 543d
6. Is it easy to make known your wish to donate your organs when you die? 863d
7. Can donors go back to their normal lives after donating a kidney? 365d

Questions about Kidney sale

8. Can people who need a kidney find someone who is willing to sell them one? 305d
9. Who sets the price for sale of a kidney? 180d
10. Do people who sell their kidneys need the money they receive? 698d
11. What do people do with the money they receive from selling their kidney? 586d
12. How can a poor person who can't afford to buy a kidney get one? 249d
13. Can someone put out a notice that they need a kidney? 972d
14. Can someone be forced to sell their kidney? 916d

Add questions of your own:

15. _____

_____

16. _____

_____

17. _____

_____

Questions about Kidney donation

1. What is a kidney and why do people have to have one?
A person's two kidneys are bean-shaped organs, each about the size of your fist, located near the middle of the back, just below the rib cage. Every day, your kidneys process about 200 quarts of blood to separate out about 2 quarts of waste products and extra water. The waste and extra water become urine. If your kidneys did not remove this waste, the waste would build up in the blood and damage your body. The kidneys also regulate blood pressure. [D+]

http://www.webmd.com/a-to-z-guides/function-kidneys

2. Do people needing a new kidney to replace a failed one die because they can't get a kidney donation in time?
Yes, in 2014, over 4,700 people in the US died while waiting for a donated kidney. [D–]

https://www.kidney.org/news/newsroom/factsheets/Organ-Donation-and-Transplantation-Stats

3. Do many people agree to donate a kidney to someone who needs one?
Rates of kidney donation vary around the world. Currently, 42% of Americans choose to be organ donors. [D+/–]

http://www.donorrecovery.org/2011/10/100-million-donors-registered-in-u-s/

4. Do enough people volunteer to donate their kidneys for there to be enough kidneys to go around to those who need them?
No. Over 100,000 people are on waiting lists to receive kidney transplants, and in 2014, there were only about 17,100 kidneys available from donors. About 5,500 kidneys were transplanted from living donors that year. [D–]

https://www.kidney.org/news/newsroom/factsheets/Organ-Donation-and-Transplantation-Stats

5. Have methods been tried to increase organ donation?
France has increased their donors to 99% by assuming that everyone wants to donate their organs unless they notify in writing that they don't want to (this is called "opting out"). [D+]

http://www.huffingtonpost.com/entry/france-organ-donors_us_586b6476e4b0eb58648a523a

6. Is it easy to make known your wish to donate your organs when you die?
Yes. Many US states encourage donations by allowing the consent to be noted on a person's driver's license. [D+]

http://www.nytimes.com/2009/09/27/business/economy/27view.html

7. Can donors go back to their normal lives after donating a kidney?
Yes, the large majority of donors recover completely after 4-6 weeks, encounter no serious health problems, and resume their normal lives. [D+]

http://www.hopkinsmedicine.org/transplant/living_donors/expect.html

Questions about Kidney sale

8. Can people who need a kidney find someone who is willing to sell them one?
Yes, it is illegal to sell organs in most nations, but a person who wants to buy a kidney can travel to another country where it is not against the law and buy one there. [S+]

https://www.theatlantic.com/business/archive/2015/10/give-a-kidney-get-a-check/412609/

9. Who sets the price for sale of a kidney?
Price must be negotiated and agreed by seller and buyer. There is no regulated or standard price. A typical price can be $30,000, but sometimes much more. [S–]

https://www.theatlantic.com/business/archive/2015/10/give-a-kidney-get-a-check/412609/

10. Do people who sell their kidneys need the money they receive?
Yes. Almost always they are very poor and have few ways to earn money. [S+]

https://www.theatlantic.com/business/archive/2015/10/give-a-kidney-get-a-check/412609/

11. What do people do with the money they receive from selling their kidney?
They are free to use it in any way they choose. [S+]

https://www.theatlantic.com/business/archive/2015/10/give-a-kidney-get-a-check/412609/

12. How can a poor person who can't afford to buy a kidney get one?
The only option is to wait for a donor and hope that there will be one soon. [S–]

http://abcnews.go.com/Health/story?id=1514702

13. Can someone put out a notice that they need a kidney?
Yes, as long as they don't offer to pay money for the kidney. [S+/–]

http://www.kidneyregistry.org/?cookie=1

14. Can someone be forced to sell their kidney?
This should never happen. However, there is no way to know if a person feels pressured to sell. [S–]

http://content.time.com/time/health/article/0,8599,1912880,00.html

---

DECISION. Weapons of mass destruction. *Some countries are believed to have or be developing weapons powerful enough to destroy all humanity. Should efforts be made to stop them by using persuasion or by using force?*

1. What are Nuclear-Weapon States? Code 997d
2. Is North Korea capable of launching a nuclear weapon that could reach the US? 237d
3. Has the US indicated its readiness to take military action against North Korea in response to North Korea's claim of possessing nuclear weapons capable of reaching the US? 571d
4. Is "preventive war" a possible course of action? 807d
5. Have secret talks with North Korea, pressuring them to abandon their nuclear weapons build-up, had results? 968d
6. Did Iraq ever possess biological or chemical weapons of mass destruction? 726d

7. Were attempts made to verify whether Iraq possessed or were developing weapons of mass destruction? 135d

8. How did the 2003 US war against Iraq begin? 854d

9. Did Iraq in fact possess the weapons of mass destruction that the US claimed in 2003? 963d

10. Has Iran been involved in developing nuclear weapons? 787d

11. Does Iran accept being forbidden to develop nuclear weapons? 862d

12. Did United Nations criticism and penalties against Iran in 2006 influence Iran's nuclear program? 907d

13. What was the US reaction following a 2011 report that Iran was continuing on a path toward nuclear weapon development? 359d

14. What would military action against Iran accomplish? 253d

15. What is the current US position on Iran's nuclear program? 419d

Add questions of your own:

16. _____

17. _____

18. _____

1. What are Nuclear-Weapon States?
Nuclear-Weapon States are nations that possess nuclear weapons able to achieve destruction of millions of people over a large area. Five such nations (US, UK, China, France, and Russia) in 1970 signed a treaty not to use these weapons unless in self-defense. Other nations (India, Pakistan, Israel, North Korea) are known to have such weapons but have not signed the treaty. [P+/F+]

https://en.wikipedia.org/wiki/List_of_states_with_nuclear_weapons

2. Is North Korea capable of launching a nuclear weapon that could reach the US?
In July 2017, North Korea tested a missile that appeared capable of reaching the West Coast of the US, an event that the US has long said it would not tolerate. [F+]

https://www.nytimes.com/2017/07/28/world/asia/north-korea-ballistic-missile.html

3. Has the US indicated its readiness to take military action against North Korea in response to North Korea's claim of possessing nuclear weapons capable of reaching the US?
In August 2017, in response to North Korea's claim of possessing nuclear weapons able to reach the US, the US president indicated on repeated occasions that the US is ready to take military action against North Korea and that "military solutions are now fully in place." [F+]

https://www.nytimes.com/2017/08/11/world/asia/trump-north-korea-locked-and-loaded.html?hp&action=click&pgtype=Homepage&clickSource=story-heading&module=a-lede-package-region&region=top-news&WT.nav=top-news

4. Is "preventive war" a possible course of action?
Attacking another country and damaging it could be claimed a preventive show of force if it discouraged that country from a bigger, more serious attack. In 2017, the US president responded to North Korea's verbal threats of attack with the threat of a "preventive" attack on North Korea — a military strike that would not destroy North Korea but would do significant damage — to show North Korea it is serious. [F+/P+]

https://www.nytimes.com/2017/08/10/opinion/susan-rice-trump-north-korea.html

5. Have secret talks with North Korea, pressuring them to abandon their nuclear weapons build-up, had results?
President Johnson in 1968 and President Clinton in 1994 both succeeded in getting North Korean leaders to participate in talks about limiting nuclear weapons. [P+]

https://www.nytimes.com/2017/08/09/us/politics/north-korea-presidents-diplomacy-trump.html

https://www.nytimes.com/2017/07/28/world/asia/north-korea-ballistic-missile.html

6. Did Iraq ever possess biological or chemical weapons of mass destruction?
In 1991 Iraq revealed to United Nations inspectors that it had a biological weapons program but claimed it was only for defensive purposes. In 1995 Iraq admitted this program was larger than previously admitted and included weapons. [P+/F+]

https://en.wikipedia.org/wiki/Iraq_and_weapons_of_mass_destruction

7. Were attempts made to verify whether Iraq possessed or were developing weapons of mass destruction?
Repeated UN inspections were undertaken but remained inconclusive and stopped for four years beginning in 1998. In 2002, UN inspectors reported that 90–95% of Iraq's WMDs had been verified as destroyed. [P+/F–]

https://www.un.org/Depts/unscom/Chronology/chronologyframe.htm

https://web.archive.org/web/20061021202822/http://www.pbs.org/newshour/bb/middle_east/july-dec98/ritter_8-31.html

https://en.wikipedia.org/wiki/Iraq_and_weapons_of_mass_destruction

8. How did the 2003 US war against Iraq begin?
In 2003 the US claimed that Iraq still possessed large hidden stockpiles of weapons of mass destruction (WMDs). This WMD possession was cited by the US as the main reason for declaring war against Iraq. [F+]

https://www.un.org/apps/news/story.asp?NewsID=6383&Cr=iraq&Cr1=inspect#.WY3MROmRC0s

https://en.wikipedia.org/wiki/Iraq_and_weapons_of_mass_destruction

9. Did Iraq in fact possess the weapons of mass destruction that the US claimed in 2003?
In 2006, US President Bush admitted "the intelligence was wrong, and [he was] just as disappointed as everybody else" when WMDs were not found." In 2015, however, it was learned that Iraq's WMDs had not been fully accounted for by earlier UN inspections. [F+/–]

http://www.washingtontimes.com/news/2006/apr/6/20060406-112119-5897r/

https://mobile.nytimes.com/2015/02/16/world/cia-is-said-to-have-bought-and-destroyed-iraqi-chemical-weapons.html?referer&_r=1

https://en.wikipedia.org/wiki/Iraq_and_weapons_of_mass_destruction

10. Has Iran been involved in developing nuclear weapons?

In 2006 the United Nations announced the claim that Iran was developing a nuclear program, in violation of agreements not to do so. The UN demanded that Iran suspend its program and imposed penalties if it did not. Iran refused, claiming that the purpose of its nuclear program was solely to produce electricity. Iran continued to seek materials needed for a nuclear program from Russia and China. [P+/F+]

https://fas.org/nuke/control/npt/text/npt3.htm

https://www.un.org/apps/news/story.asp?NewsID=19353&Cr=iran&Cr1=#.WY3XJ-mRC0s

https://en.wikipedia.org/wiki/Iran_and_weapons_of_mass_destruction#Nuclear_weapons

11. Does Iran accept being forbidden to develop nuclear weapons?

Iran claims it is unfair for Nuclear Weapon States to be the only ones allowed to possess nuclear weapons. [P+/–]

https://en.wikipedia.org/wiki/Iran_and_weapons_of_mass_destruction#Nuclear_weapons

https://web.archive.org/web/20071208223330/http://www.nti.org/d_newswire/issues/2007_4_2.html

12. Did United Nations criticism and penalties against Iran in 2006 influence Iran's nuclear program?

A 2011 report gave indications that Iran was continuing a nuclear program intended to develop nuclear weapons. [P+/F+]

http://www.iiss.org/en/publications/strategic%20dossiers/issues/iran--39-s-nuclear--chemical-and-biological-capabilities--a-net-assessment-44f8

https://en.wikipedia.org/wiki/Iran_and_weapons_of_mass_destruction#Nuclear_weapons

13. What was the US reaction following a 2011 report that Iran was continuing on a path toward nuclear weapon development?

The US made clear its acceptance of Iran's right to nuclear power for energy purposes, but it remains suspicious that Iran will use its nuclear energy program to manufacture weapons, The US joined with European countries, Russia and China in offering nuclear and other economic and technological cooperation with Iran if Iran suspends uranium enrichment. Iran is believed to have produced enough fuel to manufacture nuclear weapons, but only if the fuel goes through further enrichment. [P+]

http://www.nytimes.com/2012/01/09/world/middleeast/iran-will-soon-move-uranium-work-underground-official-says.html?pagewanted=2

https://en.wikipedia.org/wiki/Iran_and_weapons_of_mass_destruction#Nuclear_weapons

14. What would military action against Iran accomplish?

A military strike on Iran would delay but not destroy its nuclear program. [F+/–]

http://www.nytimes.com/2012/01/09/world/middleeast/iran-will-soon-move-uranium-work-underground-official-says.html?pagewanted=2

https://en.wikipedia.org/wiki/Iran_and_weapons_of_mass_destruction#Nuclear_weapons

15. What is the current US position on Iran's nuclear program?

The most recent agreement signed by Iran was signed in 2015. Since then, Iran has been accused of conducting missile tests that violate this agreement. Iran has claimed the missile tests were not designed to carry nuclear weapons, and were for energy development or defensive purposes only. The current US administration claims the 2015 agreement was too weak and wishes to abandon the agreement and demand new inspections. [P+/–]

http://www.ibtimes.com/will-trump-go-war-iran-tehran-vows-use-weapons-against-us-if-provoked-2485917

www.nytimes.com/2017/07/27/world/middleeast/trump-iran-nuclear-agreement.html

DECISION. Charity. *Your family wants to make a donation to help children. Should they give money to a family they know whose parent has just lost their job or should they send it to a community in Africa where children are starving?*

1. What financial help may someone get if they are laid off from their job? Code 451d
2. When US unemployment payments run out after six months, can they be renewed? 193d
3. What happens if a person falls behind in paying their housing costs? 159d
4. Are many children in Africa currently facing death? 713d
5. Is death in the first two years of life common in parts of the world due to inadequate food and healthcare? 667d
6. What is UNICEF? 550d

Add questions of your own:

7. _____

8. _____

9. _____

1. What financial help may someone get if they are laid off from their job?
Government programs vary across nations. In the US, a laid-off worker is likely to be eligible for unemployment payments for about six months. The amount is likely to be less than earned on the job, and the worker must regularly report to show they are searching for a job. [C+]

https://www.thebalance.com/what-is-unemployment-insurance-2064139

2. When US unemployment payments run out after six months, can they be renewed?
Generally unemployment payments end after six months and cannot be renewed. [C+]

https://www.thebalance.com/what-is-unemployment-insurance-2064139

3. What happens if a person falls behind in paying their housing costs?
If someone is paying a mortgage on a home they are buying, they can be evicted from their home if they don't make their monthly mortgage payments and the mortgage bank takes ownership of the house. If someone is renting, the landlord can evict them for nonpayment of rent. [C+]

http://www.foreclosureuniversity.com/studycenter/freereports/what_are_mortgages.php
http://www.nolo.com/legal-encyclopedia/evictions-renters-tenants-rights-29824.html

4. Are many children in Africa currently facing death?

The United Nations Security Council reported in the spring of 2017 that 2.1 billion dollars was needed to reach 12 million people in several countries in Africa to save their lives; thus far, only 6% of that amount had been donated. [A+]

https://www.nytimes.com/2017/08/12/opinion/sunday/this-is-what-hunger-looks-like-again.html

5. Is death in the first two years of life common in parts of the world due to inadequate food and healthcare?

Infant mortality is reported in the range of 150 to 200 per 1,000 live births in many parts of Africa. In the US, a comparable figure is 6 per 1,000, down from 7 per 1,000 in 2005. [A+]

http://www.encyclopedia.com/social-sciences-and-law/political-science-and-government/united-nations/unicef

http://www.nbcnews.com/health/health-news/infant-mortality-rates-fall-15-percent-u-s-n736366

6. What is UNICEF?

UNICEF is the United Nations International Children's Emergency Fund. The large majority of its funds go to improving the health of children in poor countries. Its Child Survival and Development Revolution (CSDR) focuses on inexpensive interventions to reduce child deaths; these include detecting child malnutrition, oral rehydration to prevent death by dehydration, food security, and family planning. [A+]

http://www.encyclopedia.com/social-sciences-and-law/political-science-and-government/united-nations/unicef

www.unicef.org/what-we-do#child-survival

Part Four

■ ■ ■

For Teachers

Chapter 11

■ ■ ■

Assessing Student Growth: *What Can this Curriculum Accomplish?*

This chapter, which appears only in the Teachers' Edition, is the one that teachers (and parents) will likely turn to first, for two reasons. First, you want to know what the program presented in this book will accomplish. Does it justify the time students will devote to it, amidst the many competing demands on their time? Second, how can their progress be tracked?

This chapter addresses both questions, which are related. Once we identify the forms of growth that have been observed among students participating in a program based on the curriculum described in this book, we can suggests ways in which teachers can formally or informally track their own students' progress. We begin, therefore, with a brief, non-technical summary of research findings on the progress of students engaged in the program.

Research evidence

Versions of the argumentation curriculum described in this book have been now carried out in a number of different public middle and high schools within the US primarily in the New York City area, for periods of one to three school years, with students typically participating during two class periods per week. It has also been implemented and assessed in a wide range of places internationally, including ones in Singapore, Beijing, Brazil, Cyprus, and the Dominican Republic. A number of additional implementation and assessment efforts are now underway or in the planning stages, including ones in Chengdu, China, and Seoul, Korea, and at additional schools in Singapore and Beijing. Educators in Asian countries, we have found, are in particular at this point in time strongly concerned that their students develop into strong, independent thinkers.

The students whose progress we have evaluated most extensively come from three schools in New York City in the neighborhood surrounding Columbia University, where residents range from middle to lower class. Two of the three groups attend public schools and one private. The private school is a K–8 school, and one of the public schools, Columbia Secondary School, is a grade 6–12 school, both affiliated with Columbia University. The other public middle school is nearby. The private school is well equipped with resources, while the two public schools struggle with a scarcity of funds. Demographically each of the three schools serves diverse populations, with a significant proportion of African-American and Hispanic students and students from low-income families. The proportion of low-income students is higher in the two public schools, with 60 percent or more qualifying for free or reduced-price lunch.

In total, 14 classes of 30-plus students from these schools each participated in the curriculum and in the associated assessments we report on here. Most of the classes participated for two years, five for only one year, and one for three years (allowing us to assess the "value added" of an additional year of participation). Twelve of the 14 classes came from the five successive entering classes of Columbia Secondary School between 2007 and 2011. These are the classes that provide the data we report on here. Publications reporting on other schools are included in the list at the end of the chapter.[1] Also included is the source for a report on implementation of a version of the curriculum with a more specialized population, residents of a juvenile detention center.[2] The sources listed at the end of the chapter contain full statistical and other technical details for readers wishing this information.

The Columbia Secondary classes provided an extraordinarily valuable sample for evaluating the effects of the curriculum during the five-year period our reporting covers. Each entering 6th-grade cohort at the school comprises roughly 96 students divided into three sections equivalent with respect to demographic characteristics and academic standing. Our argumentation curriculum was situated in a twice-weekly free-standing class (rather than included within the curriculum of a customary school subject) that all students enrolled in each year. It was identified as a course in philosophy. Among each cohort, only two of the three sections (and in two of the five years only one of the three) participated in our curriculum.

The remaining class sections enrolled in a parallel class taught by regular school faculty, also identified as a class in philosophy. It was equivalent in time and work investment but followed a more traditional whole-class discussion format, plus required writing assignments and some role-playing activities. These classes were loosely based on a Philosophy for Children[3] model, and students discussed many of the same topics as students in our curriculum, although without the focused pair dialogs, electronic discourse, or structured debates that our curriculum features. Instead, they focused on whole-class discussion and frequent essay writing (more than students participating in our curriculum).

We conducted initial and final assessments with these classes as well, thus allowing for close comparison with students who participated in our curriculum. This comparison is very different from the more typical control-group comparison, in which control students get no special experience while the experimental students do something new and different. Students in both groups came from the same overall school environment, as well as range of family backgrounds. All of their other courses were identical. This enabled us to conclude with considerable confidence that any differences could be attributed to experiences specific to our curriculum. Other explanations could be eliminated, such as extra attention paid to the experimental group (since both curricula were characterized as new and innovative to parents and students) or to preexisting differences between the two groups (since assignment to classes was random).

For the first four years, our dialogic curriculum was delivered entirely by our research staff, with much of this work supported by funding from the US Institute of Education Sciences, while the comparison curriculum was delivered by school faculty. During the fifth year, three of the first-year sections of our curriculum were taught by a member of the school faculty who volunteered for the assignment, with support and consultation by our team. We saw this as a next and critical step in establishing that our curriculum is deliverable by regular teachers.

Assessments were conducted just before the curriculum began and annually thereafter. Students in the comparison group participated in these assessments at the same times. We can thus compare participating students' performance to that of the comparison group, as well as tracking participating students' gains over time.

There are a number of dimensions on which we have examined students' progress. In electronic dialogs and the verbal showdown, do they show progress in how well they address one another's claims and respond with effective counterarguments and rebuttals? Do they progress in their ability to evaluate others' arguments or to choose the more effective of two possible counterarguments to a claim? Can they construct an effective hypothetical argument between a disagreeing pair? Do they become more discerning in their interpretations of evidence, the task examined in Chapter 6? We begin, however, with the skill that is of the greatest and most universal concern to teachers, construction of a written argument supporting a position on an issue. It also is a skill that has assumed a key role in the new US Common Core State Standards.[4]

Developing argumentive writing

Students and teachers alike tend toward despair over students' writing proficiency, especially in non-narrative expository writing. Students stare at the proverbial blank page needing to be filled and may themselves become filled with dread, not unrelated to that of the teacher who is faced with grading and providing timely feedback on an accumulating pile of these student efforts. Students' skill in such writing repeatedly has been judged as weak at every grade level, across K-12 and college.

Our research has shown that the individual argumentive writing of students participating in our curriculum improves as students engage in the curriculum. Moreover, it does so to a greater extent than does the writing of the comparison group described above, who had more frequent writing practice along with their whole-class discussion.[5]

We believe this is so because our dialogic focus supports the development of individual written argument by giving the latter a purpose. There is now both someone to communicate to and a purpose for communicating. In addition to the final "position" piece they write individually at the conclusion of a topic, our participants write regularly in their electronic communications to opposing pairs. This writing has a very specific and focused communicative purpose. Students also have the support of a same-side partner to collaborate with, as well as a context in which to reflect together on what they are going to say to an opposing pair. All of these factors, our studies have suggested, contribute to students' success. Experiencing a flesh-and-blood interlocutor and a purpose to the exchange they engage in leads the way for students to interiorize this dialogic frame when it comes time for them to express themselves individually in writing. Students are no longer writing to or for a teacher, seeking to produce what they think the teacher is looking for. Instead, they engage with their peers — first electronically and then in person. Later, in individual writing, this discourse remains alive, although confined to their own thought, when they envision what another might say and how they can address it.

What course does this improvement take, as reflected in students' final individual essays on successive topics? The first and most basic challenge a student faces in constructing a written argument is to recognize that an argument worth constructing has at a minimum two sides. Beginning students are typically not aware that it is critical to address both sides of the argument — the two competing claims — and show that the reasoning and evidence favoring one is greater than that favoring the other. Ignoring the opposing side never wins an argument, no matter how convincing one's own side seems. The dialogic focus of the experience students participating in our curriculum have, prior to individual writing, makes this realization difficult to avoid.

The second and more specific task then becomes one of coordinating claims with evidence bearing on them. Students cannot generate rich arguments and counterarguments in a vacuum. They need to bring to bear information relevant to the topic that will inform their thinking and discourse. The Q&As included in the present book for each of a chapter's suggested topics provide a source of such evidence for these topics. The short Q&A format in which the information is provided, and the associated questions students generate, have the value of creating a need for the information, thereby helping students to anticipate its value and as a result leaving them more disposed to make use of it.

In a two-sided argumentive framework, evidence can serve one of four basic functions:

1. *Support my position* (M+). An idea that serves to support one's own position.

2. *Weaken other's position* (O–). An idea that critiques and thereby attempts to weaken the opponent's position.

3. *Support other's position* (O+). An idea that acknowledges a strength of the opponent's position.

4. *Weaken my position* (M–). An idea that acknowledges a weakness of one's own position.

Our research on students' end-of-topic individual essays over the school year has shown that student essays progress in the sequence depicted below.[6] Students' essays initially focus only on arguments and evidence to support their own position. Second to appear are arguments and evidence that weaken the opposing position. The student at this second level has now developed a consistent stance easy to maintain: *Here are all the reasons that make my position a strong one and yours a weak one.*

Next to appear is the more challenging achievement of recognizing arguments and evidence that support the opposing position. These don't fit so well into an integrated, consistent stance. As a result, they often may be simply noted and then ignored, without an attempt to address them. The same is true of the even greater challenge of acknowledging arguments and evidence that weaken one's own position, the last to emerge. A final and critical achievement is thus needed (the final step in the sequence depicted here): inclusion of the "However" connections that attempt to connect and integrate conflicting types — for example, a *Support other* and a *Weaken other* or a *Support other* and a *Support my.*

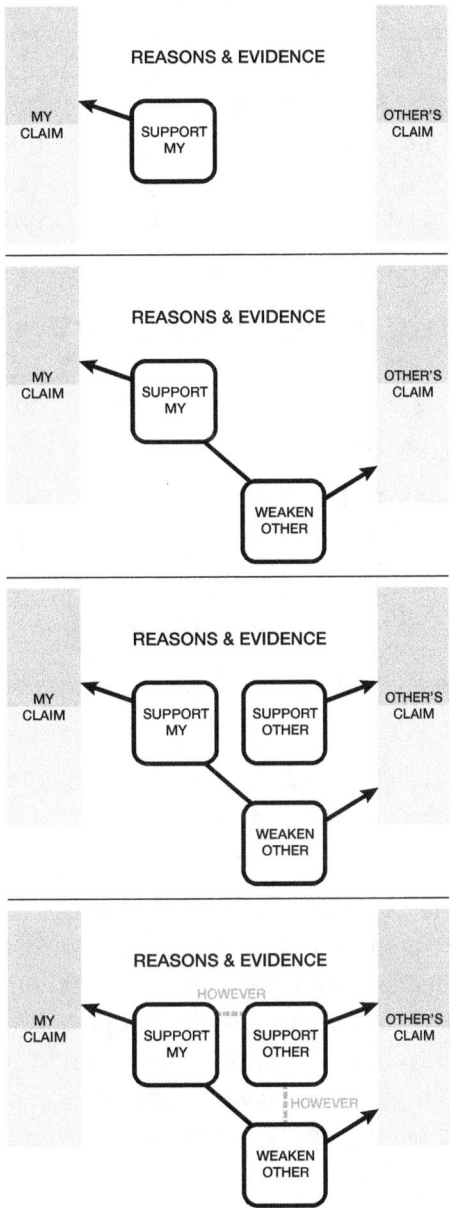

Assessing students' argumentive writing

Teachers are likely to have developed many of their own frameworks and preferences in evaluating students' non-narrative writing. What we have introduced here is intended as a complementary scheme, one that focuses squarely on the form and complexity of the thinking strategies underlying student essays. Teachers may find this scheme useful both for assessment purposes and in providing students feedback on their essays. The symbols in parentheses following each of the Q&A items in Chapters 7-10 should be understood as only suggestive in this regard and for illustrative purposes. They indicate the most common way in which a particular piece of evidence is likely to be used (supporting one side, weakening one side, supporting other side, weakening other side). Students, and indeed all writers, however, draw on evidence in unexpected ways. Hence, a student's use of any piece of evidence in an essay must be assessed on its own merits, making the best effort to understand the student's intention in drawing on that piece of evidence.

A student's essay can then be assessed as falling into one of the four types in the sequence appearing here. Below is an example of an essay falling into the first category and an example of one falling into the final, fourth category, both on the Home schooling topic from Chapter 8. For illustration purposes the essay is divided into idea units and each idea unit assigned one of the four types, M+, O–, O+, or M–. To facilitate reading them, each idea unit begins on a new line.

Example of Lowest-Level Essay

I think that Nick's parents should be allowed to home school Nick because they have the right to make the decision on how Nick should be educated. [M+]

Nick's parents are also qualified teachers. So, they can teach him effectively, and it is not that they just want to keep him home doing nothing. [M+]

Should Nick decide to go to town school on his own, his parents still have the final decision over him because Nick is 11 years old, and not of legal age 18, yet. [M+]

Also, making friends and having a social life can happen without being in school. [M+]

Nick can also learn English by just being in an environment where all he hears is English. He might learn English at a slower pace but he will learn it. [M+]

Note that in the lowest-level essay, the student expresses the parent-right perspective (the more difficult to recognize than the perspective of benefit to the child and the one beginning students more often omit). Nonetheless, the essay addresses only the alleged positives of the home-school option and never addresses the opposing position in terms of either positive or negative attributes.

In the second essay, a high-level essay on the same topic, the position (favoring home school) is also the same. The argumentative structure of the essay, however, is much more complex, containing all four of the function types (M+, O–, O+, M–) as well as multiple uses of the *However* connector that integrates them. Note in addition how the dialogic structure experienced in the dialogic engagement preceding the essay expresses itself in the essay ("Many people say...."). Note finally the assumption voiced in this essay as a *Condition* on which the writer's position is predicated.

> # Example of High-Level Essay
>
> Nick should go to home school. We live in America. In America, people have rights. [M+]
>
> Plus, Nick's parents are certified teachers. [M+]
>
> Some people say you need to know how to speak English to have a good life. [O+]
>
> [HOWEVER] Well, you don't. [M–] Think of some of the people today that only speak Greek or any other language besides English. They're well educated and are living well. Nick doesn't need to learn English.
>
> He would get a better education in his own language. [M+]
>
> If he goes to town school, he'll HAVE to learn English. [O–]
>
> He can get an "A" in Greek [M+]
>
> instead of getting a "C" or "B" in English. [O–]
>
> Many people say "How is he going to get a job when he is older"? [M–]
>
> [HOWEVER] He can open his own Greek shop. He can hire someone who speaks more than one language including Greek and English for when other people who come in that don't speak Greek. [M+]
>
> Also, he can be on a soccer team since he's good at it. [M+]
>
> Nick should keep his ties to Greece by continuing to learn and speak in Greek. [M+]
>
> Therefore, Nick shouldn't have to go to town school. He should be able to be home schooled, as long as he REALLY IS being taught. [CONDITION]

Details of how the essays of students in the middle-school samples we have studied progress over time are available in sources listed at the end of this chapter.[7] For purposes of providing students feedback on their argumentive writing, the classification of their essay overall into one of the four types in the sequence makes it possible to offer the student suggestions as to what is missing from their essay and could strengthen it. These suggestions can be made in conjunction with additional suggestions as to how to strengthen links among ideas, as well as enhance overall organization and cohesion.

Argumentive discourse

Although it has received much less attention than writing in school contexts, argumentive discourse is an activity in which we would like to see all students gain in skill. It plays an increasingly important role as students progress from K-12 education to higher education and careers. Such discourse is of course central to the curriculum presented in this book.

Students' electronic dialogs and their verbal showdown dialogs can be assessed in terms of the core criterion of the extent to which a communication is directly responsive to the immediately preceding statement by the opponent. Our research data show significant gains over time both in this respect and in the quality of these responses.[8] Novices are likely to ignore the opponent's statement and continue with their own line of thought. A contribution that is responsive to the opponent's preceding statement can be further categorized with respect to its success in questioning or criticizing the opponent's claim in a way that weakens its force. Students' counterargument efforts may be unsuccessful at first, and students can be given feedback as to how they might be strengthened.

An ideal time for this feedback to occur is during the debrief session following the showdown, when excerpts from the showdown are reviewed by the class as a whole and discussed (Chapter 4). Also worthy of close attention are counterarguments of counterarguments, i.e., rebuttals. Across how many exchanges does a dialog keep a sequence of rebuttals going? A point system for scoring the showdown, along with video examples, is available in a guidebook for teachers of the curriculum.[9] They can if they wish use it to formally score a showdown (or the earlier electronic dialogs). It should be emphasized, however, that there are no hard-and-fast rules that define such a scoring system. Rather, the system adopted should be an evolving one. Initially, a successful response can be one that addresses the opponent's immediately preceding statement. As students' skills grow, the bar can gradually be raised as to what constitutes a successful counterargument. For example, does it merely introduce an alternative possibility or does it directly lower the likely correctness of the claim the opponent has made? Most important, of course, with respect to the debrief session, is that students receive feedback on the quality of their argumentation with peers that is appropriate to their current skill levels.

Other assessment tools

Two tasks we include in this chapter offer additional ways to assess students' progress in constructing and evaluating arguments. The construction task[10] (see Box) consists of a writing assignment novice students will find difficult; hence its use should be postponed until students have gained some skill. The task is a challenging one because in writing a dialog for the two arguers the student must alternate between first adopting the position of one speaker and then the position of the other. In addition, the student must draw on the evidence provided (about city problems and about each candidates' positions on multiple issues) to support (and to challenge) speakers' claims.

There are a number of assessment criteria that can be applied to the arguments students construct in their imagined dialogs, and, again, these criteria can be adjusted to best fit students' current skill levels, both for assessment purposes and in providing students feedback on their performance. Here are some key ones:

1. Does the writer fulfill the same criterion highlighted earlier in the case of the student's own argumentation, i.e., do the constructed statements by the respective speakers directly address the immediately preceding statement of the opposing speaker?

2. Does the writer draw on the available evidence (on problems and candidate positions) to support the claims made by each speaker?

3. Does the writer integrate multiple pieces of evidence (within or across problems and candidates)?

4. Does the writer *compare* the strengths and weaknesses of both candidates, rather than focus on only one?

One could easily devise a scoring system to portray the extent to which the student writer fulfills each of these criteria, if a teacher wishes to have a quantitative score to show progress if the task is carried out on repeated occasions. Most important, however, is that the student receive feedback on how his or her constructed argument could better fulfill the task demands.

Constructing an Argument

Ana Cruz and Maria Diaz are running for mayor of their troubled large city. Among the city's problems are high housing costs, teen crime, traffic, school dropout, and unemployment.

Chuck and Doug are TV commentators arguing about who is the better candidate. Write a script of what they might say. They are both experts on the city; they are both expert arguers and evenly matched. So your script should present the most well argued debate you can construct.

Begin your script like this:
   CHUCK: Cruz should be elected mayor because she'll do better than Diaz.
   DOUG: I disagree, because xxxxxx

Then continue their argument, filling in what each one might say:
   CHUCK: xxxxxx
   DOUG: xxxxxx
   CHUCK: xxxxxx etc.

Here is some information about Cruz' positions. She promises to:
   – create job training programs
   – expand city parks
   – raise teachers' pay
   – open walk-in health clinics
   – reduce rents
   – impose a teen curfew
   – employ senior citizens in city schools

Here is some information about Diaz' positions. She promises to:
   – improve public transportation
   – open more centers for senior citizens
   – revise the high school curriculum
   – build a new athletic stadium
   – improve healthcare
   – build more housing

(You are not required to include all the above topics in your script.)

A second task, the argument choice task,[11] is in a multiple-choice format that can easily be objectively scored. For teacher convenience, in the box displaying the items, *response A is always the correct one.* The A-B response orders should therefore be varied in a version to present to students. A is the better response choice because it addresses directly and seeks to weaken, the opponent's claim. Response B could be a true statement, but it leaves the opponent's claim standing.

Argument Choice

Chris and Jose are expert arguers. They are having an argument about why students fail in school. Here are parts of their conversation. Chris always speaks first. Then two choices appear underneath what Chris says — these two choices are possible responses Jose might make. Read what Chris says; then decide and circle what response expert arguer Jose is more likely to make.

Chris says: "Students fail in school because they don't try hard enough to do well on tests."

Does Jose say A or B in response to Chris?

A. "No matter how hard students work, some just aren't good test-takers."

B. "Some students act out in class instead of paying attention to the teacher."

Chris says: "Success at school is based on work other than just tests, like essays and homework."

Does Jose say A or B in response to Chris?

A. "Some tests are so important that students can't graduate if they don't pass them."

B. "Some students have a bad attitude and don't take tests seriously."

Chris says: "If students study hard, they can learn what they need to know to pass the most important tests."

Does Jose say A or B in response to Chris?

A. "A student can be prepared enough to do well on a test, but then panic and fail."

B. "Some students have so many problems that tests don't seem that important."

Chris says: "If students have a bad attitude, it's because the teacher isn't encouraging them."

Does Jose say A or B in response to Chris?

A. "Many students fail even though they have great teachers."

B. "Some students fail because friends distract them from listening to the teacher."

continues on next page

> *Chris says:* "If students act out, it's because the teacher isn't disciplining them."
>
> *Does Jose say A or B in response to Chris?*
>
> A. "Many students fail even though they have very strict teachers."
>
> B. "Some students have problems at home and so they can't pay attention to the teacher in school."
>
> *Chris says:* "If a teacher is too strict, it can cause students to lose motivation."
>
> *Does Jose say A or B in response to Chris?*
>
> A. "Students who are motivated to do well in school will do so regardless of the teacher."
>
> B. "Some students have problems at home and so they aren't motivated to focus on what the teacher is saying."
>
> *Chris says:* "Many students have problems at home and still do well in school."
>
> *Does Jose say A or B in response to Chris?*
>
> A. "If problems with parents are bad enough, it because impossible to concentrate on schoolwork."
>
> B. "If there isn't good communication between parents and teachers, students' grades can suffer."

Managing controversy in the classroom

A final issue that warrants addressing is how comfortable the adults involved feel about having young teens discussing controversial social and political issues that at least to start they know little about.[12] Our observation of many classrooms in which students are so engaged confirms that students are entirely comfortable and eager to talk about issues that they believe really matter. They need only be monitored and reminded if needed to "Criticize Ideas, not People." Their limited knowledge expands as they engage the topic.

Teachers may feel most challenged in conducting the final whole-class debrief session following the showdown on a topic. The teacher should deflect any request from students to divulge their own position on the topic, stating firmly that this is the students' debate and the teacher and any other adults are there only as coaches. The coach's role, students can be reminded, is to help students develop their skills in good arguing and these skills do not depend on what position one holds on an issue. If a teacher hears that students after a time are still neglecting critical factors regarding an issue, the teacher might (and probably should) make the general suggestion that they need to look further into the Q&As available for the topic. As adults, we need to otherwise stand by and have the faith they will in good time construct the important ideas themselves.

Endnotes

1. Kuhn, D., Goh, W., Iordanou, K., & Shaenfield, D. (2008). Arguing on the computer: A microgenetic study of developing argument skills in a computer-supported environment. *Child Development, 79*, 1311–1329.
2. DeFuccio, M., Kuhn, D., Udell, W., & Callender, K. (2009). Developing argument skills in severely disadvantaged adolescent males in a residential setting. *Applied Developmental Science, 13*, 30–41.
3. Lipman, M. (1980). *Philosophy in the classroom*. Philadelphia: Temple University Press.
4. Common Core State Standards W.6.1.Write arguments to support claims with clear reasons and relevant evidence. [W.6.1]
5. Kuhn, D., & Crowell, A. (2011). Dialogic argumentation as a vehicle for developing young adolescents' thinking. *Psychological Science, 22*, 545–552.
6. Kuhn, D., Hemberger, L., & Khait, V. (2016). Tracing the development of argumentive writing in a discourse-rich context. *Written Communication, 33*, 92–121.
7. Hemberger, L., Kuhn, D., Matos, F., & Shi, Y. (2017). A dialogic path to evidence-based argumentive writing. *Journal of the Learning Sciences*.
8. Crowell, A., & Kuhn, D. (2014). Developing dialogic argumentation skills: A three-year intervention study. *Journal of Cognition and Development, 31*, 456–496.
9. Kuhn, D., Hemberger, L., & Khait, V. (2016). *Argue with me: Argument as a path to developing students' thinking and writing*. New York: Routledge. (2nd ed.)
10. Kuhn, D., Zillmer, N., Crowell, A., & Zavala, J. (2013). Developing norms of argumentation: Metacognitive, epistemological, and social dimensions of developing argumentive competence. *Cognition & Instruction, 31*, 456–496.
11. Goldstein, M., Crowell, A., & Kuhn, D. (2009). What constitutes skilled argumentation and how does it develop? *Informal Logic, 29*, 379–395.
12. Hess, D., & McAvoy, P. (2015). *The political classroom*. Routledge.